The Collected Short Plays of

THORNTON WILDER

The
COLLECTED
SHORT PLAYS *of*
THORNTON
WILDER

VOLUME I

Edited by Donald Gallup
and A. Tappan Wilder

With additional material by F. J. O'Neil

THEATRE COMMUNICATIONS GROUP

Wilder, Thornton, 1897–1975.
The collected shorter plays of Thornton Wilder. — 1st ed.
ISBN 1-55936-138-7 (cloth)   ISBN 1-55936-131-X (paper)
I. Title.
PS3545.I345A6   1997
812'.52—dc21   97-7734
CIP

97-1546
812
WIL
v.1

Book design and composition by Lisa Govan
Cover design by Carol Divine Carson
Cover and frontispiece photographs courtesy of
The Thornton Wilder Archive, Collection of American Literature,
Beinecke Rare Book and Manuscript Library, Yale University

First Edition, June 1997

To Donald Gallup
With Appreciation

CONTENTS

PREFACE

by A. Tappan Wilder

THORNTON WILDER'S devotion to the short play lasted from his grade school years through his sixth decade. Given the longevity of this interest—the variety of the forms and subjects with which he practiced it, and their importance for understanding Wilder's work as a whole— it is not surprising that his literary executor, Donald Gallup, proposed a collected edition of short plays the year after the author's death in 1975.

Mr. Gallup put the project aside, however, when the playwright's family decided to abide by the author's desire to withdraw several plays from both publication and production. In *Pigeons on the Granite: Memoirs of a Yale Librarian* (1988), Mr. Gallup phrased the issue this way: "I had not foreseen that Isabel, and to a certain extent also their older brother Amos, would be so governed by what they felt Thornton himself would have wanted. I began on the premise that all finished uncollected work ought to be printed, especially work that had been produced."

Near the end of her life, Isabel Wilder (1900–1995), the author's sister and long-time personal agent, changed her mind about the embargoed works. As a result, in 1994, *The Wreck on the Five-Twenty-Five* was published in the *Yale Review* together with Mr. Gallup's introductory note about Wilder's ambitious plans for fourteen shorter plays depicting "The Seven Deadly Sins" and "The Seven Ages of Man." The following year, *The Wreck* was produced successfully on the New York stage, and was subsequently published in *The Best American Short Plays, 1994–1995*.

The success of *The Wreck* opened the doors to this edition. Each of its two volumes is constructed around one of the previously published collections of Wilder's short plays, both out of print in English: *The Angel That Troubled the Waters and Other Plays* (1928) anchors Volume II (to be published in 1998); and *The Long Christmas Dinner and Other Plays in One Act* (1931) the book at hand.

In 1963, Harper & Row arranged for a new edition of the latter volume, adding to it an introduction by John Gassner (1903–1967), then Sterling Professor of Playwriting and Dramatic Literature at Yale. Mr. Gallup and Isabel Wilder most appropriately viewed this often-cited piece as part of the record. It has therefore been included here. This TCG volume also restores *Such Things Only Happen in Books* to the collected work. This play appeared in the 1931 edition but was subsequently withdrawn by the author.

With the exception of F. J. O'Neil's contributions, Donald Gallup helped prepare the material for this volume, including overseeing the first appearance of *Cement Hands*, and providing the bibliographical notes. For Volume I, he has also revised his *Yale Review* introduction to take account of this volume's broader scope.

In 1995, after twenty years, Donald Gallup stepped down as Thornton Wilder's literary executor. In addition to building up and managing the Wilder archive, he was responsible for editing three important works of interest to scholars and the broader public alike: *The Alcestiad or A Life in the Sun: A Play in Three Acts—With a Satyr Play: The Drunken Sisters* (1977), *American Characteristics and Other*

Essays (1979) and the essential tool for understanding much of Wilder's mind, and works-in-progress, *The Journals of Thornton Wilder, 1939–1961* (1985).

As curator of the Yale Collection of American Literature, Mr. Gallup shared his day with the papers of many writers besides Wilder, among them T. S. Eliot, Gertrude Stein, Eugene O'Neil, Ezra Pound and Edmund Wilson. With insight and candor, these, and other prominent figures in twentieth-century letters, come alive in *Pigeons on the Granite*.

Because the Wilders lived near Yale, Mr. Gallup knew Thornton and Isabel especially well, and often heard Thornton read from works-in-progress at the well-known address on Deepwood Drive in Hamden, Connecticut. Here is Gallup describing Wilder trying to be helpful to his future literary executor: "During [his] last years, Thornton would often greet me at Deepwood Drive with the announcement that he had destroyed another fifty pages that afternoon that I'd not have to be bothered with when he was no longer around."

It is characteristic of Donald Gallup's generosity to have insisted that I take over as editor of this book. The least I would accept, I insisted in turn, was to permit my name to rest in his shade. Whatever the duties, they allow me (with some secrecy) to perform the happy act of dedicating this volume to him on behalf of my mother, sister and I (the sister-in-law, niece and nephew of Thornton Wilder). Behind the language lies our admiration for building the Wilder archive and for the intellectual companionship, loyalty, affection and sheer pleasure he brought into Thornton and Isabel's lives.

F. J. O'Neil also heard Wilder read from his work at the house on Deepwood Drive. The two met in 1950 when Wilder was teaching at Harvard as the Charles Eliot Norton Professor of Poetry, and "Jim" O'Neil was a stage-struck undergraduate, acting in, among other plays, *The Skin of Our Teeth*. Through visits and correspondence their friendship lasted until Thornton's death. With Donald Gallup, F. J. O'Neil served as one of the ushers at Thornton's memorial service.

In 1995, Mr. O'Neil, whose theatrical career has included acting and directing, began to explore the manuscripts of the "Ages" and "Sins" plays, which Wilder had left unfinished but had not destroyed (itself a sign of the importance he attached to them). After much detective work on the surviving manuscripts written in the author's cramped handwriting style, Mr. O'Neil produced his important contribution to this volume: *Youth*, *The Rivers Under the Earth*, *A Ringing of Doorbells* and *In Shakespeare and the Bible*. The recovery of these last two plays allows us to include in this volume, for the first time, a full cycle of "The Seven Deadly Sins" plays.

In editing these four plays for this book, incorrect spellings and other minor and obvious errors, such as placement of an incorrect character name, have been corrected, and punctuation adjusted to conform to modern usage. Mr. O'Neil offers his interpretation for the ending of these plays. He does this by adding stage directions to all four plays and, in one case (*The Ringing of Doorbells*), by adding a reprise of a Wilder line. These changes are indicated by brackets and discussed in brief afterwords to each play. The complete record of Mr. O'Neil's labors will be added to the Thornton Wilder Collection at the Beinecke Rare Book and Manuscript Library at Yale University.

In addition to his well-known observation that a wastepaper basket is a writer's best friend, Wilder sometimes added that a cot is the worst enemy. A literary executor could well say that his or her charge's unpublished materials are *the* worst enemy. Beyond entertaining scholars in dark corners, should work considered unfinished by the author be permitted to see daylight?

It was not difficult to answer the question in the case of these four plays; all who have read them believe that they are worthy, at a minimum, of inclusion in this collection, and thus available to a broad public. And the maximum? The theatre, as Thornton often pointed out (and celebrated), is a collaborative enterprise. Time and the interest on the part of directors, producers and actors will reveal how these "new" plays (as well as *Bernice* and *Cement Hands*) "play" at the beginning of a new century.

It was Thornton Wilder's intention, expressed as late as 1966, that the completed cycles of the "Ages" and "Sins" plays appear first in print as a "reading book." For this reason, until 1970, Samuel French distributed only mimeographed copies of *Childhood* and *Infancy*. Now, thanks to Barbara Hogenson, the Wilder literary agent; Terry Nemeth, Steve Samuels and Kathy Sova at TCG Books; and John Guare, we have the "reading book" at last. That it includes the work of both the young playwright *and* the elder statesman makes the Wilder Centenary (forgive me) still wilder.

A. Tappan Wilder
Literary Executor
May 1997

INTRODUCTION

by John Guare

IMAGINE A MOUNT RUSHMORE for American playwrights located—why not—at 42nd Street and Broadway, the crossroads of the world. We'd surely look up to admire Thornton Wilder's professorial head, along with the massive heads of O'Neill, Miller and Williams. But would Wilder be the Teddy Roosevelt of Mount Rushmore? We don't question his being there. We're just not quite sure why.

We learned in school that Thornton Wilder is one of America's most distinguished and—that horrible word—beloved playwrights. Beloved? Well, because *Our Town* gave us an image of our American selves that we like to live with. Does *Our Town* make Thornton Wilder the theatrical equivalent of Norman Rockwell? Thornton Wilder has an odd place in the pantheon.

He was famous enough in 1953 to be on the cover of *Time* (published by his Yale classmate, Henry Luce). Under his portrait on the cover in front of a Jasper Johns-ish American flag is his quote: "The American is the first planetary mind." In 1974, in *Reader's Digest*, S. N. Behrman recalled going with Thornton Wilder to a dinner at the

White House for André Malraux during the Kennedy years. Behrman, a very successful playwright of the 1930s, praised Wilder to the *Reader's Digest* readership as "America's universal man." I can't imagine *Reader's Digest* ever publishing a celebration of Tennessee Williams.

Why do we think Wilder is important? Why do we vaguely think he's middlebrow and then, as I did, become overwhelmed by the sheer emotional size of *Our Town*, when seen in a production like Gregory Mosher's 1991 Lincoln Center Theater production with Spalding Gray as the Stage Manager?

Thornton Wilder. What do we do with this man who was a playwright, novelist, actor, teacher, musician, essayist, translator, adaptor, opera librettist and screenwriter (for what some people think is Hitchcock's finest film, *Shadow of a Doubt*)? This was a man who as a hobby—it had to be an act of love—spent years dating the four hundred extant plays of Lope de Vega. This was a man whose nickname was The Library. At his memorial service on January 18, 1976 (six weeks after his death on December 7, 1975), Ruth Gordon, his great Dolly Levi, said in her tribute: "Somebody asked [my husband] Garson Kanin where he went to college. He said he never did. He went to Thornton Wilder."

Wilder's fame relies today not on his novels, such as *The Bridge of San Luis Rey*, which brought him blockbuster fame at the age of thirty, but solely on the reputation of three plays . . . well, two major plays, which each won the Pulitzer Prize, and a third play whose fame rests on, and has been supplanted by, its transmogrification into the glitter of *Hello Dolly*.

We don't think of Thornton Wilder as a prolific playwright. Yet look at all these one-act plays being published in only the first of two volumes. And these two volumes of plays will not contain the big three, and will also *not* include *The Trumpet Shall Sound* (his 1926 New York theatrical debut directed by Richard Boleslavsky for the American

Laboratory Theatre), or his 1932 translation of André Obey's *The Rape of Lucrèce* (starring Katharine Cornell and designed by the visionary Robert Edmond Jones), or his adaptation of *A Doll's House* (directed by Jed Harris and starring Ruth Gordon, a highlight on Broadway in 1937). Has its run of 144 performances for a New York production of an Ibsen play been equaled?

It will take at least a third volume for us to finally read *The Merchant of Yonkers*, which failed on Broadway in 1938 (the same year *Our Town* opened), in spite of being directed by the legendary Max Reinhardt. Wilder swore he would validate that play one day. And he did, sixteen years later, in its reincarnation as *The Matchmaker*. Perhaps a later volume will contain portions, if not all, of the massive and unfinished *Emporium*, which occupied him so in the 1950s. Prolific for a man who said a wastepaper basket is a writer's best friend.

This collection of seventeen one-act plays is really three collections. The first batch of six plays, published in 1931 as *The Long Christmas Dinner and Other Plays in One Act*, contains three plays that are simply masterpieces: *The Long Christmas Dinner*, *The Happy Journey to Trenton and Camden* and *Pullman Car Hiawatha* (all influenced by the Japanese Noh theatre and the writing on Noh theatre by the French playwright, Paul Claudel). These three plays were the workshops, the laboratories, for *Our Town* and *The Skin of Our Teeth*. Two realistic plays from his Yale days: *Queens of France* and *Love and How to Cure It*; and a play he later disowned, *Such Things Only Happen in Books* (which could have been a George S. Kaufman/Moss Hart revue sketch) are also collected here.

It took nearly thirty years for the next two collections of one-acts to be attempted. He entitled these two cycles "The Seven Deadly Sins" and "The Seven Ages of Man." These had to be important: they just couldn't be seven deadly sins. He announced in his journals, November 24, 1958, that "maybe all my seven could be *les péchés capitaux*." In a 1961 interview with Arthur Gelb in the *New York Times*, Wilder said that he had completed "the first segment of what is expected to be my artistic summing-up," a double cycle of fourteen one-act plays. He would later say he regretted saying this.

He completed to his satisfaction only two of "The Seven Ages of Man" plays: *Infancy* and *Childhood*, which were produced in 1962 by New York's Circle in the Square, as part of an evening now called "Plays for Bleecker Street." *Youth* (Gulliver) and *The Rivers Under the Earth* (which may or may not be Middle Age, and may or may not belong to the cycle) were only recently recovered from the Wilder Archive at Yale.

He got further along with "The Seven Deadly Sins," but, after the forays of Gluttony, Lust, Sloth and Pride into the outside world, he consigned the latter two (with the exception of a German translation of Pride) to burial in his archives, along with Envy, Wrath and Avarice, which he considered unfinished. These plays are all bitter and bleak as the early plays are full of comfort. What happened to the author of those early plays who described himself thus: "the most valuable thing I inherited was a temperament that doesn't revolt against Necessity and is constantly renewed in Hope"?

Read *The Wreck on the Five-Twenty-Five* illustrating Sloth and hear Hawkins talking about his commuter train going in and out of the city to the suburbs:

> Hoping against hope that there'll be . . . a wreck, so we can crawl out of the smoking, burning cars . . . and get into one of those houses. Do you know what you see from the windows of the train? Those people— those cars that you see on the streets of Bennsville— they're just dummies. *Cardboard.* They've been up there to deceive you. What really goes on in Bennsville—inside those houses—that's what's really interesting. People with six arms and legs. People that can talk like Shakespeare. Children . . . that can beat

Einstein. Fabulous things . . . We're so expert at hiding things from one another—we're so cram-filled with things we can't say to one another that only a wreck could crack us open.

These seven plays are filled with the people who have not escaped by the skin of their teeth. These are the people of *Our Town* who lived long enough to learn the price you pay for staying smugly in your own Grover's Corners. Emily said, "Oh life, you are too wonderful." I know what these seven plays are. These are the plays if Emily had lived.

Who was Thornton Wilder? The bare bones. He was born April 17, 1897, in Madison, Wisconsin, where his father owned and edited a newspaper. His identical twin brother did not survive the birth. With the exception of two spells in China, where his father served in the consular service, Wilder spent much of his childhood in Berkeley, California (where a neighbor bought Duchamp's "Nude Descending a Staircase," which young Wilder went to see over and over), and graduated from Berkeley High School in 1915.

He went on to Oberlin and then Yale for college; then to Italy to the American Academy in Rome where he studied archaeology ("Once you have swung a pickax that will reveal the curve of a street four thousand years covered over, which was once an active well-traveled highway, you are never quite the same again."); to Lawrenceville, the elite prep school in New Jersey, where he taught for a number of years and published his first novels; then on to the lecturing at the University of Chicago.

In 1927, when he was thirty, his second published novel, *The Bridge of San Luis Rey*, set in Peru (which he hadn't visited up to that point), received a sensational response—he won his first Pulitzer Prize in 1928; he was launched. But, in 1939, he said, "All my work, all of the earlier writing has been one long apprenticeship for the theatre."

He lived on Deepwood Drive, Hamden, Connecticut, outside New Haven, in the house that *The Bridge* [*of San Luis Rey*] built; his sister Isabel acted as his amanuensis. The house was a home base as he traveled back and forth around the world.

He wrote seven novels, many plays and several screenplays. He was celebrated in America and Europe. In the 1950s, *Our Town* was even done on TV as a musical. Frank Sinatra played the Stage Manager, singing the hit song: "Love and Marriage" over and over, and Paul Newman and Eva Marie Saint were George and Emily. *The Skin of Our Teeth* was the first American play Brecht chose to run in the repertory of the Berliner Ensemble; in the mid-1950s, the United States State Department sent it on a worldwide goodwill tour with the stars Mary Martin and Helen Hayes. In 1964, *The Matchmaker* became *Hello Dolly* without his having to lift a finger, he said, and it lavished money on him for the rest of his life. In 1973 he published his seventh novel, *Theophilus North*, which remained on the best-seller list for twenty-one weeks. In 1975 he died in his sleep while taking a nap. A good life. What do we do with him?

He never went out to sea like O'Neill or Melville or on the road like Kerouac or mad like Poe or even stayed in his room like Emily Dickinson. He was never on the river like Mark Twain. He served in two wars but never fought in a battle like Stephen Crane or shot big game like Hemingway. He never drank himself to an early death like Fitzgerald. He had many friendships from Sigmund Freud (even though he was never analyzed) to Katharine Hepburn, but no serious relationships. He didn't have the political activism or the mythic private and public life of Arthur Miller. He didn't create an indelibly personal world of torment as did Tennessee Williams. Where did his life experience, his bravado, come from?

In 1928, he wrote in a foreword to his first collection of plays, *The Angel That Troubled the Waters*:

During the years that these plays were being written I was reading widely, and these pages are full of allusions to it. The art of literature springs from two curiosities, a curiosity about human beings pushed to such an extreme that it resembles love, and a love of a few masterpieces of literature so absorbing that it has all the richest elements of curiosity. I use the word *curiosity* in the French sense of a tireless awareness of things . . . The training for literature must be acquired by the artist alone, through the passionate assimilation of a few masterpieces written from a spirit somewhat like his own, and of a few masterpieces written from a spirit not at all like his own.

Wilder found his wilderness, his running off to sea, his trip up the Amazon, his polar expeditions, his Spanish civil war in the library. No wonder we can't get a handle on him. He's not the stuff of legends. The Wilder who said, "No man has a father after the age of twenty-one," had two infatuations that validated his best work. *Our Town* and *The Skin of Our Teeth* were each written under the spell of a different master, a spell so bewitching for him that it is love. Even though he prepared for *Our Town* in the three great one-acts in this volume, it was the spiritual tutelage of Gertrude Stein who gave him the intellectual validation and courage to go on and write such a seemingly homespun work as *Our Town*.

His adaptation of *A Doll's House* led him to question Ibsen, whose naturalistic language was infused with symbols "which move like great clouds behind the ordinary parlor conversations." (Noel Coward described an Ibsen play as a play with a stuffed bird on the mantelpiece screaming, "I'm the title! I'm the title!") Wilder was inspired by Gertrude Stein's clarion call:

Now listen! Can't you see that when the language was new—as it was with Chaucer and Homer—the poet could use the name of a thing and the thing was really there? He could say, "O moon," "O sea," "O love" and the moon and the sea and love were really there. And can't you see that after hundreds of years had gone by and thousands of poems had been written, he could call on those words and find that they were just wornout literary words? The excitingness of pure being had withdrawn from them; they were just rather stale literary words. Now the poet has to work in the excitingness of pure being; he has to get back that intensity into the language . . . it's not enough to be bizarre.

The Thornton Wilder, who, in 1931, had written in *The Happy Journey to Trenton and Camden*: "Goodness, smell that air, will you! It's got the whole ocean in it. —Elmer, drive careful over that bridge," was ready for the Stein he met in 1934 when she came to Chicago to lecture on "What Is English Literature?" She had not returned to America since 1903. In her, Wilder met an artist who wanted to find, as he put it: "a constant freshening of the ways of saying a thing." She validated his gift of capturing the poetry of common speech. Otherwise, would its simplicity have embarrassed him? After all, he was now Thornton Wilder. His devoted sister Isabel wrote that "the astonishing success of *The Bridge of San Luis Rey* [in 1928] . . . may be said to have ruined his life . . . it weighted [him] with a cumbersome bag of perquisites: honors, privileges . . . balanced by a loss of privacy and hazards to body, mind and spirit." Not only had he become Thornton Wilder, he had to surround himself with Stein and then James Joyce. Couldn't *The Skin of Our Teeth* stand on its own? Why did Wilder so frequently have to announce its indebtedness to *Finnegans Wake*, so much so that he was unjustly accused by Joseph Campbell and Henry Morton Robinson of having plagiarized it (a false accusation, which people claimed cost Wilder the Nobel Prize)?

He would write in his journal in 1960 that "*Finnegans*

Wake is a vast compendium of techniques to reproduce the dream state."

We have not one but two Thornton Wilders: the plain homespun Thornton of Gertrude Stein and the fantastical Ice Age Wilder of James Joyce. Who does Wilder remind me of?

And then I thought of a great American poem called "The Red Wheelbarrow" by William Carlos Williams:

> so much depends
> upon
>
> a red wheel
> barrow
>
> glazed with rain
> water
>
> beside the white
> chickens

I thought about Stein's mandate to purify the symbolic luggage around language. I remembered the detail that Wilder's identical twin brother was stillborn. Wilder didn't remind me of one person. He reminded me of two people. Let me take a page out of his 1928 preface to *The Angel That Troubled the Waters*, in which he said "no subject was too grandiose." As he resurrected the young wife who dies in *Pullman Car Hiawatha*, let me give breath to the unnamed stillborn twin.

For I remember of whom Wilder reminds me. He reminds me of not one but of two great American poets—William Carlos Williams and Ezra Pound (who happened to be classmates at the University of Pennsylvania and remained lifelong friends). The problem that confronted them in their youth was where to go for experience to feed their art. Each wanted to be a poet. How to do that? William

Carlos Williams stayed in New Jersey as a doctor and found his source of experience there, writing of Paterson, New Jersey, as faithfully and plainly and mythically as Wilder would in *Our Town*. Ezra Pound fled to Europe to leap into the world culture. To take on the virtu of Dante, of Homer; the poems of China and Java. To reinvent the canto (Canto VII):

> Eleanor (she spoiled in a British climate)
> ''Ελανδρος and 'Ελέπτολις, and
>   poor old Homer blind, blind, as a bat,
> Ear, ear for the sea-surge;
>   rattle of old men's voices.
> And then the phantom of Rome,
>   marble narrow for seats
> "Si pulvis nullus" said Ovid,
> "Erit, nullum tamen execute."

Think of the Wilder of *Pullman Car Hiawatha* and act 3 of *The Skin of Our Teeth*. Wilder didn't mind that no one would understand the Greek and Hebrew that the philosophers spoke in those plays. The audience would know it was authentic. William Carlos Williams wrote in *I Wanted to Write a Poem*:

> Innocense [sic] can never perish. I really believed that then, and I really believe it now. It is something intrinsic in a man. And I still care about simplicity. I have been outspoken all my life, but honestly outspoken. I try to say it straight, whatever is to be said.

And the brilliant rodomontade of Pound's cantos, reinventing the Japanese form. What other man would T. S. Eliot trust to edit *The Waste Land*? One former American reaching out to another former American. The disparate relationship between William Carlos Williams and Pound seems to be what Thornton Wilder contained in one man. The spirit of that lost twin.

One Thornton lived in Hamden, Connecticut, on Deepwood Drive with forays into New Haven for lunch and the library, and wrote about New Hampshire and New Jersey and Rhode Island. The other Thornton summoned up the Ice Age and Atlantic City in high extravagance, peopled with philosophers who spoke in ancient Greek and Latin and Hebrew, and wrote novels of ancient Rome, and traveled to Europe and America receiving prizes and acclaim.

Thornton Wilder is so hard to get a handle on because he embodies the basic American dilemma. In the enormous mass of America, where do we go for experience? Are we William Carlos Williams? Or are we Ezra Pound? But then isn't that the American story? It's the story of Henry James, of T. S. Eliot. Where do we go for experience? It's the theme of James's *The Ambassadors* and *The Portrait of a Lady*; of Sinclair Lewis's *Dodsworth*. Where do we go in the vastness of America—the youngest country as world powers go and the oldest country in influence? (Wilder had said if the nineteenth century was the English century then the twentieth century is the American century and that makes it the oldest country.)

Is this theme the same force in America that produced Edwin Arlington Robinson's great American archetype Miniver Cheevy who

> dreamed of Thebes and Camelot,
>   And Priam's neighbors . . .
> Miniver Cheevy, born too late,
>   Scratched his head and kept on thinking;
> Miniver coughed, and called it fate,
>   And kept on drinking.

Or worse, Richard Cory who

> . . . we thought that he was everything
> To make us wish that we were in his place . . .
> And Richard Cory, one calm summer night,
> Went home and put a bullet through his head.

At the end of *Our Town*, one of the dead tells Emily after she's returned from the living: "Now you know—that's the happy existence you wanted to go back to. Ignorance and blindness."

That ignorance and blindness is what the optimist Wilder faced in these later plays, plays in which he struggled to find a language to reflect the despair of postwar America. Thornton Wilder had the gifts to manage the difficult balancing act of being both Williams and Pound up through the Second World War. He had found a way to live in his bifurcated world, staying at home and roaming the world . . . well, Europe . . . seemingly at home in his homespun world and in his worldview world. But where do we go for the real experience? Can America gives us this? Is this the theme of all these plays?

What's exciting about having these last unpublished plays is seeing a writer trying to find a new vocabulary, a new diction, a new way of reflecting life after the war, after the dreadful fact of the atom bomb. In *The Rivers Under the Earth*, the last extant play of "The Seven Ages of Man" (we're not sure if it is part of the cycle), is the first time we see the new voice coming together, where we see in its masterfully achieved simplicity the long plays Wilder might have written had he lived another lifetime. It is this regret for the life not lived (*The Wreck on the Five-Twenty-Five*) as well as the life lived (*In Shakespeare and the Bible* and *Bernice*) that bursts through the workshop plays and beckons to the postwar plays that would never be written, the plays searching out a language for the despair, the fear, the pessimism that is America's guilty secret.

Thornton Wilder could not finish his work but that does not diminish his work. His dilemma becomes our obligation. Take the image of the parade of philosophers from

Pullman Car Hiawatha and *The Skin of Our Teeth*, and imagine that parade not of philosophers but of playwrights from Aeschylus on down, through Plautus and Hroswitha and Calderon and Marlowe and Webster and Dryden and Behn and Strindberg and Shaw and Wilde and Pinero and O'Neill and Hellman and Orton and Albee and Hansberry and Shepard and Mamet and McNally and Wilson and Kushner, to every member of The Dramatists Guild, and to the next class of playwrights leaving Yale or NYU or Juilliard or whatever drama school or no drama school, or any of you readers of this book who've written even one play you've never shown anyone—join the march across the stage. Hear each generation saying, "Finish my work. Finish what I started. These are the questions I leave behind." And we must answer theirs and leave our own unanswered questions for others to come from all over the globe and finish ours, and the generations after to finish theirs.

Theatre is always the living proof of multiculturalism. Asking again and again, how do we keep language new? How do we keep the stage uncluttered so we can see and hear what must be seen and heard. No one lives long enough to finish his or her work. These later plays of Thornton Wilder will only reveal the darkness in the early plays; the light in the early plays will only shine a light on the rueful later work. Read these plays to celebrate that purity of intention that Wilder brought to the American theatre. Read the later plays as workshops for longer plays that he did not live long enough to write. We do not know what to do with Wilder because we have not known the full scope of his theatrical work. These plays, published in celebration of the centennial of Wilder's birth, will happily redress that fact.

John Guare
New York City
May 1997

The Long Christmas Dinner

and OTHER PLAYS
IN ONE ACT

THE SIX PLAYS in this section were written by Thornton Wilder in the late 1920s, and were published by Coward-McCann and Yale University Press in 1931 in *The Long Christmas Dinner and Other Plays in One Act*. By 1946, if not earlier, Wilder had withdrawn *Such Things Only Happen in Books* from production and subsequent English and foreign language editions. Its appearance here thus restores the content of the original volume. John Gassner's 1963 introduction to these plays begins on page 311.

The Long Christmas Dinner

CHARACTERS

LUCIA, Roderick's wife
RODERICK, Mother Bayard's son
MOTHER BAYARD
COUSIN BRANDON
CHARLES, Lucia and Roderick's son
GENEVIEVE, Lucia and Roderick's daughter
LEONORA BANNING, Charles's wife
LUCIA, Leonora and Charles's daughter, Samuel's twin
SAMUEL, Leonora and Charles's son, Lucia's twin
RODERICK, Leonora and Charles's youngest son
COUSIN ERMENGARDE
SERVANTS
NURSES

SETTING

The dining room of the Bayard home.

Close to the footlights a long dining table is handsomely spread for Christmas dinner. The carver's place with a great turkey before it is at the spectator's right.

A door, left back, leads into the hall.

At the extreme left, by the proscenium pillar, is a strange portal trimmed with garlands of fruits and flowers. Directly opposite is another, edged and hung with black velvet. The portals denote birth and death.

Ninety years are to be traversed in this play which represents in accelerated motion ninety Christmas dinners in the Bayard household. The actors are dressed in inconspicuous clothes and must indicate their gradual increase in years through their acting. Most of them carry wigs of white hair which they adjust upon their heads at the indicated moment, simply and without comment. The ladies may have shawls concealed beneath the table that they gradually draw up about their shoulders as they grow older.

Throughout the play the characters continue eating imaginary food with imaginary knives and forks.

There is no curtain. The audience arriving at the theatre sees the stage set and the table laid, though still in partial darkness. Gradually the lights in the auditorium become dim and the stage brightens until sparkling winter sunlight streams through the dining-room windows.

Enter Lucia. She inspects the table, touching here a knife and there a fork. She talks to a servant girl who is invisible to us.

LUCIA: I reckon we're ready now, Gertrude. We won't ring the chimes today. I'll just call them myself. *(She goes into the hall and calls)* Roderick. Mother Bayard. We're all ready. Come to dinner.

(Enter Roderick pushing Mother Bayard in a wheelchair.)

MOTHER BAYARD: . . . and a new horse too, Roderick. I used to think that only the wicked owned two horses. A new horse and a new house and a new wife!

LUCIA: Here, Mother Bayard, you sit between us.

RODERICK: Well, Mother, how do you like it? Our first Christmas dinner in the new house, hey?

MOTHER BAYARD: Tz–Tz–Tz! I don't know what your dear father would say!

(Roderick says grace.)

My dear Lucia, I can remember when there were still Indians on this very ground, and I wasn't a young girl either. I can remember when we had to cross the Mississippi on a new-made raft. I can remember when Saint Louis and Kansas City were full of Indians.

LUCIA *(Tying a napkin around Mother Bayard's neck)*: Imagine that! There! What a wonderful day for our first Christmas dinner: a beautiful sunny morning, snow, a splendid sermon. Dr. McCarthy preaches a splendid sermon. I cried and cried.

RODERICK *(Extending an imaginary carving fork)*: Come now, what'll you have, Mother? A little sliver of white?

LUCIA: Every last twig is wrapped around with ice. You almost never see that. Can I cut it up for you, dear? *(Over her shoulder)* Gertrude, I forgot the jelly. You know—on the top shelf. Mother Bayard, I found your mother's gravy boat while we were moving. What was her name, dear? What were all your names? You were . . . a . . . Genevieve Wainright. Now your mother—

MOTHER BAYARD: Yes, you must write it down somewhere. I was Genevieve Wainright. My mother was Faith Morrison. She was the daughter of a farmer in New Hampshire who was something of a blacksmith too. And she married young John Wainright—

LUCIA *(Memorizing on her fingers)*: Genevieve Wainright. Faith Morrison.

RODERICK: It's all down in a book somewhere upstairs. We have it all. All that kind of thing is very interesting. Come, Lucia, just a little wine. Mother, a little red wine for Christmas day. Full of iron. "Take a little wine for thy stomach's sake."

LUCIA: Really, I can't get used to wine! What would my father say? But I suppose it's all right.

(Enter Cousin Brandon from the hall. He takes his place by Lucia.)

COUSIN BRANDON *(Rubbing his hands)*: Well, well, I smell turkey. My dear cousins, I can't tell you how pleasant it is to be having Christmas dinner with you all. I've lived out there in Alaska so long without relatives. Let me see, how long have you had this new house, Roderick?

RODERICK: Why, it must be . . .

MOTHER BAYARD: Five years. It's five years, children. You should keep a diary. This is your sixth Christmas dinner here.

LUCIA: Think of that, Roderick. We feel as though we had lived here twenty years.

COUSIN BRANDON: At all events it still looks as good as new.

RODERICK *(Over his carving)*: What'll you have, Brandon, light or dark? —Frieda, fill up Cousin Brandon's glass.

LUCIA: Oh, dear, I can't get used to these wines. I don't know what my father'd say, I'm sure. What'll you have, Mother Bayard?

(During the following speeches Mother Bayard's chair, without any visible propulsion, starts to draw away from the table, turns toward the right, and slowly goes toward the dark portal.)

MOTHER BAYARD: Yes, I can remember when there were Indians on this very land.

LUCIA *(Softly)*: Mother Bayard hasn't been very well lately, Roderick.

MOTHER BAYARD: My mother was a Faith Morrison. And in New Hampshire she married a young John Wainright, who was a congregational minister. He saw her in his congregation one day . . .

LUCIA: Mother Bayard, hadn't you better lie down, dear?

MOTHER BAYARD: . . . and right in the middle of his sermon he said to himself: "I'll marry that girl." And he did, and I'm their daughter.

LUCIA *(Half rising, looking after her with anxiety)*: Just a little nap, dear?

MOTHER BAYARD: I'm all right. Just go on with your dinner. I was ten, and I said to my brother . . .

(She goes out. A very slight pause.)

COUSIN BRANDON: It's too bad it's such a cold dark day today. We almost need the lamps. I spoke to Major Lewis for a moment after church. His sciatica troubles him, but he does pretty well.

LUCIA *(Dabbing her eyes)*: I know Mother Bayard wouldn't want us to grieve for her on Christmas Day, but I can't forget her sitting in her wheelchair right beside us, only a year ago. And she would be so glad to know our good news.

RODERICK *(Patting her hand)*: Now, now. It's Christmas. *(Formally)* Cousin Brandon, a glass of wine with you, sir.

COUSIN BRANDON *(Half rising, lifting his glass gallantly)*: A glass of wine with you, sir.

LUCIA: Does the Major's sciatica cause him much pain?

COUSIN BRANDON: Some, perhaps. But you know his way. He says it'll be all the same in a hundred years.

LUCIA: Yes, he's a great philosopher.

RODERICK: His wife sends you a thousand thanks for her Christmas present.

LUCIA: I forget what I gave her. —Oh, yes, the workbasket!

(Through the entrance of Birth comes a nurse wheeling a perambulator trimmed with blue ribbons. Lucia rushes toward it, the men following.)

O my wonderful new baby, my darling baby! Who ever saw such a child! Quick, nurse, a boy or a girl? A boy! Roderick, what shall we call him? Really, nurse, you've never seen such a child!

RODERICK: We'll call him Charles after your father and grandfather.

LUCIA: But there are no Charleses in the Bible, Roderick.

RODERICK: Of course, there are. Surely there are.

LUCIA: Roderick!—Very well, but he will always be Samuel to me.—What miraculous hands he has! Really, they are the most beautiful hands in the world. All right, nurse. Have a good nap, my darling child.

RODERICK: Don't drop him, nurse. Brandon and I need him in our firm.

(Exit nurse and perambulator into the hall. The others return to their chairs, Lucia taking the place left vacant by Mother Bayard and Cousin Brandon moving up beside her. Cousin Brandon puts on his white hair.)

Lucia, a little white meat? Some stuffing? Cranberry sauce, anybody?

LUCIA *(Over her shoulder)*: Margaret, the stuffing is very good today. —Just a little, thank you.

RODERICK: Now something to wash it down. *(Half rising)* Cousin Brandon, a glass of wine with you, sir. To the ladies, God bless them.

LUCIA: Thank you, kind sirs.

COUSIN BRANDON: Pity it's such an overcast day today. And no snow.

LUCIA: But the sermon was lovely. I cried and cried. Dr. Spaulding does preach such a splendid sermon.

RODERICK: I saw Major Lewis for a moment after church. He says his rheumatism comes and goes. His wife says she has something for Charles and will bring it over this afternoon.

(Enter nurse again with perambulator. Pink ribbons. Same rush toward the left.)

LUCIA: O my lovely new baby! Really, it never occurred to me that it might be a girl. Why, nurse, she's perfect.

RODERICK: Now call her what you choose. It's your turn.

LUCIA: Looloolooloo. Aië. Aië. Yes, this time I shall have my way. She shall be called Genevieve after your mother. Have a good nap, my treasure.

(She looks after it as the nurse wheels the perambulator into the hall.)

Imagine! Sometime she'll be grown up and say "Good morning, Mother. Good morning, Father."—Really, Cousin Brandon, you don't find a baby like that every day.

COUSIN BRANDON: *And* the new factory.

LUCIA: A new factory? Really? Roderick, I shall be very uncomfortable if we're going to turn out to be rich. I've been afraid of that for years. —However, we mustn't talk about such things on Christmas Day. I'll just take a little piece of white meat, thank you. Roderick, Charles is destined for the ministry. I'm sure of it.

RODERICK: Woman, he's only twelve. Let him have a free mind. *We* want him in the firm, I don't mind saying. Anyway, no time passes as slowly as this when you're waiting for your urchins to grow up and settle down to business.

LUCIA: I don't want time to go any faster, thank you. I love the children just as they are. —Really, Roderick, you know what the doctor said: one glass a meal. *(Putting her hand over his glass)* No, Margaret, that will be all.

(Roderick rises, glass in hand. With a look of dismay on his face he takes a few steps toward the dark portal.)

RODERICK: Now I wonder what's the matter with me.

LUCIA: Roderick, do be reasonable.

RODERICK *(Tottering, but with gallant irony)*: But, my dear, statistics show that we steady, moderate drinkers . . .

LUCIA *(Rises, gazing at him in anguish)*: Roderick! My dear! What . . . ?

RODERICK *(Returns to his seat with a frightened look of relief)*: Well, it's fine to be back at table with you again. How many good Christmas dinners have I had to miss upstairs? And to be back at a fine bright one, too.

LUCIA: O my dear, you gave us a very alarming time! Here's your glass of milk. —Josephine, bring Mr. Bayard his medicine from the cupboard in the library.

RODERICK: At all events, now that I'm better I'm going to start doing something about the house.

LUCIA: Roderick! You're not going to change the house?

RODERICK: Only touch it up here and there. It looks a hundred years old.

(Charles enters casually from the hall.)

CHARLES: It's a great blowy morning, Mother. The wind comes over the hill like a lot of cannon. *(He kisses his mother's hair and sits down)*

LUCIA: Charles, you carve the turkey, dear. Your father's not well. You always said you hated carving, though you *are* so clever at it.

(Father and son exchange places.)

And such a good sermon. I cried and cried. Mother Bayard loved a good sermon so. And she used to sing the Christmas hymns all around the year. Oh, dear, oh, dear, I've been thinking of her all morning!

CHARLES: Shh, Mother. It's Christmas Day. You mustn't think of such things. You mustn't be depressed.

LUCIA: But sad things aren't the same as depressing things. I must be getting old: I like them.

CHARLES: Uncle Brandon, you haven't anything to eat. Pass his plate, Hilda . . . and some cranberry sauce . . .

(Enter Genevieve. She kisses her father's temple and sits down.)

GENEVIEVE: It's glorious. Every last twig is wrapped around with ice. You almost never see that.

LUCIA: Did you have time to deliver those presents after church, Genevieve?

GENEVIEVE: Yes, Mama. Old Mrs. Lewis sends you a thousand thanks for hers. It was just what she wanted, she said. Give me lots, Charles, lots.

RODERICK *(Rising and starting toward the dark portal)*: Statistics, ladies and gentlemen, show that we steady, moderate . . .

CHARLES: How about a little skating this afternoon, Father?

RODERICK: I'll live till I'm ninety.

LUCIA: I really don't think he ought to go skating.

RODERICK *(At the very portal, suddenly astonished)*: Yes, but . . . but . . . not yet!

(He goes out.)

LUCIA *(Dabbing her eyes)*: He was so young and so clever, Cousin Brandon. *(Raising her voice for Cousin Brandon's deafness)* I say he was so young and so clever. —Never forget your father, children. He was a good man. Well, he wouldn't want us to grieve for him today.

CHARLES: White or dark, Genevieve? Just another sliver, Mother?

LUCIA (*Putting on her white hair*): I can remember our first Christmas dinner in this house, Genevieve. Twenty-five years ago today. Mother Bayard was sitting here in her wheelchair. She could remember when Indians lived on this very spot and when she had to cross the river on a new-made raft.

CHARLES: She couldn't have, Mother.

GENEVIEVE: That can't be true.

LUCIA: It certainly was true—even I can remember when there was only one paved street. We were very happy to walk on boards. (*Louder, to Cousin Brandon*) We can remember when there were no sidewalks, can't we, Cousin Brandon?

COUSIN BRANDON (*Delighted*): Oh, yes! And those were the days.

CHARLES AND GENEVIEVE (*Sotto voce, this is a family refrain*): Those were the days.

LUCIA: And the ball last night, Genevieve? Did you have a nice time? I hope you didn't *waltz*, dear. I think a girl in our position ought to set an example. Did Charles keep an eye on you?

GENEVIEVE: He had none left. They were all on Leonora Banning. He can't conceal it any longer, Mother. I think he's engaged to marry Leonora Banning.

CHARLES: I'm not engaged to marry anyone.

LUCIA: Well, she's very pretty.

GENEVIEVE: I shall never marry, Mother. —I shall sit in this house beside you forever, as though life were one long, happy Christmas dinner.

LUCIA: O my child, you mustn't say such things!

GENEVIEVE (*Playfully*): You don't want me? You don't want me?

(*Lucia bursts into tears.*)

Why, Mother, how silly you are! There's nothing sad about that—what could possibly be sad about that?

LUCIA *(Drying her eyes)*: Forgive me. I'm just unpredictable, that's all.

(Charles goes to the door and leads in Leonora Banning.)

LEONORA *(Kissing Lucia's temple)*: Good morning, Mother Bayard. Good morning, everybody. Mother Bayard, you sit here by Charles. It's really a splendid Christmas Day today.

CHARLES: Little white meat? Genevieve, Mother, Leonora?

LEONORA: Every last twig is encircled with ice. —You never see that.

CHARLES *(Shouting)*: Uncle Brandon, another? —Rogers, fill my uncle's glass.

LUCIA *(To Charles)*: Do what your father used to do. It would please Cousin Brandon so. You know *(Pretending to raise a glass)* "Uncle Brandon, a glass of wine . . ."

CHARLES *(Rising)*: Uncle Brandon, a glass of wine with you, sir.

BRANDON: A glass of wine with you, sir. To the ladies, God bless them every one.

THE LADIES: Thank you, kind sirs.

GENEVIEVE: And if I go to Germany for my music I promise to be back for Christmas. I wouldn't miss that.

LUCIA: I hate to think of you over there all alone in those strange pensions.

GENEVIEVE: But, darling, the time will pass so fast that you'll hardly know I'm gone. I'll be back in the twinkling of an eye.

(Enter left, the nurse and perambulator. Green ribbons.)

LEONORA: Oh, what an angel! The darlingest baby in the world. Do let me hold it, nurse.

(But the nurse resolutely wheels the perambulator across the stage and out the dark door.)

Oh, I did love it so!

(Charles rises, puts his arm around his wife, and slowly leads her back to the table.)

GENEVIEVE *(Softly to her mother as the other two cross)*: Isn't there anything I can do?

LUCIA *(Raises her eyebrows, ruefully)*: No, dear. Only time, only the passing of time can help in these things.

(Charles returns to the table.)

Don't you think we could ask Cousin Ermengarde to come and live with us here? There's plenty for everyone and there's no reason why she should go on teaching the first grade for ever and ever. She wouldn't be in the way, would she, Charles?

CHARLES: No, I think it would be fine. —A little more potato and gravy, anybody? A little more turkey, Mother?

(Brandon rises and starts slowly toward the dark portal.
Lucia rises and stands for a moment with her face in her hands.)

COUSIN BRANDON *(Muttering)*: It was great to be in Alaska in those days . . .

GENEVIEVE *(Half rising, and gazing at her mother in fear)*: Mother, what is . . . ?

LUCIA *(Hurriedly)*: Hush, my dear. It will pass. —Hold fast to your music, you know. *(As Genevieve starts toward her)* No, no. I want to be alone for a few minutes.

(She turns and starts after Cousin Brandon toward the right.)

CHARLES: If the Republicans collected all their votes instead of going off into cliques among themselves, they might prevent his getting a second term.

GENEVIEVE: Charles, Mother doesn't tell us, but she hasn't been very well these days.

CHARLES: Come, Mother, we'll go to Florida for a few weeks.

(Exit Brandon.)

LUCIA *(Smiling at Genevieve and waving her hand)*: Don't be foolish. Don't grieve.

*(Lucia clasps her hands under her chin. Her lips move, whispering. She walks serenely into the portal.
Genevieve stares after her, frozen.)*

GENEVIEVE *(Sinks down at the table, her face buried in her arms)*: But what will I do? What's left for me to do?

(At the same moment the nurse and perambulator enter from the left. Pale yellow ribbons. Leonora rushes to it.)

LEONORA: O my darlings … twins … Charles, aren't they glorious! Look at them. Look at them.

CHARLES *(Bending over the basket)*: Which is which?

LEONORA: I feel as though I were the first mother who ever had twins. —Look at them now! But why wasn't Mother Bayard allowed to stay and see them!

GENEVIEVE *(Rising suddenly distraught, loudly)*: I don't want to go on. I can't bear it.

CHARLES *(Goes to her quickly. They sit down. He whispers to her earnestly, taking both her hands)*: But Genevieve,

Genevieve! How frightfully Mother would feel to think that . . . Genevieve!

GENEVIEVE *(Shaking her head wildly)*: I never told her how wonderful she was. We all treated her as though she were just a friend in the house. I thought she'd be here forever.

LEONORA *(Timidly)*: Genevieve darling, do come one minute and hold my babies' hands. We shall call the girl Lucia after her grandmother—will that please you? Do just see what adorable little hands they have.

(Genevieve collects herself and goes over to the perambulator. She smiles brokenly into the basket.)

GENEVIEVE: They are wonderful, Leonora.

LEONORA: Give him your finger, darling. Just let him hold it.

CHARLES: And we'll call the boy Samuel. —Well, now everybody come and finish your dinners. Don't drop them, nurse; at least don't drop the boy. We need him in the firm.

LEONORA *(Stands looking after them as the nurse wheels them into the hall)*: Someday they'll be big. Imagine! They'll come in and say "Hello, Mother!" *(She makes clucking noises of rapturous consternation.)*

CHARLES: Come, a little wine, Leonora, Genevieve? Full of iron. Eduardo, fill the ladies' glasses. It certainly is a keen, cold morning. I used to go skating with Father on mornings like this and Mother would come back from church saying—

GENEVIEVE *(Dreamily)*: I know: saying, "Such a splendid sermon. I cried and cried."

LEONORA: Why did she cry, dear?

GENEVIEVE: That generation all cried at sermons. It was their way.

LEONORA: Really, Genevieve?

GENEVIEVE: They had had to go since they were children and I suppose sermons reminded them of their fathers and mothers, just as Christmas dinners do us. Especially in an old house like this.

LEONORA: It really is pretty old, Charles. And so ugly, with all that ironwork filigree and that dreadful cupola.

GENEVIEVE: Charles! You aren't going to change the house!

CHARLES: No, no. I won't give up the house, but great heavens! It's fifty years old. This spring we'll remove the cupola and build a new wing toward the tennis courts.

(From now on Genevieve is seen to change. She sits up more straightly. The corners of her mouth become fixed. She becomes a forthright and slightly disillusioned spinster. Charles becomes the plain businessman and a little pompous.)

LEONORA: And then couldn't we ask your dear old Cousin Ermengarde to come and live with us? She's really the self-effacing kind.

CHARLES: Ask her now. Take her out of the first grade.

GENEVIEVE: We only seem to think of it on Christmas Day with her Christmas card staring us in the face.

(Enter left, nurse and perambulator. Blue ribbons.)

LEONORA: Another boy! Another boy! Here's a Roderick for you at last.

CHARLES: Roderick Brandon Bayard. A regular little fighter.

LEONORA: Goodbye, darling. Don't grow up too fast. Yes, yes. Aië, aië, aië—stay just as you are. Thank you, nurse.

GENEVIEVE *(Who has not left the table, repeats dryly)*: Stay just as you are.

(Exit nurse and perambulator. The others return to their places.)

LEONORA: Now I have three children. One, two, three. Two boys and a girl. I'm collecting them. It's very exciting. *(Over her shoulder)* What, Hilda? Oh, Cousin Ermengarde's come! Come in, Cousin.

(Leonora goes to the hall and welcomes Cousin Ermengarde, who already wears her white hair.)

ERMENGARDE *(Shyly)*: It's such a pleasure to be with you all.

CHARLES *(Pulling out her chair for her)*: The twins have taken a great fancy to you already, Cousin.

LEONORA: The baby went to her at once.

CHARLES: Exactly how are we related, Cousin Ermengarde? —There, Genevieve, that's your specialty. —First a little more turkey and stuffing, Mother? Cranberry sauce, anybody?

GENEVIEVE: I can work it out: Grandmother Bayard was your ...

ERMENGARDE: Your Grandmother Bayard was a second cousin of my Grandmother Haskins through the Wainrights.

CHARLES: Well, it's all in a book somewhere upstairs. All that kind of thing is awfully interesting.

GENEVIEVE: Nonsense. There are no such books. I collect my notes off gravestones, and you have to scrape a good deal of moss—let me tell you—to find one great-grandparent.

CHARLES: There's a story that my Grandmother Bayard crossed the Mississippi on a raft before there were any bridges or ferryboats. She died before Genevieve and I were born. Time certainly goes very fast in a great new country like this. Have some more cranberry sauce, Cousin Ermengarde.

ERMENGARDE *(Timidly)*: Well, time must be passing very slowly in Europe with this dreadful, dreadful war going on.

CHARLES: Perhaps an occasional war isn't so bad after all. It clears up a lot of poisons that collect in nations. It's like a boil.

ERMENGARDE: Oh, dear, oh, dear!

CHARLES *(With relish)*: Yes, it's like a boil. —Ho! ho! Here are your twins.

(The twins appear at the door into the hall. Sam is wearing the uniform of an ensign. Lucia is fussing over some detail on it.)

LUCIA: Isn't he wonderful in it, Mother?

CHARLES: Let's get a look at you.

SAM: Mother, don't let Roderick fool with my stamp album while I'm gone.

LEONORA: Now, Sam, do write a letter once in a while. Do be a good boy about that, mind.

SAM: You might send some of those cakes of yours once in a while, Cousin Ermengarde.

ERMENGARDE *(In a flutter)*: I certainly will, my dear boy.

CHARLES: If you need any money, we have agents in Paris and London, remember.

LEONORA: Do be a good boy, Sam.

SAM: Well, good-bye . . .

(Sam goes briskly out through the dark portal, tossing his unneeded white hair through the door before him.
Lucia sits down at the table with lowered eyes.)

ERMENGARDE *(After a slight pause, in a low, constrained voice, making conversation)*: I spoke to Mrs. Fairchild for a moment coming out of church. Her rheumatism's a little better, she says. She sends you her warmest thanks for the Christmas present. The workbasket, wasn't it? —It was an admirable sermon. And our stained-glass window looked so beautiful, Leonora, so beautiful. Everybody spoke of it and so affectionately of Sammy. *(Leonora's hand goes to her mouth)* Forgive me, Leonora, but it's better to speak of him than not to speak of him when we're all thinking of him so hard.

LEONORA (*Rising, in anguish*): He was a mere boy. He was a mere boy, Charles.

CHARLES: My dear, my dear.

LEONORA: I want to tell him how wonderful he was. We let him go so casually. I want to tell him how we all feel about him. —Forgive me, let me walk about a minute. —Yes, of course, Ermengarde—it's best to speak of him.

LUCIA (*In a low voice to Genevieve*): Isn't there anything I can do?

GENEVIEVE: No, no. Only time, only the passing of time can help in these things.

(*Leonora, straying about the room, finds herself near the door to the hall at the moment that her son Roderick enters. He links his arm with hers and leads her back to the table.*)

RODERICK: What's the matter, anyway? What are you so glum about? The skating was fine today.

CHARLES: Sit down, young man. I have something to say to you.

RODERICK: Everybody was there. Lucia skated in the corners with Dan Creighton the whole time. When'll it be, Lucia, when'll it be?

LUCIA: I don't know what you mean.

RODERICK: Lucia's leaving us soon, Mother. Dan Creighton, of all people.

CHARLES (*Ominously*): Roderick, I have something to say to you.

RODERICK: Yes, Father.

CHARLES: Is it true, Roderick, that you made yourself conspicuous last night at the country club—at a Christmas Eve dance, too?

LEONORA: Not now, Charles, I beg of you. This is Christmas dinner.

RODERICK (*Loudly*): No, I didn't.

LUCIA: Really, Father, he didn't. It was that dreadful Johnny Lewis.

CHARLES: I don't want to hear about Johnny Lewis. I want to know whether a son of mine . . .

LEONORA: Charles, I beg of you . . .

CHARLES: The first family of this city!

RODERICK *(Rising)*: I hate this town and everything about it. I always did.

CHARLES: You behaved like a spoiled puppy, sir, an ill-bred spoiled puppy.

RODERICK: What did I do? What did I do that was wrong?

CHARLES: You were drunk and you were rude to the daughters of my best friends.

GENEVIEVE *(Striking the table)*: Nothing in the world deserves an ugly scene like this. Charles, I'm ashamed of you.

RODERICK: Great God, you gotta get drunk in this town to forget how dull it is. Time passes so slowly here that it stands still, that's what's the trouble.

CHARLES: Well, young man, we can employ your time. You will leave the university and you will come into the Bayard factory on January second.

RODERICK *(At the door into the hall)*: I have better things to do than to go into your old factory. I'm going somewhere where time passes, my God!

(He goes out into the hall.)

LEONORA: *(Rising)*: Roderick, Roderick, come here just a moment. —Charles where can he go?

LUCIA *(Rising)*: Shh, Mother. He'll come back. Now I have to go upstairs and pack my trunk.

LEONORA: I won't have any children left!

LUCIA: Shh, Mother. He'll come back. He's only gone to California or somewhere. Cousin Ermengarde has done most of my packing—thanks a thousand times, Cousin Ermengarde. *(She kisses her mother)* I won't be long. *(She runs out into the hall)*

(Genevieve and Leonora put on their white hair.)

ERMENGARDE: It's a very beautiful day. On the way home from church I stopped and saw Mrs. Foster a moment. Her arthritis comes and goes.

LEONORA: Is she actually in pain, dear?

ERMENGARDE: Oh, she says it'll all be the same in a hundred years!

LEONORA: Yes, she's a brave little stoic.

CHARLES: Come now, a little white meat, Mother?—Mary, pass my cousin's plate.

LEONORA: What is it, Mary? —Oh, here's a telegram from them in Paris! "Love and Christmas greetings to all." I told them we'd be eating some of their wedding cake and thinking about them today. It seems to be all decided that they will settle down in the east, Ermengarde. I can't even have my daughter for a neighbor. They hope to build before long somewhere on the shore north of New York.

GENEVIEVE: There is no shore north of New York.

LEONORA: Well, east or west or whatever it is.

(Pause.)

CHARLES: My, what a dark day.

(He puts on his white hair. Pause.)

How slowly time passes without any young people in the house.

LEONORA: I have three children somewhere.

CHARLES *(Blunderingly offering comfort)*: Well, one of them gave his life for his country.

LEONORA *(Sadly)*: And one of them is selling aluminum in China.

GENEVIEVE *(Slowly working herself up to a hysterical crisis)*: I can stand everything but this terrible soot everywhere. We should have moved long ago. We're surrounded by factories. We have to change the window curtains every week.

LEONORA: Why, Genevieve!

GENEVIEVE: I can't stand it. I can't stand it any more. I'm going abroad. It's not only the soot that comes through the very walls of this house; it's the *thoughts,* it's the thought of what has been and what might have been here. And the feeling about this house of the years *grinding away.* My mother died yesterday—not twenty-five years ago. Oh, I'm going to live and die abroad! Yes, I'm going to be the American old maid living and dying in a pension in Munich or Florence.

ERMENGARDE: Genevieve, you're tired.

CHARLES: Come, Genevieve, take a good drink of cold water. Mary, open the window a minute.

GENEVIEVE: I'm sorry. I'm sorry.

(Genevieve hurries tearfully out into the hall.)

ERMENGARDE: Dear Genevieve will come back to us, I think.

(She rises and starts toward the dark portal.)

You should have been out today, Leonora. It was one of those days when everything was encircled with ice. Very pretty, indeed.

(Charles rises and starts after her.)

CHARLES: Leonora, I used to go skating with Father on mornings like this. I wish I felt a little better.

LEONORA: What! Have I got two invalids on my hands at once? Now, Cousin Ermengarde, you must get better and help me nurse Charles.

ERMENGARDE: I'll do my best.

(She turns at the very portal and comes back to the table.)

CHARLES: Well, Leonora, I'll do what you ask. I'll write the puppy a letter of forgiveness and apology. It's Christmas Day. I'll cable it. That's what I'll do.

(He goes out the dark door.)

LEONORA *(Drying her eyes)*: Ermengarde, it's such a comfort having you here with me. Mary, I really can't eat anything. Well, perhaps, a sliver of white meat.

ERMENGARDE *(Very old)*: I spoke to Mrs. Keene for a moment coming out of church. She asked after the young people. —At church I felt very proud sitting under our windows, Leonora, and our brass tablets. The Bayard aisle—it's a regular Bayard aisle and I love it.

LEONORA: Ermengarde, would you be very angry with me if I went and stayed with the young people a little this spring?

ERMENGARDE: Why, no. I know how badly they want you and need you. Especially now that they're about to build a new house.

LEONORA: You wouldn't be angry? This house is yours as long as you want it, remember.

ERMENGARDE: I don't see why the rest of you dislike it. I like it more than I can say.

LEONORA: I won't be long. I'll be back in no time and we can have some more of our readings aloud in the evening. *(She kisses her and goes into the hall)*

(Ermengarde left alone, eats slowly and talks to Mary.)

ERMENGARDE: Really, Mary, I'll change my mind. If you'll ask Bertha to be good enough to make me a little eggnog. A dear little eggnog. —Such a nice letter this morning from Mrs. Bayard, Mary. Such a nice letter. They're having their first Christmas dinner in the new house. They must be very happy. They call her Mother Bayard, she says, as though she were an old lady. And she says she finds it more comfortable to come and go in a wheelchair. —Such a dear letter . . . And Mary, I can tell you a secret. It's still a great secret, mind! They're expecting a grandchild. Isn't that good news! Now I'll read a little.

(She props a book up before her, still dipping a spoon into a custard from time to time. She grows from very old to immensely old. She sighs. The book falls down. She finds a cane beside her, and soon totters into the dark portal, murmuring:)

"Dear little Roderick and little Lucia."

END OF PLAY

Queens of France

CHARACTERS

MARIE-SIDONIE CRESSAUX
M'SU CAHUSAC
MADAME PUGEOT
MAMSELLE POINTEVIN

SETTING

A lawyer's office in New Orleans, 1869.

The office door to the street is hung with a reed curtain, through which one obtains a glimpse of a public park in sunshine.

A small bell tinkles. After a pause it rings again.

Marie-Sidonie Cressaux pushes the reeds apart and peers in. She is an attractive young woman equal to any situation in life except a summons to a lawyer's office.

M'su Cahusac, a dry little man with sharp black eyes, enters from an inner room.

MARIE-SIDONIE *(Indicating a letter in her hand)*: You . . . you have asked me to come and see you.

M. CAHUSAC *(Severe and brief)*: Your name, madame?

MARIE-SIDONIE: Mamselle Marie-Sidonie Cressaux, m'su.

M. CAHUSAC *(After a pause)*: Yes. Kindly be seated, mamselle.

(He goes to his desk and opens a great many drawers, collecting documents from each. Presently having assembled a large bundle, he returns to the center of the room and says abruptly:)

Mamselle, this interview is to be regarded by you as strictly confidential.

MARIE-SIDONIE: Yes, m'su.

M. CAHUSAC *(After looking at her sternly a moment)*: May I ask if mamselle is able to bear the shock of surprise, of good or bad news?

MARIE-SIDONIE: Why . . . yes, m'su.

M. CAHUSAC: Then if you are Mamselle Marie-Sidonie Cressaux, the daughter of Baptiste-Anténor Cressaux, it is my duty to inform you that you are in danger.

MARIE-SIDONIE: I am in danger, m'su?

(He returns to his desk, opens further drawers, and returns with more papers. She follows him with bewildered eyes.)

M. CAHUSAC: Mamselle, in addition to my duties as a lawyer in this city, I am the representative here of a historical society in Paris. Will you please try and follow me, mamselle? This historical society has been engaged in tracing the descendants of the true heir to the French throne. As you know, at the time of the Revolution, in 1795, to be exact, mamselle, the true, lawful, and legitimate heir to the French throne disappeared. It was rumored that this boy, who was then ten years old, came to America and lived for a time in New Orleans. We now know that the rumor was true. We now know that he here begot legitimate issue, that this legitimate issue in turn begot legitimate issue, and that—*(Marie-Sidonie suddenly starts searching for something in her shopping bag)* Mamselle, may I have the honor of your attention a little longer?

MARIE-SIDONIE *(Choking)*: My fan—my, my fan, m'su. *(She finds it and at once begins to fan herself wildly. Suddenly she cries out)* M'su, what danger am I in?

M. CAHUSAC *(Sternly)*: If mamselle will exercise a moment's—one moment's—patience, she will know all . . . That legitimate issue here begot legitimate issue, and the royal line of France has been traced to a certain *(He consults his documents)* Baptiste-Anténor Cressaux.

MARIE-SIDONIE *(Her fan stops and she stares at him)*: Ba't—Ba'tiste! . . .

M. CAHUSAC *(Leaning forward with menacing emphasis)*: Mamselle, can you *prove* that you are the daughter of Baptiste-Anténor Cressaux?

MARIE-SIDONIE: Why . . . Why . . .

M. CAHUSAC: Mamselle, have you a certificate of your parents' marriage?

MARIE-SIDONIE: Yes, m'su.

M. CAHUSAC: If it turns out to be valid, and if it is true that you have no true lawful and legitimate brothers—

MARIE-SIDONIE: No, m'su.

M. CAHUSAC: Then, mamselle, I have nothing further to do than to announce to you that you are the true and long-lost heir to the throne of France.

(He draws himself up, approaches her with great dignity, and kisses her hand. Marie-Sidonie begins to cry. He goes to the desk, pours out a glass of water and, murmuring "Your Royal Highness," offers it to her.)

MARIE-SIDONIE: M'su Cahusac, I am very sorry . . . But there must be some mistake. My father was a poor sailor . . . a . . . a poor sailor.

M. CAHUSAC *(Reading from his papers)*: . . . A distinguished and esteemed navigator.

MARIE-SIDONIE: . . . A poor sailor . . .

M. CAHUSAC *(Firmly)*: . . . Navigator . . .

(Pause. Marie-Sidonie looks about, stricken.)

MARIE-SIDONIE *(As before, suddenly and loudly)*: M'su, what danger am I in?

M. CAHUSAC *(Approaching her and lowering his voice)*: As Your Royal Highness knows, there are several families in New Orleans that claim, without documents *(He rattles the vellum and seals in his hand)*, without proof—that pretend to the blood royal. The danger from them, however, is not great. The real danger is from France. From the impassioned Republicans.

MARIE-SIDONIE: Impass . . .

M. CAHUSAC: But Your Royal Highness has only to put Herself into my hands.

MARIE-SIDONIE *(Crying again)*: Please do not call me "Your Royal Highness."

M. CAHUSAC: You . . . give me permission to call you Madame de Cressaux?

MARIE-SIDONIE: Yes, m'su. Mamselle Cressaux. I am Marie-Sidonie Cressaux.

M. CAHUSAC: Am I mistaken . . . hmm . . . in saying that you have children?

MARIE-SIDONIE *(Faintly)*: Yes, m'su. I have three children.

(M. Cahusac looks at her thoughtfully a moment and returns to his desk.)

M. CAHUSAC: Madame, from now on thousands of eyes will be fixed upon you, the eyes of the whole world, madame.

I cannot urge you too strongly to be very discreet, to be very circumspect.

MARIE-SIDONIE *(Rising, abruptly, nervously)*: M'su Cahusac, I do not wish to have anything to do with this. There is a mistake somewhere. I thank you very much, but there is a mistake somewhere. I do not know where. I must go now.

M. CAHUSAC *(Darts forward)*: But, madame, you do not know what you are doing. Your rank cannot be dismissed as easily as that. Do you not know that in a month or two, all the newspapers in the world, including the New Orleans *Times-Picayune*, will publish your name? The first nobles of France will cross the ocean to call upon you. The bishop of Louisiana will call upon you . . . the mayor . . .

MARIE-SIDONIE: No, no.

M. CAHUSAC: You will be given a great deal of money—and several palaces.

MARIE-SIDONIE: No, no.

M. CAHUSAC: And a guard of soldiers to protect you.

MARIE-SIDONIE: No, no.

M. CAHUSAC: You will be made president of Le Petit Salon and queen of the Mardi Gras . . . Another sip of water, Your Royal Highness.

MARIE-SIDONIE: Oh, m'su, what shall I do? . . . Oh, m'su, save me! —I do not want the bishop or the mayor.

M. CAHUSAC: You ask me what you shall do?

MARIE-SIDONIE: Oh, yes, oh, my God!

M. CAHUSAC: For the present, return to your home and lie down. A little rest and a little reflection will tell you what you have to do. Then come and see me Thursday morning.

MARIE-SIDONIE: I think there must be a mistake somewhere.

M. CAHUSAC: May I be permitted to ask Madame de Cressaux a question: Could I have the privilege of presenting Her—until the great announcement takes place—with a small gift of . . . money?

MARIE-SIDONIE: No, no.

M. CAHUSAC: The historical society is not rich. The historical society has difficulty in pursuing the search for the last documents that will confirm madame's exalted rank, but they would be very happy to advance a certain sum to madame, subscribed by her devoted subjects.

MARIE-SIDONIE: Please no. I do not wish any. I must go now.

M. CAHUSAC: Let me beg madame not to be alarmed. For the present a little rest and reflection . . .

(The bell rings. He again bends over her hand, murmuring ". . . obedient servant and devoted subject . . .")

MARIE-SIDONIE *(In confusion)*: Good-bye, good morning, M. Cahusac. *(She lingers at the door a moment, then returns and says in great earnestness)* Oh, M. Cahusac, do not let the bishop come and see me. The mayor, yes—but not the bishop.

(Enter Madame Pugeot, a plump little bourgeoise in black. Exit Marie-Sidonie.

M. Cahusac kisses the graciously extended hand of Madame Pugeot.)

MME. PUGEOT: Good morning, M. Cahusac.

M. CAHUSAC: Your Royal Highness.

MME. PUGEOT: What business can you possibly be having with that dreadful Marie Cressaux! Do you not know that she is an abandoned woman?

M. CAHUSAC: Alas, we are in the world, Your Royal Highness. For the present I must earn a living as best I can. Mamselle Cressaux is arranging about the purchase of a house and garden.

MME. PUGEOT: Purchase, M. Cahusac, phi! You know very well that she has half a dozen houses and gardens already. She persuades every one of her lovers to give her a little house and garden. She is beginning to own the whole parish of Saint-Magloire.

M. CAHUSAC: Will Your Royal Highness condescend to sit down? *(She does)* And how is the royal family this morning?

MME. PUGEOT: Only so-so, m'su Cahusac.

M. CAHUSAC: The Archduchess of Tuscany?

MME. PUGEOT *(Fanning herself with a turkey's wing)*: A cold. One of her colds. I sometimes think the dear child will never live to see her pearls.

M. CAHUSAC: And the Dauphin, Your Royal Highness?

MME. PUGEOT: Still, still amusing himself in the city, as young men will. Wine, gambling, bad company. At least it keeps him out of harm.

M. CAHUSAC: And the Duke of Burgundy?

MME. PUGEOT: Imagine! The poor child has a sty in his eye!

M. CAHUSAC: Tchk-tchk! *(With solicitude)* In which eye, madame?

MME. PUGEOT: In the left!

M. CAHUSAC: Tchk-tchk! And the Prince of Lorraine and the Duke of Berry?

MME. PUGEOT: They are fairly well, but they seem to mope in their cradle. Their first teeth, my dear chamberlain.

M. CAHUSAC: And your husband, madame?

MME. PUGEOT *(Rises, walks back and forth a moment, then stands still)*: From now on we are never to mention him again—while we are discussing these matters. It is to be understood that he is my husband in a manner of speaking only. He has no part in my true life. He has chosen to scoff at my birth and my rank, but he will see what he will see . . . Naturally I have not told him about the proofs that you and I have collected. I have not the heart to let him see how unimportant he will become.

M. CAHUSAC: Unimportant, indeed!

MME. PUGEOT: So remember, we do not mention him in the same breath *with these matters*!

M. CAHUSAC: You must trust me, madame. *(Softly, with significance)* And *your* health, Your Royal Highness?

MME. PUGEOT: Oh, very well, thank you. Excellent. I used

to do quite poorly, as you remember, but since this wonderful news I have been more than well, God be praised.

M. CAHUSAC *(As before, with lifted eyebrows)*: I beg of you to do nothing unwise. I beg of you . . . The little new life we are all anticipating . . .

MME. PUGEOT: Have no fear, my dear chamberlain. What is dear to France is dear to me.

M. CAHUSAC: When I think, madame, of how soon we shall be able to announce your rank—when I think that this time next year you will be enjoying all the honors and privileges that are your due, I am filled with a pious joy.

MME. PUGEOT: God's will be done, God's will be done.

M. CAHUSAC: At all events, I am particularly happy to see that Your Royal Highness is in the best of health, for I have had a piece of disappointing news.

MME. PUGEOT: Chamberlain, you are not going to tell me that Germany has at last declared war upon my country?

M. CAHUSAC: No, madame.

MME. PUGEOT: You greatly frightened me last week. I could scarcely sleep. Such burdens as I have! My husband tells me that I cried out in my sleep the words: *"Paris, I come!"*

M. CAHUSAC: Sublime, madame!

MME. PUGEOT: *"Paris, I come,"* like that. I cried out twice in my sleep: *"Paris, I come."* Oh, these are anxious times; I am on my way to the cathedral now. This Bismarck does not understand me. We must avoid a war at all costs, M. Cahusac . . . Then what is your news?

M. CAHUSAC: My anxiety at present is more personal. The historical society in Paris is now confirming the last proofs of your claim. They have secretaries at work in all the archives: Madrid, Vienna, Constantinople . . .

MME. PUGEOT: Constantinople!

M. CAHUSAC: All this requires a good deal of money and the society is not rich. We have been driven to a painful decision. The society must sell one of the royal jewels or one of the royal *fournitures* which I am guarding upstairs. The historical society has written me, madame, ordering me to send them at once—the royal christening robe.

MME. PUGEOT: Never!

M. CAHUSAC: The very robe under which Charlemagne was christened, the Charles, the Henris, the Louis, to lie under a glass in the Louvre. *(Softly)* And this is particularly painful to me because I had hoped—it was, in fact, the dream of my life—to see at least one of your children christened under all those fleurs-de-lis.

MME. PUGEOT: It shall not go to the Louvre. I forbid it.

M. CAHUSAC: But what can I do? I offered them the scepter. I offered them the orb. I even offered them the mug which Your Royal Highness has already purchased. But no! The christening robe it must be.

MME. PUGEOT: It shall not leave America! *(Clutching her handbag)* How much are they asking for it?

M. CAHUSAC: Oh, madame, since it is the Ministry of Museums and Monuments they are asking a great many thousands of francs.

MME. PUGEOT: And how much would they ask their Queen?

M. CAHUSAC *(Sadly)*: Madame, madame, I cannot see you purchasing those things which are rightly yours.

MME. PUGEOT: I will purchase it. I shall sell the house on the Chausée Sainte Anne.

M. CAHUSAC *(Softly)*: If Your Majesty will give five hundred dollars of Her money I shall add five hundred of my own.

MME. PUGEOT *(Shaken)*: Five hundred. Five hundred . . . Well, you will be repaid many times, my dear chamberlain, when I am restored to my position *(She thinks a moment)* Tomorrow at three. I shall bring you the papers for the sale of the house. You will do everything quietly. My husband will be told about it in due time.

M. CAHUSAC: I understand. I shall be very discreet.

(The bell rings. M. Cahusac turns to the door as Mamselle Pointevin starts to enter.)

I shall be free to see you in a few moments, mamselle. Madame Pugeot has still some details to discuss with me.

MLLE. POINTEVIN: I cannot wait long, m'su Cahusac.

M. CAHUSAC: A few minutes in the park, thank you, mamselle.

(Exit Mamselle Pointevin.)

MME. PUGEOT: Has that poor girl business with a lawyer, M. Cahusac? A poor schoolteacher like that?

M. CAHUSAC *(Softly)*: Mamselle Pointevin has taken it into her head to make her will.

MME. PUGEOT *(Laughs superiorly)*: Three chairs and a broken plate. *(Rising)* Well, tomorrow at three . . . I am now going to the cathedral. I do not forget the great responsibilities for which I must prepare myself—the army, the navy, the treasury, the appointment of bishops. When I am dead, my dear chamberlain—

M. CAHUSAC: Madame!

MME. PUGEOT: No, no!—even I must die some day . . . When I am dead, when I am laid with my ancestors, let it never be said of me . . . By the way, where shall I be laid?

M. CAHUSAC: In the church of Saint Denis, Your Royal Highness?

MME. PUGEOT: Not in Notre Dame?

M. CAHUSAC: No, madame.

MME. PUGEOT *(Meditatively)*: Not in Notre Dame. Well *(Brightening)* we will cross these bridges when we get to them. *(Extending her hand)* Good morning and all my thanks, my dear chamberlain.

M. CAHUSAC: . . . Highness's most obedient servant and devoted subject.

MME. PUGEOT *(Beautifully filling the doorway)*: Pray for us.

> *(Exit Madame Pugeot. M. Cahusac goes to the door and bows to Mamselle Pointevin in the street.)*

M. CAHUSAC: Now mamselle, if you will have the goodness to enter.

> *(Enter Mamselle Pointevin, a tall and indignant spinster.)*

MLLE. POINTEVIN: M'su Cahusac, it is something new for you to keep me waiting in the public square while you carry on your wretched little business with a vulgar woman like Madame Pugeot. When I condescend to call upon you, my good man, you will have the goodness to receive me at once. Either I am, or I am not, Henriette, Queen of France, Queen of Navarre and Aquitania. It is not fitting that we cool our heels on a public bench among the nursemaids of remote New Orleans. It is hard enough for me to *hide myself* as a schoolmistress in this city, without having to suffer further humiliations at your hands. Is there no respect due to the blood of Charlemagne?

M. CAHUSAC: Madame . . .

MLLE. POINTEVIN: Or, sir, are you bored and overfed on the company of queens?

M. CAHUSAC: Madame . . .

MLLE. POINTEVIN: You are busy with the law. Good! Know, then, *La loi—c'est moi. (Sitting down and smoothing out her skirts)* Now what is it you have to say?

M. CAHUSAC *(Pauses a moment, then approaches her with tightly pressed lips and narrowed eyes)*: Your Royal Highness, I have received a letter from France. There is some discouraging news.

MLLE. POINTEVIN: No! I cannot afford to buy another thing. I possess the scepter and the orb. Sell the rest to the Louvre, if you must. I can buy them back when my rank is announced.

M. CAHUSAC: Alas!

MLLE. POINTEVIN: What do you mean "alas"?

M. CAHUSAC: Will Your Royal Highness condescend to read the letter I have received from France?

MLLE. POINTEVIN (*Unfurls the letter, but continues looking before her, splendidly*): Have they no bread? Give them cake. (*She starts to read, is shaken, suddenly returns it to him*) It is too long. It is too long . . . What does it say?

M. CAHUSAC: It is from the secretary of the historical society. The society remains convinced that you are the true and long-sought heir to the throne of France.

MLLE. POINTEVIN: Convinced? Convinced? I should hope so.

M. CAHUSAC: But to make this conviction public, madame, to announce it throughout the newspapers of the world, including the New Orleans *Times-Picayune* . . .

MLLE. POINTEVIN: Yes, go on!

M. CAHUSAC: To establish your claim among all your rivals. To establish your claim beyond any possible ridicule . . .

MLLE. POINTEVIN: Ridicule!

M. CAHUSAC: All they lack is one little document. One little but important document. They had hoped to find it in the archives of Madrid. Madame, it is not there.

MLLE. POINTEVIN: It is not there? Then where is it?

M. CAHUSAC: We do not know, Your Royal Highness. We are in despair.

MLLE. POINTEVIN: Ridicule, M. Cahusac!

(*She stares at him, her hand on her mouth.*)

M. CAHUSAC: It may be in Constantinople. It may be in Vienna. Naturally we shall continue to search for it. We shall continue to search for generations, for centuries, if need be. But I must confess this is a very discouraging blow.

MLLE. POINTEVIN: Generations! Centuries! But I am not a young girl, m'su Cahusac. Their letter says over and over again that I am the heir to the throne. (*She begins to cry*)

(M. Cahusac discreetly proffers her a glass of water.)

Thank you.

M. CAHUSAC *(Suddenly changing his tone, with firmness)*: Madame, you should know that the society suspects the lost document to be in your possession. The society feels sure that the document has been handed down from generation to generation in your family.

MLLE. POINTEVIN: In my possession!

M. CAHUSAC *(Firmly)*: Madame, are you concealing something from us?

MLLE. POINTEVIN: Why . . . no.

M. CAHUSAC: Are you playing with us, as a cat plays with a mouse?

MLLE. POINTEVIN: No, indeed I'm not.

M. CAHUSAC: Why is that paper not in Madrid, or in Constantinople or in Vienna? *Because it is in your house.* You live in what was once your father's house, do you not?

MLLE. POINTEVIN: Yes, I do.

M. CAHUSAC: Go back to it. Look through every old trunk . . .

MLLE. POINTEVIN: Every old trunk!

M. CAHUSAC: Examine especially the linings. Look through all the tables and desks. Pry into the joints. You will find perhaps a secret drawer, a secret panel.

MLLE. POINTEVIN: M'su Cahusac!

M. CAHUSAC: Examine the walls. Examine the boards of the floor. It may be hidden beneath them.

MLLE. POINTEVIN: I will. I'll go now.

M. CAHUSAC: Have you any old clothes of your father?

MLLE. POINTEVIN: Yes, I have.

M. CAHUSAC: It may be sewn into the lining.

MLLE. POINTEVIN: I'll look.

M. CAHUSAC: Madame, in what suit of clothes was your father buried?

MLLE. POINTEVIN: In his best, m'su.

(She gives a sudden scream under her hand as this thought strikes home. They stare at one another significantly.)

M. CAHUSAC: Take particular pains to look under all steps. These kinds of documents are frequently found under steps. You will find it. If it is not in Madrid, it is there.

MLLE. POINTEVIN: But if I can't find it! *(She sits down, suddenly spent)* No one will ever know that I am the Queen of France. *(Pause)* I am very much afraid, M'su Cahusac, that I shall never find that document in my four rooms. I know every inch of them. But I shall look. *(She draws her hand across her forehead, as though awaking from a dream)* It is all very strange. You know, M'su Cahusac, I think there may have been a mistake somewhere. It was so beautiful while it lasted. It made even schoolteaching a pleasure, m'su . . . And my memoirs. I have just written my memoirs up to the moment when your wonderful announcement came to me—the account of my childhood *incognito*, the little girl in Louisiana who did not guess the great things before her. But before I go, may I ask something of you? Will you have the historical society write me a letter saying that they seriously think I may be . . . the person . . . the person they are looking for? I wish to keep the letter in the trunk with the orb and . . . with the scepter. You know . . . the more I think of it, the more I think there must have been a mistake somewhere.

M. CAHUSAC: The very letter you have in mind is here, madame. *(He gives it to her)*

MLLE. POINTEVIN: Thank you. And M'su Cahusac, may I ask another favor of you?

M. CAHUSAC: Certainly, madame.

MLLE. POINTEVIN: Please, never mention this . . . this whole affair to anyone in New Orleans.

M. CAHUSAC: Madame, not unless you wish it.

MLLE. POINTEVIN: Good morning—good morning, and thank you. *(Her handkerchief to one eye, she goes out)*

(M. Cahusac goes to his desk.

The bell rings. The reed curtain is parted and a Negro boy pushes in a wheelchair containing a woman of some hundred years of age. She is wrapped in shawls, like a mummy, and wears a scarf about her head, and green spectacles on her nose. The mummy extends a hand which M. Cahusac kisses devotedly, murmuring, "Your Royal Highness.")

END OF PLAY

Pullman Car Hiawatha

CHARACTERS

	THE STAGE MANAGER
Compartment Three:	AN INSANE WOMAN, Mrs. Churchill
	A MALE ATTENDANT, Mr. Morgan
	THE FEMALE ATTENDANT, A trained nurse
Compartment Two:	PHILIP
Compartment One:	HARRIET, Philip's young wife
Lower One:	A MAIDEN LADY
Lower Three:	A MIDDLE-AGED DOCTOR
Lower Five:	A STOUT, AMIABLE WOMAN OF FIFTY
Lower Seven:	AN ENGINEER, Bill, going to California
Lower Nine:	AN ENGINEER, Fred
	THE PORTER, Harrison
	GROVER'S CORNERS, OHIO
	THE FIELD
	THE TRAMP
	PARKERSBURG, OHIO
	THE WORKMAN, Mr. Krüger, a ghost

THE WORKER, a watchman

A MECHANIC

The Hours: TEN O'CLOCK, ELEVEN O'CLOCK, TWELVE O'CLOCK

The Planets: SATURN, VENUS, JUPITER, EARTH

The Archangels: GABRIEL, MICHAEL

SETTING

A Pullman car making its way from New York to Chicago, December 1930.

At the back of the stage is a balcony or bridge or runway leading out of sight in both directions. Two flights of stairs descend from it to the stage. There is no further scenery.

At the rise of the curtain The Stage Manager is making lines with a piece of chalk on the floor of the stage by the footlights.

THE STAGE MANAGER: This is the plan of a Pullman car. Its name is Hiawatha and on December twenty-first it is on its way from New York to Chicago. Here at your left are three compartments. Here is the aisle and five lowers. The berths are all full, uppers and lowers, but for the purposes of this play we are limiting our interest to the people in the lower berths on the further side only.

The berths are already made-up. It is half past nine. Most of the passengers are in bed behind the green curtains. They are dropping their shoes on the floor, or wrestling with their trousers, or wondering whether they dare hide their valuables in the pillow slips during the night.

All right! Come on, everybody!

(The actors enter carrying chairs. Each improvises his berth by placing two chairs "facing one another" in his chalk-marked space. They then sit in one chair, profile to the audience, and rest their feet on the other. This must do for lying in bed. The passengers in the compartments do the same.)

LOWER ONE: Porter, be sure and wake me up at quarter of six.

THE PORTER: Yes, ma'am.

LOWER ONE: I know I shan't sleep a wink, but I want to be told when it's quarter of six.

THE PORTER: Yes, ma'am.

LOWER SEVEN *(Putting his head through the curtains)*: Hsst! Porter! Hsst! How the hell do you turn on this other light?

THE PORTER *(Fussing with it)*: I'm afraid it's outta order, suh. You'll have to use the other end.

THE STAGE MANAGER *(Falsetto, substituting for some woman in an upper berth)*: May I ask if someone in this car will be kind enough to lend me some aspirin?

THE PORTER *(Rushing about)*: Yes, ma'am.

LOWER NINE *(One of the engineers, descending the aisle and falling into Lower Five)*: Sorry, lady, sorry. Made a mistake.

LOWER FIVE *(Grumbling)*: Never in all my born days!

LOWER ONE *(In a shrill whisper)*: Porter! Porter!

THE PORTER: Yes, ma'am.

LOWER ONE: My hot water bag's leaking. I guess you'll have to take it away. I'll have to do without it tonight. How awful!

LOWER FIVE *(Sharply to the passenger above her)*: Young man, you mind your own business, or I'll report you to the conductor.

THE STAGE MANAGER *(Substituting for Upper Five)*: Sorry, ma'am, I didn't mean to upset you. My suspenders fell down and I was trying to catch them.

LOWER FIVE: Well, here they are. Now go to sleep. Everybody seems to be rushing into my berth tonight. *(She puts her head out)* Porter! Porter! Be a good soul and bring me a glass of water, will you? I'm parched.

LOWER NINE: Bill!

(No answer.)

Bill!

LOWER SEVEN: Yea? Wha'd'ya want?

LOWER NINE: Slip me one of those magazines, willya?

LOWER SEVEN: Which one d'ya want?

LOWER NINE: Either one. *Detective Stories.* Either one.

LOWER SEVEN: Aw, Fred. I'm just in the middle of one of 'em in *Detective Stories.*

LOWER NINE: That's all right. I'll take the *Western.* —Thanks.

THE STAGE MANAGER *(To the actors)*: All right! —Sh! Sh! Sh!
(To the audience) Now I want you to hear them thinking.

(There is a pause and then they all begin a murmuring-swishing noise, very soft. In turn each one of them can be heard above the others.)

LOWER FIVE *(The Woman of Fifty)*: Let's see: I've got the doll for the baby. And the slip-on for Marietta. And the fountain pen for Herbert. And the subscription to *Time* for George . . .

LOWER SEVEN *(Bill)*: God! Lillian, if you don't turn out to be what I think you are, I don't know what I'll do. —I guess it's bad politics to let a woman know that you're going all the way to California to see her. I'll think up a song-and-dance about a business trip or something. Was I ever as hot and bothered about anyone like this before? Well, there was Martha. But that was different. I'd better try and read or I'll go cuckoo. "How did you know it was ten o'clock when the visitor left the house?" asked the detective. "Because at ten o'clock," answered the girl, "I always turn out the lights in the conservatory and in the back hall. As I was coming

down the stairs I heard the master talking to someone at the front door. I heard him say, 'Well, good night...'"
—Gee, I don't feel like reading; I'll just think about Lillian. That yellow hair. Them eyes!...

LOWER THREE *(The Doctor reads aloud to himself the most hair-raising material from a medical journal, every now and then punctuating his reading with an interrogative "So?")*

LOWER ONE *(The Maiden Lady)*: I know I'll be awake all night. I might just as well make up my mind to it now. I can't imagine what got hold of that hot water bag to leak on the train of all places. Well now, I'll lie on my right side and breathe deeply and think of beautiful things, and perhaps I can doze off a bit.

(And lastly:)

LOWER NINE *(Fred)*: That was the craziest thing I ever did. It's set me back three whole years. I could have saved up thirty thousand dollars by now, if I'd only stayed over here. What business had I got to fool with contracts with the goddam Soviets. Hell, I thought it would be interesting. Interesting, what the hell! It's set me back three whole years. I don't even know if the company'll take me back. I'm green, that's all. I just don't grow up.

(The Stage Manager strides toward them with lifted hand, crying, "Hush," and their whispering ceases.)

THE STAGE MANAGER: That'll do! —Just one minute. Porter!
THE PORTER *(Appearing at the left)*: Yessuh.
THE STAGE MANAGER: It's your turn to think.

(The Porter is very embarrassed.)

Don't you want to? You have a right to.

THE PORTER *(Torn between the desire to release his thoughts and his shyness)*: Ah . . . ah . . . I'm only thinkin' about my home in Chicago and . . . and my life insurance.

THE STAGE MANAGER: That's right.

THE PORTER: . . . Well, thank you . . . Thank you.

(The Porter slips away, blushing violently, in an agony of self-consciousness and pleasure.)

THE STAGE MANAGER *(To the audience)*: He's a good fellow, Harrison is. Just shy.

(To the actors again) Now the compartments, please.

(The berths fall into shadow.

Philip is standing at the door connecting his compartment with his wife's.)

PHILIP: Are you all right, angel?

HARRIET: Yes. I don't know what was the matter with me during dinner.

PHILIP: Shall I close the door?

HARRIET: Do see whether you can't put a chair against it that will hold it half open without banging.

PHILIP: There.—Good night, angel. If you can't sleep, call me and we'll sit up and play Russian Bank.

HARRIET: You're thinking of that awful time when we sat up every night for a week . . . But at least I know I shall sleep tonight. The noise of the wheels has become sort of nice and homely. What state are we in?

PHILIP: We're tearing through Ohio. We'll be in Indiana soon.

HARRIET: I know those little towns full of horse blocks.

PHILIP: Well, we'll reach Chicago very early. I'll call you. Sleep tight.

HARRIET: Sleep tight, darling.

(Philip returns to his own compartment. In Compartment Three, the male attendant tips his chair back against the

wall and smokes a cigar. The trained nurse knits a stocking. The insane woman leans her forehead against the windowpane, that is, stares into the audience.)

THE INSANE WOMAN (*Her words have a dragging, complaining sound, but lack any conviction*): Don't take me there. Don't take me there.

THE FEMALE ATTENDANT: Wouldn't you like to lie down, dearie?

THE INSANE WOMAN: I want to get off the train. I want to go back to New York.

THE FEMALE ATTENDANT: Wouldn't you like me to brush your hair again? It's such a nice feeling.

THE INSANE WOMAN (*Going to the door*): I want to get off the train. I want to open the door.

THE FEMALE ATTENDANT (*Taking one of her hands*): Such a noise! You'll wake up all the nice people. Come and I'll tell you a story about the place we're going to.

THE INSANE WOMAN: I don't want to go to that place.

THE FEMALE ATTENDANT: Oh, it's lovely! There are lawns and gardens everywhere. I never saw such a lovely place. Just lovely.

THE INSANE WOMAN (*Lies down on the bed*): Are there roses?

THE FEMALE ATTENDANT: Roses! Red, yellow, white . . . just everywhere.

THE MALE ATTENDANT (*After a pause*): That musta been Cleveland.

THE FEMALE ATTENDANT: I had a case in Cleveland once. Diabetes.

THE MALE ATTENDANT (*After another pause*): I wisht I had a radio here. Radios are good for *them*. I had a patient once that had to have the radio going every minute.

THE FEMALE ATTENDANT: Radios are lovely. My married niece has one. It's always going. It's wonderful.

THE INSANE WOMAN (*Half rising*): I'm not beautiful. I'm not beautiful as she was.

THE FEMALE ATTENDANT: Oh, I think you're beautiful! Beautiful.—Mr. Morgan, don't you think Mrs. Churchill is beautiful?

THE MALE ATTENDANT: Oh, fine lookin'! Regular movie star, Mrs. Churchill.

(The Insane Woman looks inquiringly at them and subsides. Harriet groans slightly. Smothers a cough. She gropes about with her hand and finds the bell.
The Porter knocks at her door.)

HARRIET *(Whispering)*: Come in. First, please close the door into my husband's room. Softly. Softly.

THE PORTER *(A plaintive porter)*: Yes, ma'am.

HARRIET: Porter, I'm not well. I'm sick. I must see a doctor.

THE PORTER: Why ma'am, they ain't no doctor . . .

HARRIET: Yes, when I was coming out from dinner I saw a man in one of the seats on *that* side, reading medical papers. Go and wake him up.

THE PORTER *(Flabbergasted)*: Ma'am, I cain't wake anybody up.

HARRIET: Yes, you can. Porter. Porter. Now don't argue with me. I'm very sick. It's my heart. Wake him up. Tell him it's my heart.

THE PORTER: Yes, ma'am.

(He goes into the aisle and starts pulling the shoulder of the man in Lower Three.)

LOWER THREE: Hello. Hello. What is it? Are we there?

(The Porter mumbles to him.)

I'll be right there. —Porter, is it a young woman or an old one?

THE PORTER: I dunno, suh. I guess she's kinda old, suh, but not so very old.

LOWER THREE: Tell her I'll be there in a minute and to lie quietly.

(The Porter enters Harriet's compartment. She has turned her head away.)

THE PORTER: He'll be here in a minute, ma'am. He says you lie quiet.

(Lower Three stumbles along the aisle muttering: "Damn these shoes!")

SOMEONE'S VOICE: Can't we have a little quiet in this car, please?

LOWER NINE *(Fred)*: Oh, shut up!

(The Doctor passes The Porter and enters Harriet's compartment. He leans over her, concealing her by his stooping figure.)

LOWER THREE: She's dead, Porter. Is there anyone on the train traveling with her?

THE PORTER: Yessuh. Dat's her husband in dere.

LOWER THREE: Idiot! Why didn't you call him? I'll go in and speak to him.

(The Stage Manager comes forward.)

THE STAGE MANAGER: All right. So much for the inside of the car. That'll be enough of that for the present. Now for its position geographically, meteorologically, astronomically, theologically considered.

Pullman Car Hiawatha, ten minutes of ten. December twenty-first, 1930. All ready.

(Some figures begin to appear on the balcony.)

No, no. It's not time for The Planets yet. Nor The Hours. *(They retire)*

(The Stage Manager claps his hands. A grinning boy in overalls enters from the left behind the berths.)

GROVER'S CORNERS, OHIO *(In a foolish voice as though he were reciting a piece at a Sunday school entertainment)*: I represent Grover's Corners, Ohio. Eight hundred twenty-one souls. "There's so much good in the worst of us and so much bad in the best of us, that it ill behooves any of us to criticize the rest of us." Robert Louis Stevenson. Thankya.

(He grins and goes out right.
Enter from the same direction somebody in shirt sleeves. This is a field.)

THE FIELD: I represent a field you are passing between Grover's Corners, Ohio, and Parkersburg, Ohio. In this field there are fifty-one gophers, two hundred and six field mice, six snakes and millions of bugs, insects, ants and spiders. All in their winter sleep. "What is so rare as a day in June? Then, if ever, come perfect days." *The Vision of Sir Launfal,* William Cullen—I mean James Russell Lowell. Thank you.

(Exit.
Enter a tramp.)

THE TRAMP: I just want to tell you that I'm a tramp that's been traveling under this car, Hiawatha, so I have a right to be in this play. I'm going from Rochester, New York, to Joliet, Illinois. It takes a lotta people to make a world. "On the road to Mandalay, where the flying fishes play and the sun comes up like thunder, over China, 'cross the bay." Frank W. Service. It's bitter cold. Thank you.

(Exit.
Enter a gentle old farmer's wife with three stringy young people.)

PARKERSBURG, OHIO: I represent Parkersburg, Ohio. Twenty-six hundred and four souls. I have seen all the dreadful havoc that alcohol has done and I hope no one here will ever touch a drop of the curse of this beautiful country.

(She beats a measure and they all sing unsteadily:)

"Throw out the lifeline! Throw out the lifeline! Someone is sinking today-ay . . ."

(The Stage Manager waves them away tactfully.
Enter a workman.)

THE WORKMAN: Ich bin der Arbeiter der hier sein Leben verlor. Bei der Sprengung für diese Brücke über die Sie in dem Moment fahren—*(The engine whistles for a trestle crossing)*—erschlug mich ein Felsbrock. Ich spiele jetzt als Geist in diesem Stück mit. "Vor sieben und achtzig Jahren haben unsere Väter auf diesem Kontinent eine neue Nation hervorgebracht . . ."

THE STAGE MANAGER *(Helpfully, to the audience)*: I'm sorry; that's in German. He says that he's the ghost of a workman who was killed while they were building the trestle over which the car Hiawatha is now passing— *(The engine whistles again)* —and he wants to appear in this play. A chunk of rock hit him while they were dynamiting. —His motto you know: "Three score and seven years ago our fathers brought forth upon this continent a new nation dedicated . . ." and so on. Thank you, Mr. Krüger.

(Exit the ghost.
      Enter another worker.)

THE WORKER: I'm a watchman in a tower near Parkers-
      burg, Ohio. I just want to tell you that I'm not asleep
      and that the signals are all right for this train. I hope you
      all have a fine trip. "If you can keep your head when all
      about you are losing theirs and blaming it on you . . ."
      Rudyard Kipling. Thank you.

(He exits.
      The Stage Manager comes forward.)

THE STAGE MANAGER: All right. That'll be enough of that.
      Now the weather.

(Enter a mechanic.)

A MECHANIC: It is eleven degrees above zero. The wind is
      north-northwest, velocity: fifty-seven. There is a field
      of low barometric pressure moving eastward from
      Saskatchewan to the eastern coast. Tomorrow it will be
      cold with some snow in the middle western states and
      northern New York. *(He exits)*
THE STAGE MANAGER: All right. Now for The Hours.
      (Helpfully to the audience) The minutes are gossips; the
      hours are philosophers; the years are theologians. The
      hours are philosophers with the exception of Twelve
      O'clock who is also a theologian. —Ready Ten O'clock!

*(The Hours are beautiful girls dressed like Elihu Vedder's
Pleiades. Each carries a great gold Roman numeral. They
pass slowly across the balcony at the back, moving from
right to left.)*

What are you doing, Ten O'clock? Aristotle?
TEN O'CLOCK: No, Plato, Mr. Washburn.

THE STAGE MANAGER: Good.—"Are you not rather convinced that he who thus . . ."

TEN O'CLOCK: "Are you not rather convinced that he who thus sees Beauty as only it can be seen will be specially favored? And since he is in contact not with images but with reality . . ." *(She continues the passage in a murmur as Eleven O'clock appears)*

ELEVEN O'CLOCK: "What else can I, Epictetus, do, a lame old man, but sing hymns to God? If then I were a nightingale, I would do the nightingale's part. If I were a swan, I would do a swan's. But now I am a rational creature . . ." *(Her voice also subsides to a murmur. Twelve O'clock appears)*

THE STAGE MANAGER: Good. —Twelve O'clock, what have you?

TWELVE O'CLOCK: Saint Augustine and his mother.

THE STAGE MANAGER: So. —"And we began to say: If to any the tumult of the flesh were hushed . . ."

TWELVE O'CLOCK: "And we began to say: If to any the tumult of the flesh were hushed; hushed the images of earth; of waters and of air . . ."

THE STAGE MANAGER: Faster. —"Hushed also the poles of Heaven."

TWELVE O'CLOCK: "Yea, were the very soul to be hushed to herself."

THE STAGE MANAGER: A little louder, Miss Foster.

TWELVE O'CLOCK *(A little louder)*: "Hushed all dreams and imaginary revelations . . ."

THE STAGE MANAGER *(Waving them back)*: All right. All right. Now The Planets. December twenty-first, 1930, please.

(The Hours unwind and return to their dressing rooms at the right.

The Planets appear on the balcony. Some of them take their place halfway on the steps. These have no words, but each has a sound. One has a pulsating, zinging sound. Another has a thrum. One whistles ascending and descending scales. Saturn does a slow, obstinate humming sound on two repeated low notes:)

Louder, Saturn. —Venus, higher. Good. Now, Jupiter. —Now the Earth.

(The Stage Manager turns to the beds on the train.)

Come, everybody. This is the Earth's sound.

(The towns, workmen, etc., appear at the edge of the stage. The passengers begin their "thinking" murmur.)

Come, Grover's Corners. Parkersburg. You're in this. Watchman. Tramp. This is the Earth's sound.

(He conducts it as the director of an orchestra would. Each of the towns and workmen does his motto.
The Insane Woman breaks into passionate weeping. She rises and stretches out her arms to The Stage Manager.)

THE INSANE WOMAN: Use me. Give me something to do.

(He goes to her quickly, whispers something in her ear, and leads her back to her guardians. She is unconsoled.)

THE STAGE MANAGER: Now shh—shh—shh! Enter The Archangels.
    (To the audience) We have now reached the theological position of Pullman Car Hiawatha.

(The towns and workmen have disappeared. The Planets, offstage, continue a faint music. Two young men in blue serge suits enter along the balcony and descend the stairs at the right. As they pass each bed the passenger talks in his sleep.

Gabriel points out Bill to Michael who smiles with raised eyebrows. They pause before Lower Five, and Michael makes the sound of assent that can only be rendered "Hn-Hn."

The remarks that the characters make in their sleep are not all intelligible, being lost in the sound of sigh or groan or whisper by which they are conveyed. But we seem to hear:)

LOWER NINE *(Loud)*: Some people are slower than others, that's all.

LOWER SEVEN *(Bill)*: It's no fun, y'know. I'll try.

LOWER FIVE *(The lady of the Christmas presents, rapidly)*: You know best, of course. I'm ready whenever you are. One year's like another.

LOWER ONE: I can teach sewing. I can sew.

(They approach Harriet's compartment.
The Insane Woman sits up and speaks to them.)

THE INSANE WOMAN: Me?

(The Archangels shake their heads.)

What possible use can there be in my simply waiting? —Well, I'm grateful for anything. I'm grateful for being so much better than I was. The old story, the terrible story, doesn't haunt me as it used to. A great load seems to have been taken off my mind. —But no one understands me any more. At last I understand myself perfectly, but no one else understands a thing I say. — So I must wait?

(The Archangels nod, smiling.)

(Resignedly, and with a smile that implies their complicity) Well, you know best. I'll do whatever is best; but everyone is so childish, so absurd. They have no logic. These people are all so mad . . . These people are like children; they have never suffered.

(She returns to her bed and sleeps. The Archangels stand beside Harriet. The Doctor has drawn Philip into the next compartment and is talking to him in earnest whispers.

Harriet's face has been toward the wall; she turns it slightly and speaks toward the ceiling.)

HARRIET: I wouldn't be happy there. Let me stay dead down here. I belong here. I shall be perfectly happy to roam about my house and be near Philip. —You know I wouldn't be happy there.

(Gabriel leans over and whispers into her ear. After a short pause she bursts into fierce tears.)

I'm ashamed to come with you. I haven't done anything. I haven't done anything with my life. Worse than that: I was angry and sullen. I never realized anything. I don't dare go a step in such a place.

(They whisper to her again.)

But it's not possible to forgive such things. I don't want to be forgiven so easily. I want to be punished for it all. I won't stir until I've been punished a long, long time. I want to be freed of all that—by punishment. I want to be all new.

(They whisper to her. She puts her feet slowly on the ground.)

But no one else could be punished for me. I'm willing to face it all myself. I don't ask anyone to be punished for me.

(They whisper to her again. She sits long and brokenly looking at her shoes, thinking it over.)

It wasn't fair. I'd have been willing to suffer for it myself—if I could have endured such a mountain.

(She smiles.)

Oh, I'm ashamed! I'm just a stupid and you know it. I'm just another American.—But then what wonderful things must be beginning now. You really want me? You really want me?

(They start leading her down the aisle of the car.)

Let's take the whole train. There are some lovely faces on this train. Can't we all come? You'll never find anyone better than Philip. Please, please, let's all go.

(They reach the steps. The Archangels interlock their arms as a support for her as she leans heavily on them, taking the steps slowly. Her words are half singing and half babbling.)

But look at how tremendously high and far it is. I've a weak heart. I'm not supposed to climb stairs. "I do not ask to see the distant scene: One step enough for me." It's like Switzerland. My tongue keeps saying things. I can't control it. —Do let me stop a minute: I want to say good-bye.

(She turns in their arms.)

Just a minute, I want to cry on your shoulder.

(She leans her forehead against Gabriel's shoulder and laughs long and softly.)

Good-bye, Philip. —I begged him not to marry me, but he would. He believed in me just as you do. —Good-bye, 1312 Ridgewood Avenue, Oaksbury, Illinois. I hope I remember all its steps and doors and wallpapers forever. Good-bye, Emerson Grammar School on the corner of Forbush Avenue and Wherry Street. Good-bye, Miss

Walker and Miss Cramer who taught me English and Miss Matthewson who taught me biology. Good-bye, First Congregational Church on the corner of Meyerson Avenue and Sixth Street and Dr. McReady and Mrs. McReady and Julia. Good-bye, Papa and Mama . . .

(She turns.)

Now I'm tired of saying good-bye. —I never used to talk like this. I was so homely I never used to have the courage to talk. Until Philip came. I see now. I see now. I understand everything now.

(The Stage Manager comes forward.)

THE STAGE MANAGER *(To the actors)*: All right. All right. —Now we'll have the whole world together, please. The whole solar system, please.

(The complete cast begins to appear at the edges of the stage. He claps his hands.)

The whole solar system, please. Where's The Tramp? —Where's The Moon?

(He gives two raps on the floor, like the conductor of an orchestra attracting the attention of his forces, and slowly lifts his hand. The human beings murmur their thoughts; The Hours discourse; The Planets chant or hum. Harriet's voice finally rises above them all, saying:)

HARRIET: "I was not ever thus, nor asked that Thou
　　　Shouldst lead me on, and spite of fears,
　　　Pride ruled my will: Remember not past years."

(The Stage Manager waves them away.)

THE STAGE MANAGER: Very good. Now clear the stage, please. Now we're at Englewood Station, South Chicago. See the university's towers over there! The best of them all.

LOWER ONE *(The Maiden Lady)*: Porter, you promised to wake me up at quarter of six.

THE PORTER: Sorry, ma'am, but it's been an awful night on this car. A lady's been terrible sick.

LOWER ONE: Oh! Is she better?

THE PORTER: No'm. She ain't one jot better.

LOWER FIVE: Young man, take your foot out of my face.

THE STAGE MANAGER *(Again substituting for Upper Five)*: Sorry, lady, I slipped—

LOWER FIVE *(Grumbling not unamiably)*: I declare, this trip's been one long series of insults.

THE STAGE MANAGER: Just one minute, ma'am, and I'll be down and out of your way.

LOWER FIVE: Haven't you got anybody to darn your socks for you? You ought to be ashamed to go about that way.

THE STAGE MANAGER: Sorry, lady.

LOWER FIVE: You're too stuck up to get married. That's the trouble with you.

LOWER NINE: Bill! Bill!

LOWER SEVEN: Yea? Wha'd'ya want?

LOWER NINE: Bill, how much d'ya give the porter on a train like this? I've been outta the country so long . . .

LOWER SEVEN: Hell, Fred, I don't know myself.

THE PORTER: CHICAGO, CHICAGO. All out. This train don't go no further.

(The passengers jostle their way out and an army of old women with mops and pails enter and prepare to clean up the car.)

END OF PLAY

Love and How to Cure It

CHARACTERS

LINDA, a dancer, sixteen
JOEY WESTON, a comedian
ROWENA STOKER, a comedic actress and singer,
    Linda's aunt
ARTHUR WARBURTON, Linda's admirer

SETTING

The stage of the Tivoli Palace of Music, Soho, London,
April 1895.

The stage is dark save for a gas jet forward left and an oil lamp on the table at the back right.
  Bare, dark, dusty and cold.
  Linda, dressed in a white ballet dress, is practicing steps and bending exercises. She is a beautiful, impersonal, remote, almost sullen girl of barely sixteen.

At the table in the distance sit Joey, a stout comedian, and Rowena, a mature soubrette. Joey is reading aloud from a pink theatrical and sporting weekly and Rowena is darning a stocking. When they speak the touch of cockney in their diction is insufficiently compensated by touches of exaggerated elegance.

There is silence for a time, broken only by the undertone of the reading and the whispered counting of Linda at her practice. Then:

ROWENA *(Calling to Linda)*: They've put off the rehearsal. Mark my words. It's after half past eight now. They must have got word to the others somehow. Or else we understood the day wrong. —Go on, Joey.

(Joey reads for a few minutes, then Rowena calls again:)

Linda, the paper says Marjorie FitzMaurice has an engagement. An Ali Baba and the Forty Thieves company that Moss has collected for Folkstone, Brighton and the piers. She must have got better. —You'd better take a rest, dearie. You'll be all blowed. —Go on, Joey, that's a good boy.

LINDA *(Gravely describing an arc waist-high with her toe)*: It's nine o'clock. I can hear the chimes.

(Apparently Joey has finished the paper. He stretches and yawns. Rowena puts down her work, picks up her chair and brings it toward the footlights, and starts firmly supervising Linda's movements.)

ROWENA: One, two, three; one, two, three. Whatever are you doing with your hands, child? Madame Angellelli didn't teach you anything like that. Bend them back like you was discovering a flower by surprise. That's right. —Upsidaisy! That's the way. —Now that's enough kicks for one night. If you must do any more, just stick to the knee-highs.

(She yawns and pats her yawn.)

There's no rehearsal. We might just as well go home. It was all a mistake somehow.

LINDA *(Almost upside down)*: No, no. I don't want to go home. Besides, I'm hungry. Ask Joey to go around the corner and buy some fish and chips.

ROWENA: Goodness, I never saw such an eater. Well, I have two kippers here I was going to set on for breakfast.

 (Calling) Joey, there's a stove downstairs still, isn't there?

JOEY: Yes.

ROWENA *(To Linda)*: There you are! We could have a little supper and ask Joey. I have a packet of tea in my bag. How would you like that, angel?

LINDA: Lovely.

ROWENA: Joey, how would you like a little supper on the stage with kipper and tea and everything nice?

JOEY: Like it! I'm that starved I could eat bones and all. Wot's more, I'll cook it for you. I'm the best little cooker of a kipper for a copper you could 'ope to see.

ROWENA *(Meditatively)*: You could use that in a song some-day, Joey. —Shall I let him cook it, Linda?

LINDA: Yes, let him cook it.

JOEY: I'll just go next door and get a spoonful of butter.

ROWENA: There's sixpence. Get some milk for the tea, too. Put some water on as you go out and I'll be down in a minute to make the tea.

JOEY: Won't be a minute, my dears.

(He hurries out.
 There is a pause. Linda stops her exercise and examines attentively each of the soles of her slippers in turn.)

ROWENA: Joey must have cooked thousands of kippers in his day. All those last years when his wife was ill, he cooked everything for her. Good old Joey! He's all lost without her. And he wants me to talk about her all the time, only he doesn't want to bring her into the conversation first. You know, Henrietta du Vaux was wonderful, but I can't talk about her forever.

(Another pause.)

Linda, whatever are you thinking about all the time?

LINDA: Nothing.

ROWENA: Don't you say "Nothing." Come now, tell your auntie. What is it you keep turning over in your mind all the time?

LINDA *(Indifferently)*: Well, almost nothing—except that I'm going to be shot any minute.

ROWENA: Don't say such things, dearie. No one's going to shoot you. You ought to be ashamed to say such things.

LINDA *(Pointing scornfully to the door)*: He's out waiting in the street this very minute.

ROWENA: Why, he went back to his university didn't he? He's a student. They don't let them come to London whenever they want.

LINDA: Oh, I don't care! Let him shoot me. I wish I'd never seen him. What was he doing, anyway—worming his way into Madame Angellelli's soirees. He'd oughta stayed among his own people.

ROWENA: I'm going out into the street this minute to see if he's there. I can get the police after him for hounding a poor girl so. What's his name?

LINDA: Arthur Warburton. I tell you I don't care if he shoots me.

ROWENA *(Sharply)*: Now I won't have you saying things like that! Now mind! If he's out there Joey'll go and get him and we'll have a talk. When did you see him last?

LINDA: Sunday. We had tea at Richmond and went boating on the river.

ROWENA: Did you let him kiss you?

LINDA: I let him kiss me once when we floated under some willow trees. And then he kept talking so hotheaded that I didn't let him kiss me again, and I liked him less and less. All the way back on the bus, I didn't pay any attention to him; just looked into the street and said yes and no; and then I told him I was too busy to see him this week. I don't want to see him again.—Aunt Rowena, he breathes so hard.

ROWENA: He didn't look like he was rough and nasty.

LINDA: He's not rough and nasty. He just . . . suffers.

ROWENA: I know 'em.

LINDA: Aunt Rowena, isn't there any way discovered to make a man get over loving you. Can it be cured?

(Rowena does not answer. She walks meditatively back to the table in the corner.)

ROWENA: Give me a hand, will you, with this table. We'll bring it nearer to the gas jet. I'd better go downstairs and see what Joey's doing to everything. *(They bring the table forward)* Dearie, what makes you say such things? What makes you say he's thinking of shooting you?

LINDA: He looked all . . . all crazy and said I oughtn't to be alive. He said if I didn't marry him . . .

ROWENA: *Marry him!* He asked you to marry him? Linda, you are a funny girl not to tell me these things before. Why do you keep everything so secret, dearie?

LINDA: I didn't think that was a secret. I don't want to marry him.

ROWENA *(Passing her thumb along her teeth and looking at Linda narrowly)*: Well, now try and remember what he said about shooting.

LINDA: He was standing at the door saying good-bye. I was playing with the key in my hand to show him I was in a hurry to be done with him. He said he couldn't think of anything but me—that he couldn't live without me and so on. Then he asked me was there someone else I loved instead of him, and I said no. And he said how about the

Italian fellow at Madame Angellelli's soiree, and I said no, not in a thousand years. He meant Mario. And then he started to cry and take on terrible. —Imagine being jealous of Mario.

ROWENA: I'll teach that young man a lesson. That's what I'll do.

LINDA: Then he was trembling all over, and he took up the edge of my coat and cried: People like me ought not to be alive. Nature ought not to allow such soulless beauties like I.

(Linda has risen on her toes, holding out her arms, and has started drifting away with little rapid steps. From the back of the stage she calls scornfully:)

I ought not to be alive, he said. I ought not to be alive.

(Pause.)

ROWENA: Someone's pounding on the street door down there. Joey must have dropped the latch.

LINDA: It's Arthur.

ROWENA: Don't be foolish.

LINDA: I know in my bones it's him.

(Joey appears at the back.)

JOEY: There's a gentleman to see you, Linda. Says his name is Warburton.

LINDA: Yes. Send him up.

JOEY: Kipper is almost ready. Water's boiling, Rowena. What are you going to do about this visitor?

ROWENA: Listen, dearie, I want to look at this Arthur again. You ask him pretty to have supper with us.

LINDA: Oh, Aunt Rowena, I couldn't eat!

ROWENA: This is serious. This is serious, Linda. Now you ask him to supper and send him around the corner for some bitters. In the meantime I'll catch a minute to tell Joey how we must watch him.

LINDA: I don't care if he shoots me. It's nothing to me.

(In the gloom at the back Arthur appears. He is wearing an opera hat and cape. He is very miserable. He expects and dreads Linda's indifference but hopes that some miraculous change of heart may occur any minute.)

ARTHUR *(Tentatively)*: Good evening, Linda.

LINDA: Hello, Arthur. Arthur, I'd like you to meet my aunt, Mrs. Rowena Stoker.

ARTHUR: It's a great pleasure to meet you, Mrs. Stoker. I hope I'm not intruding. I was just passing by and I thought . . . *(His voice trails off)*

ROWENA: We thought there was going to be a rehearsal of the new pantomime we're engaged for, Mr. Warburton. But nobody's showed up, so like as not we mistook the day. Linda's just been practicing a few steps for practice, haven't you, dovie?

LINDA *(By rote)*: Arthur, we were just going to have a little supper. We hope you'll have some with us. Just a kippered herring and some tea.

ARTHUR: That's awfully good of you. I've just come from dinner. But I hope you won't mind if I sit by you, Mrs. Stoker.

ROWENA: Suit yourself, I always say. It isn't very attractive in an empty theatre. But you must have something, oh yes.

LINDA: Perhaps you'd like to do us a favor, Arthur. Joey's downstairs doing the cooking and can't go. Perhaps you'd like to go down to the corner and bring us a jug of ale and bitters.

ROWENA: I have a shilling here somewhere.

LINDA: Aunt Rowena, perhaps Arthur is dressed too grand to go to a pub . . .

ROWENA: The pubs in this street is used to us coming in in all kinds of costumes, Mr. Warburton. They'll think you're rehearsing for a society play.

ARTHUR *(Who has refused the shilling, and is all feverish willingness)*: I'll be right back. I'll only be a minute, Mrs. Stoker.

(He hurries out.)

ROWENA: The poor boy is off his head for fair. Makes me feel all *old* just to see him. But I imagine he's quite a nice young man when he's got his senses. But never mind, Linda, nobody wants you to marry anybody you don't want to marry. —Has he been drinking, dearie, or does he just look that way?

LINDA: He just looks that way.

(Enter Joey, with cups, knives, forks, etc.)

JOEY: Where's the duke?

ROWENA: He's gone to the corner for some ale and bitters. Thank God, he's eaten already. Now Joey, listen. This young man is off his head about Linda, crazy for fair. Now this is serious. Linda says he talks wild and might even be thinking of shooting her. *(Joey whistles)* Well, the papers are full of such things, Joey. And plays are full of it. It might be. It might be.

JOEY: Well, I've heard about such things, but it never happened in my family.

ROWENA: Just the same we must take steps. Joey, I'll have him take his cape off. You take it downstairs and see if there's anything in the pocket.

JOEY: What in the pocket?

ROWENA: Why . . . one of those small guns.

LINDA: Yes, of course, there's one in his pocket. I know there is.

ROWENA: It would be in his cape so as not to bulge his other pockets. Listen, Joey, if there is a gun there, you take out the bullets, and then put the gun back into his pocket empty. See? Then bring the cape back again. If this boy is going to shoot Linda, he's going to shoot her tonight, so we can have a good heart-to-heart talk about it.

JOEY: Yes, and then call the police, that's what!

ROWENA: No, this is a thing police and prisons can't cure. Now, Joey, if you find a gun in his pocket and have done what I told you, you come back on the stage whistling one of your songs. Whistle your song about bank holidays. You know: "*My holiday girl on a holiday bus.*"

JOEY: Right-o!

ROWENA: Now, Linda, you act just natural. Let him have his murder and get it out of his system. Yes, you know I like the boy and I don't hold it against him. When we're twenty-one years old we all have a few drops of crazy melodrama in us.

LINDA *(Suddenly)*: Oh, I hate him, I 'ate 'im! Why can't he let me be?

ROWENA: Yes, yes. That's love.

LINDA *(On the verge of hysterics)*: Auntie, can't it be cured? Can't you make him just forget me?

ROWENA: Well, dovie, they say there are some ways. Some say you can make fun of him and mock him out of it. And some say you can show yourself up at your worst or pretend you're worse than you are. But I say there's only one way to cure that kind of love when it's feverish and all upset. *(She pauses groping for her thought)* Only love can cure love. Only being interested . . . only being real interested and fond of him can . . . can . . . *(She gives it up)*

It's all right, dearie. Don't you get jumpy. It's a lucky chance to get the thing cleared up. Only remember this: I like him. I like him. He's just somebody's boy that's not well for a few weeks.

LINDA: He breathes too hard.

(Enter Arthur, followed by Joey. Arthur's hands are laden with bundles and bottles.)

ROWENA: Why, Mr. Warburton, I never see such a load. Whatever did you find to bring? Fries? Salami, and I don't know what all. This *is* a feast. Take off your coat, Mr. Warburton. Joey, help Mr. Warburton off with his coat. Take it and hang it on the peg downstairs.

ARTHUR *(With concern)*: I think I'll keep the coat, thanks.

ROWENA *(As Joey attacks it)*: Oh, no, no! You won't need your coat. There's nothing worse than sitting about in a heavy coat.

(Arthur follows it with his eyes, as Joey bears it off.)

But Linda, you've been exercising. You slip that scarf about you, dearie, and draw up your chair. Well, this is going to be nice. What's nicer than friends sitting down to a bite to eat? And extra nice for you, Mr. Warburton, because you ought to be in your university, or am I mistaken?

ARTHUR: Yes, I ought to be at Cambridge.

ROWENA: Fancy that! It must be exciting to break the rule so boldly. Ah, well, life is so dull that it does us good every now and then to *make* a little excitement. Now, Mr. Warburton, you'll change your mind and have a little snack with us. A slice of salami?

ARTHUR: I don't think I could eat anything. I'll have a little ale.

ROWENA *(Busying herself over the table)*: That's right.

ARTHUR: *(Ventures a word to Linda)*: Madame Angellelli is having a soiree Thursday, Linda. Don't you go any more?

LINDA: No, I don't like them.

ARTHUR: I wondered where you were last Thursday. Madame Angellelli expected you every minute.

LINDA: I don't like them.

(Silence.)

ROWENA: What can be keeping Joey over the kipper? Have you seen Joey on the stage, Mr. Warburton? —Joey Weston he is.

ARTHUR: No, I don't think I have.

ROWENA: Oh, very fine, he is! Quite the best comedian in the pantomimes. But surely you must have seen his wife. She was Henrietta du Vaux. She was the most popular soubrette in all England, and very famous, she was. He lost her two years ago, Henrietta du Vaux. Everybody loved her. It was a terrible loss. Shh—here he comes!

(Enter Joey with the kipper and the tea. He is jubilantly whistling a tune that presently breaks out into the words: "A holiday girl on a holiday bus.")

What a noise you do make, Joey, for fair. Anybody'd think you were happy about something. Well, now, Mr. Warburton, you'll excuse us if we sit down and fall right to.

(Arthur sits at the left turned toward them. Joey faces the audience, with Rowena and Linda facing one another, Rowena at his right and Linda at his left.)

JOEY: It's cold here, Rowena, after the kitchen.

ROWENA: Yes, it's colder than I thought for. Joey, go and get Mr. Warburton's coat for him. I think he'll want it after all.

ARTHUR: Yes, I'd better keep it by me.

(He follows Joey to the door and takes the coat from him.)

ROWENA *(While the men are at the door)*: How do you feel, dearie?

LINDA: I hate it. I wish I were home.

ROWENA: Joey, this is good. You're a good cook.

(They eat absorbedly for a few moments; then Rowena gazes out into the vault of the dark theatre.)

Oh, this old theatre has seen some wonderful nights! I'll never forget you, Joey, in *Robinson Crusoe the Second*. I'll never forget you standing right there and pretending you saw a ghost. I hurt myself laughing.

JOEY: No, it wasn't me. It was Henrietta. She sang *The Sultan of Bagdad* three hundred times in this very house. On these very same boards. Three hundred times the house went crazy when she sang *The Houseboat Song*. They'd sit so quiet you'd think they were holding their breaths, and then they'd break out into shouts and cries. Henrietta du Vaux was my wife, Mr. Warburton. She was the best soubrette in England since Nell Gwynne, sir.

ROWENA: I can hear her now, Joey. She was as good a friend as she was a singer.

JOEY: After the show I would be waiting for her at the corner, Mr. Warburton. *(He points to the corner)* Do you know the corner, sir?

ARTHUR *(Fascinated)*: Yes.

JOEY: I did not always have an engagement and the manager did not think it right to have a husband waiting in the theatre to take the soubrette home. So I waited for her at that corner. She slipped away from all that applause, sir, to go home with a husband that did not always have an engagement.

ROWENA: Joey, I won't have you saying that. You're one of the best comics in England. —Joey, you're tired. Rest yourself a bit.

JOEY: No, Rowena, I want to say this about her: She never felt her success. And she had a hundred ways of pretending that she was no success at all. "Joey," she'd say, "I got it all wrong tonight." And then she'd ask me how she should do it.

ROWENA: Do draw up a chair, Mr. Warburton, and have a bite for good feelings' sake. We're all friends here. Linda, put a piece of sausage on some bread for him, with your own hands.

ARTHUR: Well, thanks, thank you very much.

JOEY *(With increasing impressiveness)*: And when she was ill, she knew that her coughing hurt me. And she'd suffer four times over trying to hold back her coughing. "Cough, Henrietta," I'd say, "if it makes you more comfortable." But no!—she'd act like I was the sick person that had to be taken care of.

(Turning on Arthur with gravity and force) I read in the papers about people who shoot the persons they love. I don't know what to think. What is it but that they want to be *noticed*, noticed even if they must shoot to get noticed? It's themselves—it's themselves they love.

(Joey stares at Arthur so fixedly that Arthur breathes an all but involuntary "Yes," then rises abruptly and says:)

ARTHUR: I must go now. You've been very kind.

ROWENA *(Rising)*: Joey, come downstairs with me a minute and help me open that old chest. I think we can find Henrietta's shield and spear from *The Palace of Ice* and other things. The lock's been broken for years.

JOEY: All right, Rowena. Let's look.

ROWENA: We won't be a minute. You go on eating.

(They go out.)

ARTHUR: I won't trouble you any more, Linda. I want you to be happy, that's all.

LINDA: You don't trouble me, Arthur.

ARTHUR: What he said is true. I want to be noticed. I wish you liked me, Linda. I mean I wish you liked me more. I wish I could prove to you that I'd do anything for you. That I could bring to you all . . . that . . . that he was describing . . . I won't be a trouble to you any more. *(He turns)* I can prove it to you, Linda. I've been waiting at that corner for hours, just walking up and down. And I'd planned, Linda, to prove that I couldn't live without you . . . and if you were going to be cold and . . . didn't like me, Linda, I was going to shoot myself right here . . . to prove to you.

(He puts the revolver on the table.)

To prove to you. —But you've all been so kind to me. And that . . . and Mr. Weston told about his wife. I think just loving isn't wasted.

(He weeps silently.)

LINDA *(Horrified)*: Arthur! I wish you wouldn't!
ARTHUR: I imagine I'm . . . I'm young still. —Good-bye and thanks. Good-bye.

(He hurries out.
    Linda shudders with distaste; peers at the revolver; starts to walk about the room and presently is sketching steps again. Joey and Rowena return.)

ROWENA: Was that he that went out? What happened, Linda?
LINDA *(Interrupting her drill, indifferently)*: He said good-bye forever. He left the gun to prove to me something or other. Thank you for nothing.
ROWENA: Linda, I hope you said a nice word to him.
LINDA: Thank you for nothing, I said.
ROWENA: Well, young lady, you're only sixteen. Wait till your turn comes. We'll have to take care of you.
LINDA: Don't let's talk about it. It makes me tired. So hot and excited and breathing so hard. Mario would never act like that. Mario . . . Mario doesn't even seem to notice you when you're there . . .

END OF PLAY

Such Things Only Happen in Books

CHARACTERS

JOHN, a young novelist
GABRIELLE, his wife
DOCTOR BUMPAS, the local doctor
MR. GRAHAM, John's friend, around fifty

SETTING

An old house in a New Hampshire village.

This is John's library and study and living room in one. It is a spring evening. John is playing solitaire on a card table before the hearth and Gabrielle is sewing.

Silence.

John finishes a game, takes up his fountain pen, makes a notation on a piece of paper beside him, and starts shuffling the cards.

JOHN: Five.

GABRIELLE: What, dear?

JOHN: Five.

GABRIELLE: Oh! . . . Even that's more than the average.

JOHN: The average is two. Listen to the scores this evening: zero, two, five, three, zero, one, four, zero, three, one six, zero, zero, zero, three, zero, six, and now five. The full fifty-two come out every twenty-one times. So that from now on my chances for getting it out increase seven point three two every game.

GABRIELLE *(Not understanding, but thinking that this is an unfortunate announcement)*: Tchk—Tchk!

(Pause.)

JOHN: The doctor's still upstairs, isn't he?

GABRIELLE: Yes.

JOHN: It does seem that he's taking an awfully long time.

GABRIELLE: Yes, every other day he changes the dressing on the wounds, or burns, or whatever you call it. It takes about half an hour. I offered to help him but he didn't seem to need me. He'll call down the stairs if he needs us.

JOHN: Well, he certainly is taking a long time. Does it hurt Katie when the dressing is changed?

GABRIELLE: Not any more. *(Pause)* When's this man coming?

JOHN: About half past eight, I imagine. He may not come at all. He had to work tonight on some sort of report. I just told him to drop around if he'd like and we'd have a game of chess.

GABRIELLE: On his first call like that, I really ought to have thought about getting together something special for him to eat.

JOHN: No, no. I told him you and I always had some cocoa about half past ten—cocoa and biscuits, I said.

GABRIELLE: Well, it's too bad Katie's laid up. I wonder he didn't hear about Katie. The whole town seems to know about her pouring all that boiling water over her legs.

JOHN: Here's another zero, I'm afraid—though it promised very well.

GABRIELLE: How'd you meet this man?

JOHN: Where I meet everybody. At the post office Sunday morning waiting for the mail. People stop in on the way home from church and everybody falls into conversation with everybody else.

GABRIELLE: That's the way you met Miss Buckingham. The unexplained Miss Buckingham. The Miss Buckingham whom I soundly disliked. Why on earth she wanted to poke into this house is still a mystery to me.

JOHN: Anyway she's left town for good now. She's gone back to Australia. —On the whole, though, dear, you don't mind my bringing home stray acquaintances from time to time, do you?

GABRIELLE: Oh, no indeed! Usually I like it.

JOHN: We authors should make it our business to multiply just such acquaintances.

GABRIELLE: By all means. I like it.

JOHN: Besides, this Mr. . . . Mr. . . .

GABRIELLE: Graham.

JOHN: Yes, this Mr. Graham asked to come. He said he'd often admired the house sitting up among its elms. I told him it was over two hundred years old and that it had a story. These westerners take a great fancy to our New Hampshire local color. —Really, Gabrielle, the doctor's taking an awfully long time upstairs.

GABRIELLE: Did you tell Mr. Graham the story about the house?

JOHN: No. Anyway I don't really know it. Two young people frightened their father to death—killed him or frightened him to death. I must ask one of the old citizens about it. Every old house in the state claims its murder. Thank God I have too much literary conscience to write another novel about an old New England house.

GABRIELLE: Just the same, let's ask the doctor to tell us all about it. He'll know.

JOHN *(Examining his game)*: Well, I guess this is stuck. It really looked as though it were coming out. I can see that if I moved just one card it would open up a lot of combinations.

GABRIELLE *(Without malice)*: But you have too much conscience.

JOHN: Yes. —You see it's like fiction. You have to adjust the cards to make a plot. In life most people live along without plots. A plot breaks through about once in every twenty-one times.

GABRIELLE: Well, then, I think a plot is just about due.

JOHN: Not unless we push back the cards and look under. —At all events, this one's no good. I'll take my pipe out into the garden and walk about.

GABRIELLE: Well, keep one eye on the gate, will you? I don't want to open the door to this Mr. Graham without being introduced.

JOHN: All right. I'll walk up and down in front of the house so I won't miss him. I'll leave the front door open; you might whistle to me when the doctor comes downstairs. *(He leans over the tobacco jar filling his pipe)* Plots. Plots. If I had no conscience I could choose any one of these plots that are in everybody's novels and in nobody's lives. These poor battered old plots. Enoch Arden returns and looks through the window and sees his wife married to another.

GABRIELLE: I've always loved that one.

JOHN: The plot that murderers always steal back to the scene of their crime and gloat over the place.

GABRIELLE: Oh, John! How wonderful. They'll come back to this house. Imagine!

JOHN: The plot that all married women of thirty-five have lovers.

GABRIELLE: Otherwise known as the Marseillaise.

JOHN: They're as pathetic and futile as the type-jokes— you know: that mothers-in-law are unpleasant, that . . . that cooks feed chicken and turkey to policemen and other callers in the kitchen . . .

GABRIELLE: Katie! Katie! —Once every twenty-one times these plots really do happen in real life, you say?

JOHN: Once in a thousand. Books and plays are a quiet, harmless fraud about life . . .

GABRIELLE: Well, now, don't get excited, dear, or you won't be able to work.

JOHN: All right. One pipeful.

(He goes out into the garden. The debonair young Doctor comes in from the right. Hat and coat and satchel. He looks inquiringly at Gabrielle. She makes a sign to him that John is before the house. She looks out of the door, is reassured, and smiles. The Doctor takes her in his arms. They kiss with conjugal tranquillity.)

GABRIELLE: Ouch!

DR. BUMPAS: Ouch! *Ouch!*

GABRIELLE: How's Katie?

DR. BUMPAS: Katie, ma'am, will get better. I've got to run along.

GABRIELLE: Oh, stay a minute!

DR. BUMPAS: Very busy. Patients dying like flies.

GABRIELLE: Tchk—Tchk!

DR. BUMPAS: You wouldn't detain me, would you, on my errands of mercy? Hundreds, ma'am, are waiting for my step on the stair.

(He puts down his coat and hat and satchel and kisses her again.)

Twins are popping all over the place—every now and then an appendix goes ttttttt-bang. Where'd you get that dress? Very chic, very eye-filling. —Can I trust you with a secret, Gabrielle? Would you like to know a secret?

GABRIELLE: Yes, but hurry. —Don't coquette about it. I told John I'd whistle to him when you came downstairs.

DR. BUMPAS: It's about Katie.

GABRIELLE: Goodness. Katie has no secrets.

DR. BUMPAS: And promise me it won't make any difference between you and Katie. Katie's a fine girl. If you were a stuffy old woman you'd probably fetch up a lot of indignation. And promise not to tell your husband.

GABRIELLE: Oh, I never tell John anything! It would prevent his working.

DR. BUMPAS: Katie just confessed to me how the accident happened. *(A short laugh)* Weren't you surprised that a strong careful girl like Katie could spill a kettle of boiling water over her legs?

GABRIELLE: I certainly was. I thought it very funny indeed.

DR. BUMPAS: Well, it was her brother that did it.

GABRIELLE: I didn't know she had a brother.

DR. BUMPAS: He's been in prison for eight years with four to go. Forgeries and embezzlements and things. But not a bad fellow, you know. Used to be an orderly in my hospital in Boston. Well, three months ago he escaped from prison. Sirens at midnight *(He whines the alarm)*, bloodhounds *(He barks)*, but he escaped. Gabrielle, did you ever use to hear noises in your kitchen at night?

GABRIELLE: I certainly did. I certainly did. But, then, this house is full of noises. I'd just turn over in bed and say: Not until that ghost comes into this room will I do anything about it.

DR. BUMPAS: Well, it wasn't a ghost. It was Katie's brother. Katie's brother has been hidden, living in your house for three months.

GABRIELLE: Without our knowing it! Why Katie's a monster.

DR. BUMPAS: Oh, Katie's in anguish about it. What Katie suffered from burns was nothing compared to what Katie suffered from conscience. Katie is as honest as the day. Every single time that Katie fed her brother a dinner out of your kitchen she went without a dinner herself. And the rest of his meals she paid for out of her own pocket money.

GABRIELLE: My, isn't life complicated!

DR. BUMPAS: That night she had boiled some water to wash the brother's shirts and socks. He lifted the kettle off the stove and, not being used to hot handles, he dropped it and the water fell all over Katie's knees. I can tell you all this now because he has safely crossed over into Canada to get some work. And now I too must go.

GABRIELLE: You must see John a minute. *(She whistles)* It's a lovely evening. The rain has stopped. John's expecting a visitor tonight, to play chess. Do you know a westerner named Graham?

(Enter John.)

JOHN: Hello, doctor, you've been a long time about it. How's Katie?

DR. BUMPAS: Katie'll get well. She'll be up and about in a few days.

(The Doctor takes up his things.)

JOHN: Can't you stay a while? Gabrielle'll make us some cocoa.

DR. BUMPAS: Cocoa! Are people still drinking cocoa? —No, I've got to hurry on. Patients dying like flies. Must look in at the hospital again.

GABRIELLE: Oh, I know! Every time he enters the door of the hospital, the building almost leaves the ground.

DR. BUMPAS: I galvanize'm. I galvanize'm. —How's your new book getting on?

JOHN: Nothing begun yet. Groping about for a plot.

DR. BUMPAS: Life's full of plots.

JOHN: We like to think so. But when you come down to it, the rank and file—rich and poor—live much as we do. Not much plot. Work and a nice wife and a nice house and a nice Katie.

DR. BUMPAS: No, no, no—life's full of plots. Swarming with 'em.

JOHN: Here's Mr. Graham now.

(John goes to the door and shakes hands with a reticent bearded man of about fifty. Presentations.)

MR. GRAHAM: I just stopped by to meet your wife and to explain that I'll have to come another time, if you'll be so good as to ask me.

GABRIELLE: Oh, I'm sorry.

MR. GRAHAM: Tonight I must work. I've been ordered to send in a report and I shall probably work all night. *(Looking about)* It's a very interesting, a very attractive house.

JOHN: And it has a story. I was just going to ask Dr. Bumpas to tell it to us.

DR. BUMPAS: Let's see . . . what was their name?

GABRIELLE: They call it the Hamburton place.

DR. BUMPAS: That's it. It must have been some thirty years ago. There was an old father, rich, hateful, miserly, beard and everything. And he buried a lot of money under the floor or between the bricks. *(He points to the hearth)* There was a son and daughter he kept in rags. Yes, sir, rags, and they lived on potato peelings. They wanted just enough money to get some education and something to wear. And one night they meant to frighten him—they tied him with rope or something to frighten him into releasing some money. Some say they meant to kill him; anyway he died in this very room.

GABRIELLE: What became of the children?

DR. BUMPAS: They disappeared. Tell the truth, no one tried very hard to find them.

GABRIELLE: Did they get any money?

DR. BUMPAS: We hope so. Let's hope they found some. Most of it lies down there in the bank to this day.

JOHN: Well, there you have it.

MR. GRAHAM: Very interesting.

GABRIELLE: Come now, can't you both stay and have a cup of cocoa? It won't take a minute.

DR. BUMPAS: Patients dying like flies. Very glad to have met you, Mr. Graham. —Zzzzt. Off I go.

(He goes out.)

JOHN: All these houses collect folklore like moss. *(To Gabrielle)* You see there's nothing one can make out of a story like that—it's too naïf.

GABRIELLE: Excuse me, one minute. I hear Katie's cowbell. We have a maid upstairs sick in bed, Mr. Graham. When she needs me she rings a cowbell.

(She goes out right.)

MR. GRAHAM: But I must go too. You'll say good night for me. —One question before I go. Did you know a Miss Buckingham, by any chance?

JOHN: Yes, oh, yes. Miss Buckingham came and spent an evening with us here. Yes, she used to be a trained nurse in South Africa, or Australia. She went back there. Did you know her?

MR. GRAHAM: Yes, I used to know her.

JOHN: She liked this house too. She asked to come and see it.

MR. GRAHAM: And she went back to Australia? That's what I wanted to know.

(Gabrielle's voice calls, "John! John!")

JOHN: There's my wife calling me upstairs. —You probably can get Miss Buckingham's address at Mrs. Thorpe's boardinghouse. She stayed there. —I'm coming! You'll excuse me. Just come any time, Mr. Graham, and we'll have a game.

(John hurries out.
Mr. Graham, who has been at the front door, reenters, crosses the room with grave caution to the front right corner.

He slowly picks up one corner of the carpet and stares at a mottled portion of the floor. He lowers the carpet and goes out into the street.

    John and Gabrielle return.)

JOHN: I guess she'll be comfortable now.

GABRIELLE: Here you see: here's our evening free after all.

JOHN: Didn't even have the excitement of a game of chess.
Well, I like it best this way.

(He sits down to his cards again. Gabrielle takes up her sewing, then rises and stands behind him watching the game over his shoulder.)

GABRIELLE: There! That jack on the ten releases the ace.

JOHN: But even then we're at a standstill.

GABRIELLE: I don't see why that game shouldn't come out oftener. *(Pause)* I don't think you see all the moves.

JOHN: I certainly do see all the moves that are to be seen.
—You don't expect me to look under the cards, do you?

(He sweeps the cards toward him and starts to shuffle.)

One more game and then we'll have some cocoa.

END OF PLAY

The Happy Journey
to Trenton and Camden

AUTHOR'S NOTE

THE FORM in which this play is cast is not an innovation but a revival. The healthiest ages of the theatre have been marked by the fact that there was the least literally representative scenery. The sympathetic participation of the audience was most engaged when their collaborative imagination was called upon to supply a large part of the background.

It is perhaps a sad commentary on the kind of people who go in for amateur stage production to say that in the many productions of the play I have seen, Ma Kirby has been permitted, or directed, to play her role sentimentally, and the closing moments have been drenched in tears, ostentatious piety and a kind of heroic self-pity. The play is a testimonial of homage to the average American mother who brings up her children as instinctively as a bird builds its nest and whose strength lies in the fact that whatever stress arrives from the circumstances of life, she strives to maintain an atmosphere of forward-looking industry and readiness.

Thornton Wilder
New Haven, Connecticut
April 13, 1942

CHARACTERS

THE STAGE MANAGER
MA, Mrs. Kate Kirby
ARTHUR, her son
CAROLINE, her daughter
PA, Ma's husband Elmer
BEULAH, the Kirbys' married daughter who lives in
    Camden, New Jersey

SETTING

The Kirby house; then the Kirby family car trip from Newark to Camden, New Jersey.

No scenery is required for this play. Perhaps a few dusty flats may be seen leaning against the brick wall at the back of the stage.

The Stage Manager not only moves forward and withdraws the few properties that are required, but he reads from a typescript the lines of all the minor characters. He reads them clearly, but with little attempt at characterization, scarcely troubling himself to alter his voice, even when he responds in the person of a child or a woman.

As the curtain rises The Stage Manager is leaning lazily against the proscenium pillar at the audience's left. He is smoking.

Arthur is playing marbles in the center of the stage.

> *Caroline is at the remote back right talking to some girls who are invisible to us.*
>
> *Ma Kirby is anxiously putting on her hat before an imaginary mirror.*

MA: Where's your pa? Why isn't he here? I declare we'll never get started.

ARTHUR: Ma, where's my hat? I guess I don't go if I can't find my hat.

MA: Go out into the hall and see if it isn't there. Where's Caroline gone to now, the plagued child?

ARTHUR: She's out waitin' in the street talkin' to the Jones girls. —I just looked in the hall a thousand times, Ma, and it isn't there. *(He spits for good luck before a difficult shot and mutters:)* Come on, baby.

MA: Go and look again, I say. Look carefully.

> *(Arthur rises, runs to the right, turns around swiftly, returns to his game, flinging himself on the floor with a terrible impact and starts shooting an aggie.)*

ARTHUR: No, Ma, it's not there.

MA *(Serenely)*: Well, you don't leave Newark without that hat, make up your mind to that. I don't go no journeys with a hoodlum.

ARTHUR: Aw, Ma!

> *(Ma comes down to the footlights and talks toward the audience as through a window.)*

MA: Oh, Mrs. Schwartz!

THE STAGE MANAGER *(Consulting his script)*: Here I am, Mrs. Kirby. Are you going yet?

MA: I guess we're going in just a minute. How's the baby?

THE STAGE MANAGER: She's all right now. We slapped her on the back and she spat it up.

MA: Isn't that fine! —Well now, if you'll be good enough to give the cat a saucer of milk in the morning and the

evening, Mrs. Schwartz, I'll be ever so grateful to you.
—Oh, good afternoon, Mrs. Hobmeyer!

THE STAGE MANAGER: Good afternoon, Mrs. Kirby, I hear
you're going away.

MA *(Modest)*: Oh, just for three days, Mrs. Hobmeyer, to
see my married daughter, Beulah, in Camden. Elmer's
got his vacation week from the laundry early this year,
and he's just the best driver in the world.

(Caroline comes "into the house" and stands by her mother.)

THE STAGE MANAGER: Is the whole family going?

MA: Yes, all four of us that's here. The change ought to be
good for the children. My married daughter was downright sick a while ago—

THE STAGE MANAGER: Tchk—Tchk—Tchk! Yes. I remember you tellin' us.

MA: And I just want to go down and see the child. I ain't
seen her since then. I just won't rest easy in my mind
without I see her.

    (To Caroline) Can't you say good afternoon to Mrs.
Hobmeyer?

CAROLINE *(Blushes and lowers her eyes and says woodenly)*:
Good afternoon, Mrs. Hobmeyer.

THE STAGE MANAGER: Good afternoon, dear. —Well, I'll
wait and beat these rugs after you're gone, because I
don't want to choke you. I hope you have a good time
and find everything all right.

MA: Thank you, Mrs. Hobmeyer, I hope I will. —Well, I
guess that milk for the cat is all, Mrs. Schwartz, if
you're sure you don't mind. If anything should come
up, the key to the back door is hanging by the icebox.

CAROLINE: Ma! Not so loud.

ARTHUR: Everybody can hear yuh.

MA: Stop pullin' my dress, children. *(In a loud whisper)* The
key to the back door I'll leave hangin' by the icebox and
I'll leave the screen door unhooked.

THE STAGE MANAGER: Now have a good trip, dear, and give my love to Loolie.

MA: I will, and thank you a thousand times.

(She returns "into the room.")

What can be keeping your pa?

ARTHUR: I can't find my hat, Ma.

(Enter Elmer holding a hat.)

ELMER: Here's Arthur's hat. He musta left it in the car Sunday.

MA: That's a mercy. Now we can start. —Caroline Kirby, what you done to your cheeks?

CAROLINE *(Defiant, abashed)*: Nothin'.

MA: If you've put anything on 'em, I'll slap you.

CAROLINE: No, Ma, of course I haven't. *(Hanging her head)* I just rubbed 'em to make 'em red. All the girls do that at high school when they're goin' places.

MA: Such silliness I never saw. Elmer, what kep' you?

ELMER *(Always even-voiced and always looking out a little anxiously through his spectacles)*: I just went to the garage and had Charlie give a last look at it, Kate.

MA: I'm glad you did. I wouldn't like to have no breakdown miles from anywhere. Now we can start. Arthur, put those marbles away. Anybody'd think you didn't want to go on a journey to look at yuh.

(They go out through the "hall," take the short steps that denote going downstairs, and find themselves in the street.)

ELMER: Here, you boys, you keep away from that car.

MA: Those Sullivan boys put their heads into everything.

(The Stage Manager has moved forward four chairs and a low platform. This is the automobile. It is in the center of

the stage and faces the audience. The platform slightly raises the two chairs in the rear. Pa's hands hold an imaginary steering wheel and continually shift gears. Caroline sits beside him. Arthur is behind him and Ma behind Caroline.)

CAROLINE *(Self-consciously)*: Good-bye, Mildred. Good-bye, Helen.

THE STAGE MANAGER: Good-bye, Caroline. Good-bye, Mrs. Kirby. I hope y'have a good time.

MA: Good-bye, girls.

THE STAGE MANAGER: Good-bye, Kate. The car looks fine.

MA *(Looking upward toward a window)*: Oh, good-bye, Emma! *(Modestly)* We think it's the best little Chevrolet in the world. —Oh, good-bye, Mrs. Adler!

THE STAGE MANAGER: What, are you going away, Mrs. Kirby?

MA: Just for three days, Mrs. Adler, to see my married daughter in Camden.

THE STAGE MANAGER: Have a good time.

(Now Ma, Caroline and The Stage Manager break out into a tremendous chorus of good-byes. The whole street is saying good-bye. Arthur takes out his peashooter and lets fly happily into the air. There is a lurch or two and they are off.)

ARTHUR *(In sudden fright)*: Pa! Pa! Don't go by the school. Mr. Biedenbach might see us!

MA: I don't care if he does see us. I guess I can take my children out of school for one day without having to hide down back streets about it.

(Elmer nods to a passerby.
    Ma asks without sharpness:)

Who was that you spoke to, Elmer?

ELMER: That was the fellow who arranges our banquets down to the lodge, Kate.

MA: Is he the one who had to buy four hundred steaks? *(Pa nods)* I declare, I'm glad I'm not him.

ELMER: The air's getting better already. Take deep breaths, children.

(They inhale noisily.)

ARTHUR: Gee, it's almost open fields already. *"Weber and Heilbronner Suits for Well-Dressed Men."* Ma, can I have one of them some day?

MA: If you graduate with good marks perhaps your father'll let you have one for graduation.

CAROLINE *(Whining)*: Oh, Pa! Do we have to wait while that whole funeral goes by?

(Pa takes off his hat.
   Ma cranes forward with absorbed curiosity.)

MA: Take off your hat, Arthur. Look at your father. —Why, Elmer, I do believe that's a lodge brother of yours. See the banner? I suppose this is the Elizabeth branch.

(Elmer nods. Ma sighs: Tchk—tchk—tchk.
   They all lean forward and watch the funeral in silence, growing momentarily more solemnized. After a pause, Ma continues almost dreamily:)

Well, we haven't forgotten the funeral that we went on, have we? We haven't forgotten our good Harold. He gave his life for his country, we mustn't forget that. *(She passes her finger from the corner of her eye across her cheek. There is another pause)* Well, we'll all hold up the traffic for a few minutes some day.

THE CHILDREN *(Very uncomfortable)*: Ma!

MA *(Without self-pity)*: Well I'm "ready," children. I hope everybody in this car is "ready." *(She puts her hand on Pa's shoulder)* And I pray to go first, Elmer. Yes. *(Pa touches her hand)*

CAROLINE: Ma, everybody's looking at you.

ARTHUR: Everybody's laughing at you.

MA: Oh, hold your tongues! I don't care what a lot of silly people in Elizabeth, New Jersey, think of me. —Now we can go on. That's the last.

(There is another lurch and the car goes on.)

CAROLINE: *"Fit-Rite Suspenders. The Working Man's Choice."* Pa, why do they spell Rite that way?

ELMER: So that it'll make you stop and ask about it, Missy.

CAROLINE: Papa, you're teasing me. —Ma, why do they say *"Three Hundred Rooms Three Hundred Baths?"*

ARTHUR: *"Miller's Spaghetti: The Family's Favorite Dish."* Ma, why don't you ever have spaghetti?

MA: Go along, you'd never eat it.

ARTHUR: Ma, I like it now.

CAROLINE *(With gesture)*: Yum-yum. It looks wonderful up there. Ma, make some when we get home?

MA *(Dryly)*: "The management is always happy to receive suggestions. We aim to please."

(The whole family finds this exquisitely funny. The children scream with laughter. Even Elmer smiles. Ma remains modest.)

ELMER: Well, I guess no one's complaining, Kate. Everybody knows you're a good cook.

MA: I don't know whether I'm a good cook or not, but I know I've had practice. At least I've cooked three meals a day for twenty-five years.

ARTHUR: Aw, Ma, you went out to eat once in a while.

MA: Yes. That made it a leap year.

(This joke is no less successful than its predecessor. When the laughter dies down, Caroline turns around in an ecstasy of well-being, and kneeling on the cushions says:)

CAROLINE: Ma, I love going out in the country like this. Let's do it often, Ma.

MA: Goodness, smell that air will you! It's got the whole ocean in it. —Elmer, drive careful over that bridge. This must be New Brunswick we're coming to.

ARTHUR *(Jealous of his mother's successes)*: Ma, when is the next comfort station?

MA *(Unruffled)*: You don't want one. You just said that to be awful.

CAROLINE *(Shrilly)*: Yes, he did, Ma. He's terrible. He says that kind of thing right out in school and I want to sink through the floor, Ma. He's terrible.

MA: Oh, don't get so excited about nothing, Miss Proper! I guess we're all yewman-beings in this car, at least as far as I know. And, Arthur, you try and be a gentleman. —Elmer, don't run over that collie dog. *(She follows the dog with her eyes)* Looked kinda peaked to me. Needs a good honest bowl of leavings. Pretty dog, too. *(Her eyes fall on a billboard)* That's a pretty advertisement for Chesterfield cigarettes, isn't it? Looks like Beulah, a little.

ARTHUR: Ma?

MA: Yes.

ARTHUR: Can't I take a paper route *("Route" rhymes with "out")* with the Newark *Daily Post*?

MA: No, you cannot. No, sir. I hear they make the paper-boys get up at four-thirty in the morning. No son of mine is going to get up at four-thirty every morning, not if it's to make a million dollars. Your *Saturday Evening Post* route on Thursday mornings is enough.

ARTHUR: Aw, Ma.

MA: No, sir. No son of mine is going to get up at four-thirty and miss the sleep God meant him to have.

ARTHUR *(Sullenly)*: Hhm! Ma's always talking about God. I guess she got a letter from him this morning.

(Ma rises, outraged.)

MA: Elmer, stop that automobile this minute. I don't go another step with anybody that says things like that. Arthur, you get out of this car. Elmer, you give him a dollar bill. He can go back to Newark, by himself. I don't want him.

ARTHUR: What did I say? There wasn't anything terrible about that.

ELMER: I didn't hear what he said, Kate.

MA: God has done a lot of things for me and I won't have Him made fun of by anybody. Get out of the car this minute.

CAROLINE: Aw, Ma—don't spoil the ride.

MA: No.

ELMER: We might as well go on, Kate, since we've got started. I'll talk to the boy tonight.

MA *(Slowly conceding)*: All right, if you say so, Elmer. But I won't sit beside him. Caroline, you come, and sit by me.

ARTHUR *(Frightened)*: Aw, Ma, that wasn't so terrible.

MA: I don't want to talk about it. I hope your father washes your mouth out with soap and water. —Where'd we all be if I started talking about God like that, I'd like to know! We'd be in the speakeasies and nightclubs and places like that, that's where we'd be. —All right, Elmer, you can go on now.

CAROLINE: What did he say, Ma? I didn't hear what he said.

MA: I don't want to talk about it.

(They drive on in silence for a moment, the shocked silence after a scandal.)

ELMER: I'm going to stop and give the car a little water, I guess.

MA: All right, Elmer. You know best.

ELMER *(To a garage hand)*: Could I have a little water in the radiator—to make sure?

THE STAGE MANAGER *(In this scene alone he lays aside his script and enters into a role seriously)*: You sure can. *(He punches the tires)* Air, all right? Do you need any oil or gas?

ELMER: No, I think not. I just got fixed up in Newark.

MA: We're on the right road for Camden, are we?

THE STAGE MANAGER: Yes, keep straight ahead. You can't miss it. You'll be in Trenton in a few minutes.

(He carefully pours some water into the hood.)

Camden's a great town, lady, believe me.

MA: My daughter likes it fine—my married daughter.

THE STAGE MANAGER: Yea? It's a great burg all right. I guess I think so because I was born near there.

MA: Well, well. Your folks still live there?

THE STAGE MANAGER: No, my old man sold the farm and they built a factory on it. So the folks moved to Philadelphia.

MA: My married daughter Beulah lives there because her husband works in the telephone company.—Stop pokin' me, Caroline!—We're all going down to see her for a few days.

THE STAGE MANAGER: Yea?

MA: She's been sick, you see, and I just felt I had to go and see her. My husband and my boy are going to stay at the Y.M.C.A. I hear they've got a dormitory on the top floor that's real clean and comfortable. Had you ever been there?

THE STAGE MANAGER: No. I'm Knights of Columbus myself.

MA: Oh.

THE STAGE MANAGER: I used to play basketball at the Y though. It looked all right to me.

(He has been standing with one foot on the rung of Ma's chair. They have taken a great fancy to one another. He reluctantly shakes himself out of it and pretends to examine the car again, whistling.)

Well, I guess you're all set now, lady. I hope you have a good trip; you can't miss it.

EVERYBODY: Thanks. Thanks a lot. Good luck to you.

(The car jolts and lurches.)

MA *(With a sigh)*: The world's full of nice people. —That's what I call a nice young man.

CAROLINE *(Earnestly)*: Ma, you oughtn't to tell 'em all everything about yourself.

MA: Well, Caroline, you do your way and I'll do mine. —He looked kinda pale to me. I'd like to feed him up for a few days. His mother lives in Philadelphia and I expect he eats at those dreadful Greek places.

CAROLINE: I'm hungry. Pa, there's a hot dog stand. K'n I have one?

ELMER: We'll all have one, eh, Kate? We had such an early lunch.

MA: Just as you think best, Elmer.

ELMER: Arthur, here's half a dollar. Run over and see what they have. Not too much mustard either.

*(Arthur descends from the car and goes off stage right.
Ma and Caroline get out and walk a bit.)*

MA: What's that flower over there? I'll take some of those to Beulah.

CAROLINE: It's just a weed, Ma.

MA: I like it. —My, look at the sky, wouldya! I'm glad I was born in New Jersey. I've always said it was the best state in the Union. Every state has something no other state has got.

*(They stroll about humming.
Presently Arthur returns with his hands full of imaginary hot dogs which he distributes.
He is still very much cast down by the recent scandal. He finally approaches his mother and says falteringly:)*

ARTHUR: Ma, I'm sorry. I'm sorry for what I said. *(He bursts into tears and puts his forehead against her elbow)*

MA: There. There. We all say wicked things at times. I know you didn't mean it like it sounded.

(He weeps still more violently than before.)

Why, now, now! I forgive you, Arthur, and tonight before you go to bed you . . . *(She whispers)* You're a good boy at heart, Arthur, and we all know it.

(Caroline starts to cry too.
  Ma is suddenly joyously alive and happy.)

Sakes alive, it's too nice a day for us all to be cryin'. Come now, get in. Caroline, go up in front with your father. Ma wants to sit with her beau. I never saw such children. Your hot dogs are all getting wet. Now chew them fine, everybody. —All right, Elmer, forward march. —Caroline, whatever are you doing?

CAROLINE: I'm spitting out the leather, Ma.

MA: Then say: Excuse me.

CAROLINE: Excuse me, please.

MA: What's this place? Arthur, did you see the post office?

ARTHUR: It said Lawrenceville.

MA: Hhn. School kinda. Nice. I wonder what that big yellow house set back was. —Now it's beginning to be Trenton.

CAROLINE: Papa, it was near here that George Washington crossed the Delaware. It was near Trenton, Mama. He was first in war and first in peace and first in the hearts of his countrymen.

MA *(Surveying the passing world, serene and didactic)*: Well, the thing I like about him best was that he never told a lie.

(The children are duly cast down.
  There is a pause.)

There's a sunset for you. There's nothing like a good sunset.

ARTHUR: There's an Ohio license in front of us. Ma, have you ever been to Ohio?

MA: No.

(*A dreamy silence descends upon them.*
Caroline sits closer to her father.
Ma puts her arm around Arthur.)

ARTHUR: Ma, what a lotta people there are in the world, Ma. There must be thousands and thousands in the United States. Ma, how many are there?

MA: I don't know. Ask your father.

ARTHUR: Pa, how many are there?

ELMER: There are a hundred and twenty-six million, Kate.

MA (*Giving a pressure about Arthur's shoulder*): And they all like to drive out in the evening with their children beside 'em.

(*Another pause.*)

Why doesn't somebody sing something? Arthur, you're always singing something; what's the matter with you?

ARTHUR: All right. What'll we sing? (*He sketches:*)

In the Blue Ridge mountains of Virginia,
On the trail of the lonesome pine . . .

No, I don't like that any more. Let's do:

I been workin' on de railroad

(*Caroline joins in:*)

All de liblong day.
I been workin' on de railroad
Just to pass de time away.

(*Finally even Ma is singing. Even Pa is singing.*
Then Ma suddenly jumps up with a wild cry:)

MA: Elmer, that signpost said Camden, I saw it.

ELMER: All right, Kate, if you're sure.

(Much shifting of gears, backing, and jolting.)

MA: Yes, there it is. Camden—five miles. Dear old Beulah. —Now, children, you be good and quiet during dinner. She's just got out of bed after a big sorta operation, and we must all move around kinda quiet. First you drop me and Caroline at the door and just say hello, and then you menfolk go over to the Y.M.C.A. and come back for dinner in about an hour.

CAROLINE *(Shutting her eyes and pressing her fists passionately against her nose)*: I see the first star. Everybody make a wish.

> Star light, star bright,
> First star I seen tonight.
> I wish I may, I wish I might
> Have the wish I wish tonight.

(Then solemnly) Pins. Mama, you say "needles." *(She interlocks little fingers with her mother)*

MA: Needles.

CAROLINE: Shakespeare. Ma, you say "Longfellow."

MA: Longfellow.

CAROLINE: Now it's a secret and I can't tell it to anybody. Ma, you make a wish.

MA *(With almost grim humor)*: No, I can make wishes without waiting for no star. And I can tell my wishes right out loud too. Do you want to hear them?

CAROLINE *(Resignedly)*: No, Ma, we know 'em already. We've heard 'em. *(She hangs her head affectedly on her mother's left shoulder and says with unmalicious mimicry)* You want me to be a good girl and you want Arthur to be honest in word and deed.

MA *(Majestically)*: Yes. So mind yourself.

ELMER: Caroline, take out that letter from Beulah in my coat pocket by you and read aloud the places I marked with red pencil.

CAROLINE *(Working)*: "A few blocks after you pass the two big oil tanks on your left . . ."

EVERYBODY *(Pointing backward)*: There they are!

CAROLINE: ". . . you come to a corner where there's an A & P store on the left and a firehouse kitty-corner to it . . ."

(They all jubilantly identify these landmarks.)

". . . turn right, go two blocks, and our house is Weyerhauser Street Number 471."

MA: It's an even nicer street than they used to live in. And right handy to an A & P.

CAROLINE *(Whispering)*: Ma, it's better than our street. It's richer than our street. —Ma, isn't Beulah richer than we are?

MA *(Looking at her with a firm and glassy eye)*: Mind yourself, missy. I don't want to hear anybody talking about rich or not rich when I'm around. If people aren't nice I don't care how rich they are. I live in the best street in the world because my husband and children live there.

(She glares impressively at Caroline a moment to let this lesson sink in, then looks up, sees Beulah and waves.)

There's Beulah standing on the steps lookin' for us.

*(Beulah has appeared and is waving.
They all call out: "Hello, Beulah—Hello."
Presently they are all getting out of the car.)*

BEULAH: Hello, Mama. —Well, lookit how Arthur and Caroline are growing!

MA: They're bursting all their clothes!

BEULAH *(Kisses her father long and affectionately)*: Hello, Papa. Good old Papa. You look tired, Pa—

MA: —Yes, your pa needs a rest. Thank Heaven, his vacation has come just now. We'll feed him up and let him sleep late. Pa has a present for you, Loolie. He would go and buy it.

BEULAH: Why, Pa, you're terrible to go and buy anything for me. Isn't he terrible?

MA: Well, it's a secret. You can open it at dinner.

BEULAH *(Puts her arm around his neck and rubs her nose against his temple)*: Crazy old Pa, goin' buyin' things! It's me that ought to be buyin' things for you, Pa.

ELMER: Oh, no! There's only one Loolie in the world.

BEULAH *(Whispering, as her eyes fill with tears)*: Are you glad I'm still alive, Pa?

(She kisses him abruptly and goes back to the house steps.)

ELMER: Where's Horace, Loolie?

BEULAH: He was kep' over a little at the office. He'll be here any minute. He's crazy to see you all.

MA: All right. You men go over to the Y and come back in about an hour.

BEULAH *(As her father returns to the wheel, she stands out in the street beside him)*: Go straight along, Pa, you can't miss it. It just stares at ya.

(The Stage Manager removes the automobile with the help of Elmer and Arthur, who go off waving their good-byes.)

Well, come on upstairs, Ma, and take off your things.
    Caroline, there's a surprise for you in the backyard.

CAROLINE: Rabbits?

BEULAH: No.

CAROLINE: Chickens?

BEULAH: No. Go and see.

(Caroline runs offstage.
  Beulah and Ma gradually go upstairs.)

There are two new puppies. You be thinking over whether you can keep one in Newark.

MA: I guess we can. It's a nice house, Beulah. You just got a *lovely* home.

BEULAH: When I got back from the hospital, Horace had moved everything into it, and there wasn't anything for me to do.

MA: It's lovely.

(The Stage Manager pushes out a bed from the left. Its foot is toward the right. Beulah sits on it, testing the springs.)

BEULAH: I think you'll find this comfortable, Ma.

MA *(Taking off her hat)*: Oh, I could sleep on a heapa shoes, Loolie! I don't have no trouble sleepin'. *(She sits down beside her)* Now let me look at my girl. Well, well, when I last saw you, you didn't know me. You kep' saying: "When's Mama comin'? When's Mama comin'?" But the doctor sent me away.

BEULAH *(Puts her head on her mother's shoulder and weeps)*: It was awful, Mama. It was awful. She didn't even live a few minutes, Mama. It was awful.

MA *(Looking far away)*: God thought best, dear. God thought best. We don't understand why. We just go on, honey, doin' our business. *(Then almost abruptly—passing the back of her hand across her cheek)* Well, now, what are we giving the men to eat tonight?

BEULAH: There's a chicken in the oven.

MA: What time didya put it in?

BEULAH *(Restraining her)*: Aw, Ma, don't go yet. I like to sit here with you this way. You always get the fidgets when we try and pet ya, Mama.

MA *(Ruefully, laughing)*: Yes, it's kinda foolish. I'm just an old Newark bag-a-bones. *(She glances at the backs of her hands)*

BEULAH *(Indignantly)*: Why, Ma, you're good-lookin'! We always said you were good-lookin'. —And besides, you're the best ma we could ever have.

MA *(Uncomfortable)*: Well, I hope you like me. There's nothin' like being liked by your family. —Now I'm going downstairs to look at the chicken. You stretch out here for a minute and shut your eyes. —Have you got everything laid in for breakfast before the shops close?

BEULAH: Oh, you know! Ham and eggs.

(They both laugh.)

MA: I declare I never could understand what men see in ham and eggs. I think they're horrible. —What time did you put the chicken in?

BEULAH: Five o'clock.

MA: Well, now, you shut your eyes for ten minutes.

(Beulah stretches out and shuts her eyes.
Ma descends the stairs absentmindedly singing:)

> There were ninety and nine that safely lay
> In the shelter of the fold,
> But one was out on the hills away,
> Far off from the gates of gold . . .

END OF PLAY

PART
II

Plays for Bleecker Street

(PLAYS IN ONE ACT
FOR AN ARENA STAGE)

IN 1956, Thornton Wilder began a series of short plays for the arena stage that grew into an ambitious attempt to write two cycles of plays depicting "The Seven Deadly Sins" and "The Seven Ages of Man." In his lifetime, Wilder completed and released six of the projected fourteen plays—*Childhood, Infancy, Someone from Assisi* (Lust), *The Drunken Sisters* (Gluttony), *Bernice* (Pride) and *The Wreck on the Five-Twenty-Five* (Sloth)— but withdrew the latter two after a single performance of each in Berlin in 1957.

This section includes these six plays as well as five additional plays that appear here in print for the first time. These are works that Wilder never completed, but left in various drafts as part of his archive. F. J. O'Neil, an actor and director, who knew Wilder, is responsible for the research and editing of *A Ringing of Doorbells* (Envy), *In Shakespeare and the Bible* (Wrath), *The Rivers Under the Earth* (probably middle age) and *Youth*. The fifth play, *Cement Hands* (Avarice), makes its debut thanks to Donald Gallup, Thornton Wilder's former literary executor. With the exception of a single public reading of *Cement Hands*, these five plays have never been performed.

The name "Plays for Bleecker Street: Plays in One-Act for an Arena Stage" refers to the title given *Infancy, Childhood* and *Someone from Assisi*, which premiered in 1962 at Circle in the Square in New York. It seems more than appropriate to identify this first published collection of Wilder's last works as a dramatist (eleven plays is all we shall have, though he had hoped to premiere all fourteen) with the title given by the theatre that in part inspired his work on the "Sins" and "Ages" cycles.

"The Seven Deadly Sins" plays are presented in an order Wilder described in his journals in 1959 rather than in strict canonical order.

INTRODUCTORY NOTE

by Donald Gallup

This note previously appeared in a slightly different form in the Yale Review *in October 1994.*

A T SARATOGA SPRINGS in 1956, Thornton Wilder began a series of "Four-Minute Plays for Four Persons," in continuation of his "Three-Minute Plays for Three Persons," most of which were written during his undergraduate days at Oberlin and Yale. (The best were published in 1928 as *The Angel That Troubled the Waters and Other Plays*.) As he commented in his journal on 2 December 1956, "The self-imposition of a scheme [is] always seen as an aid, even when as with Joyce one sees it becoming an appalling exacting discipline."

The Drunken Sisters (published in the *Atlantic Monthly* in November 1957, and eventually as the satyr play to conclude *The Alcestiad*) and *In Shakespeare and the Bible* (never completed to the author's satisfaction) may have been the first of the new series to be written, both soon developing beyond the four-minute limit, though still "shorter than one-act plays should be for practical purposes." *The Wreck on the*

Five-Twenty-Five was begun at 5:00 A.M. on 17 November, and *Bernice* in the afternoon of the 23rd. As Thornton Wilder worked on these plays, he considered possible subjects for addition to the series. Surveying what he had written, he observed in his journal on 13 December 1956:

> What I particularly like about all these, including the *manqué* ones, is the completeness of their expression as plays for a theatre in the round. This quality is at its best in *The Wreck*, precisely because it is about "looking through windows"; but in each of the later ones I seem to acquire—without that adventitious aid—a deeper exploration of the mode. Now I want to make some more—and, oh, Muse, I want one or two in lighter vein to go with these horrors.

At St. Moritz, on 14 June 1957, Thornton Wilder began *The Rivers Under the Earth*. In his journal he wrote:

> . . . what was clearest was the felicity for the arena stage of this nocturnal scene by Lake Geneva, fireflies, bonfires, and the "rocks" dispersed about the scene . . . I hope this comes out all right. It seems to me now to be the promise of a beautiful and hushed and intimative play.

Five days later, he reported:

> Well, I've about finished . . . This play presents an enormous difficulty: it must be, by its very nature, two-thirds exposition. I have to plant all those "buried associations" which, like time-bombs, explode in rapid succession in the closing third . . .

Later in 1957, when the American National Theatre and Academy asked to include his work in a program of American plays for the dedication of the new Congress Hall in West Berlin (built for cultural and scientific meetings by the

Benjamin Franklin Foundation), Thornton Wilder offered *The Wreck on the Five-Twenty-Five* and *Bernice* from the new series, along with *The Happy Journey to Trenton and Camden* (first published in 1931). Seven one-act plays were presented, in English, with Thornton Wilder as master of ceremonies, on 20 September 1957, before an audience of twelve hundred. There were two by Tennessee Williams: *This Property Is Condemned* and *Portrait of a Madonna*, the latter with Lillian Gish (for whom the play was written). Then came Eugene O'Neill's *Before Breakfast*, with Eileen Heckart and James Daly, and William Saroyan's monologue *Ever Been in Love with a Midget?* The three plays by Wilder ended the evening: first *Bernice*, with Ethel Waters and the author himself; then *The Wreck on the Five-Twenty-Five*, with Lillian Gish and Hiram Sherman; and finally *The Happy Journey*, with the author as the Stage Manager and Ethel Waters as Ma Kirby.

According to the *Times* (London) of 23 September 1957, *The Wreck* was "far and away the best" of the Wilder plays:

> Suburban frustration and lack of communication are familiar enough themes, but Mr. Wilder handles them with a subtle eye and brings his symbols and universals into the drawing-room without falsification on either level, a feat which is made to seem less remarkable than it is by the skill with which it is done.

The *Times*'s critic dismissed *Bernice* as "cliché"—and went on to deplore as "the only lapse" in the program a "treacly religious ditty ["His Eye Is on the Sparrow"] imposed on the last piece [*The Happy Journey*] by Miss Ethel Waters." (Ethel Waters had sung the hymn to great acclaim during the Broadway run of Carson McCullers's *The Member of the Wedding*. She complained that there was no God in *Bernice*.)

But the general reception of both the new plays ("applauded as theatre but deprecated as life," according to the *New York Times*) was disappointing to Thornton Wilder. Although he did permit a German translation of *Bernice* to appear three years later in *Die Neue Rundschau*, he refused to allow any other publication or production of either play.

On board the SS *Vulcania* on his way to Europe in November 1958, Thornton Wilder resumed intensive work on the one-act plays. He had already begun a seventh for the series, a comic play dealing with avarice (originally called *The Cabots* and eventually *Cement Hands*) when he read in Jean Paris's book on James Joyce the suggestion that four of the stories in *Dubliners* exemplify four of the Seven Deadly Sins in the canonical order. As he reported in his journal on 24 November:

> ... it suddenly swept over me that maybe all my seven could be *les péchés capitaux*. And in a few minutes I saw that I could save and finish and deepen those two plays which I thought were to be discarded [*The Ringing of Doorbells* and *In Shakespeare and the Bible*], and that the three I had written could very well fit into such a series ...
>
> *Bernice* [Pride] would require the addition of only a few lines: that the "born alone" of these two was to be born disdainful of others, superior, secret, and prideful. *The Ringing of Doorbells* [Envy] now comes to life and meaning and will be very strong (though ... I do not see its concluding moments). As I groped in the extremely difficult problem of "exemplifying" ... [Lust], there came back to my mind that notion I had long had of doing a St. Francis before the conversion: that saints are monsters of nature that have hesitated, been good and evil at their extremes. This [*Someone from Assisi*] promises to be a most extraordinary play, indeed, and full of matter not often said. I do not yet see how *In Shakespeare and the Bible* can be directed towards a statement about ... [Wrath]; I may have to find another story, but such lies latent there: that wrath against a person is wrath against the universe; that— as I say so often of the Irish—they are grandiose

before they find the pretext for the quarrel. *The Drunken Sisters* [Gluttony] acquires a new charm when we see it in this framework. *The Wreck on the Five-Twenty-Five* [Sloth] will require the addition of a few words to show that the type of despair into which the hero falls is, precisely, in Dante's sense, an unwillingness to accept the gifts of life: "Sullen we were in the bright air." [The quotation is from the *Inferno*, canto 7, lines 121–24 (Circle V, Of the Wrathful and the Sullen). Thornton Wilder's *Dante*, in the Temple Classics edition, has the Italian text underlined by him and gives this English equivalent: "Fixed in the slime, they say: 'Sullen were we / in the sweet air, that is gladdened by the Sun, / carrying lazy smoke within our hearts; // now lie we sullen here in the black mire.'"]

In Salzburg two weeks later he expressed his satisfaction:

How right I was to hit on this serial idea. The plays become *gonflé* with the concept and the author is relieved of the necessity of underscoring it.

The difficulty of *Someone from Assisi* is to carry the burden of two tremendous elements as subordinate to elements that must overweigh them, i.e., brief summarized sketches of the characteristics of a St. Francis and a St. Clara as merely contributive to the idea of the Erotic as Destroyer and the Erotic as Creative.

By the spring of 1959 the order and titles for "The Seven Deadly Sins" series had been firmly established:

"SEVEN PLAYS IN ONE ACT FOR AN ARENA STAGE":
"The Seven Deadly Sins"

The Drunken Sisters (Gluttony)
Bernice (Pride)
The Wreck on the Five-Twenty-Five (Sloth)

A Ringing of Doorbells (Envy)
In Shakespeare and the Bible (Wrath)
Someone from Assisi (Lust)
Cement Hands (Avarice)

In this period Thornton Wilder had begun to go to the Circle in the Square in New York, and was impressed with the skill demonstrated by José Quintero, the director, in using this surrounded platform. Because he had always intended his one-act plays for the arena stage, he had agreed, in May 1959, that the Circle in the Square could present them. He hoped they would begin "in the fall" if he could "write finis" to them.

But a year later, in May 1960, "The Seven Deadly Sins" plays were still not complete; an entirely new series—"The Seven Ages of Man"—had been added; and, as his journal entry for 16 May shows, further new ideas were being contemplated:

I would like this series of Seven Ages plays to be also a repertory of different kinds of plays. Could I do this "Youth" as a Noh, or as a *commedia dell'arte*, or as a Raimund *Volksstuck*, and so on? Of course, this Youth-confronting-Age could take its place toward the end of the series, too.

Thornton Wilder had recorded in his journal on 31 January 1957, at an early stage in his work on the one-act plays, that "precisely the claim of the arena stage—the beauty and power of the arena stage—is that it diminishes all that is not in the high sense poetic." And he forced himself to admit on 17 May 1960 that

... the thing that bores me with the whole project [for *High Noon*] now is that there's no "poetry" in it ... The play *Childhood* is full of poetry. And I now see that *Infancy* has even more; and both beyond any conscious

intention on my part. This project for *High Noon*, at
the present stage of adumbration, is merely a notion,
fanciful enough but not of the kind of fancy which
can enlist my enthusiasm. Unless, with more medita-
tion, a new factor enters, it must probably be relegated
to that groaning wastepaper basket of mistaken
departures.

Fresh impetus came with Thornton Wilder's decision to
allow Circle in the Square to present *Childhood*, *Infancy*
and *Someone from Assisi* (Lust) as the first of the Wilder
"Plays for Bleecker Street." In the *New York Times* on
6 November 1961, Arthur Gelb reported that the two series
would be the author's "artistic summing up." The title chosen for the first bill underlined the fact that the cycles were
written specifically for the playhouse on Bleecker Street.
(Gelb quoted the author as saying that being able to work
for the arena stage had renewed his creative energies.) As
other one-act plays are completed, "they will be added to
the repertory of the Circle in the Square. José Quintero,
Circle's director, and Theodore Mann, its producer, antic-
ipate that the fourteen plays will be presented over a period
of six years."

"Plays for Bleecker Street" opened on 11 January 1962
(it had been postponed from 18 December 1961) and ran for
some 350 performances, finally closing on 11 November.
Although Thornton Wilder was reported in the *New York
Times Magazine* of 15 April 1962 as agreeing that the plays
were "a success," he insisted to Flora Lewis in the same
interview that he had "years of full-time work ahead on
these projects alone." In the event, only the three plays presented in 1962 ever reached the New York stage.

For a period of two and a half years beginning in 1963,
Thornton Wilder authorized Samuel French to license the
three Bleecker Street plays for performance by those amateur groups who could perform them on an arena-type
stage, or thrust stage which permits the audience to sit on

at least three sides of the stage, bringing them closer to the acting area.

For the use of such groups, Samuel French offered the plays "in manuscript"—that is, as scripts reproduced from typed copy. Regular acting editions of *Infancy* and *Childhood* were published on 17 June 1970, although *Someone from Assisi* continued to be offered only "in manuscript."

Childhood was televised by the CBC (1966, repeated 1969) and *Childhood* and *Infancy* on educational television (1966, repeated 1970). All three plays have been performed in several countries.

Of the planned fourteen plays, Thornton Wilder actually completed six, had a seventh—*Cement Hands* (Avarice)—in a satisfactory enough stage to be read to friends, and "all but finished" an eighth—*Youth* (Gulliver)—and a ninth—*The Rivers Under the Earth* (Middle Age).

Only notes and fragmentary drafts for the others remain to provide evidence of how nobly the project was conceived. With *The Emporium* and the book of the Norton Lectures at Harvard, the two cycles take their place in the imposing array of Wilder enterprises that, to our great loss, never came to fruition.

DONALD GALLUP, Thornton Wilder's literary executor from 1975–1995, served from 1947 to 1980 as curator of the Yale Collection of American Literature at the Beinecke Rare Book and Manuscript Library.

The Seven Deadly Sins

ONE

The Drunken Sisters

(Gluttony)

CHARACTERS

CLOTHO
LACHESIS   *The Three Fates*
ATROPOS
APOLLO

SETTING

The time of Admetus, King of Thessaly.

The Three Fates, largely hidden by their voluminous draperies, are seated on a bench. They wear the masks of old women, touched by the grotesque but with vestiges of nobility. Seated are Clotho with her spindle, Lachesis with the bulk of the thread of life on her lap, and Atropos with her scissors. They rock back and forth as they work, passing the threads from right to left. The audience watches them for a time in silence, broken only by a faint humming from Clotho.

CLOTHO: What is it that goes first on four legs, then on two legs? Don't tell me! Don't tell me!

LACHESIS *(Bored)*: You know it!

CLOTHO: Let me pretend that I don't know it.

ATROPOS: There are no new riddles. We know them all.

LACHESIS: How boring our life is without riddles! Clotho, make up a riddle.

CLOTHO: Be quiet, then, and give me a moment to think . . . What is it that . . . What is it that . . . ?

(Enter Apollo, disguised.)

APOLLO *(To the audience)*: These are the great sisters—the Fates. Clotho weaves the threads of life; Lachesis measures the length of each; Atropos cuts them short. In their monotonous work of deciding our lives they are terribly bored, and like so many people who are bored, they find great pleasure in games—in enigmas and riddles. Naturally they can't play cards, because their hands are always busy with the threads of life.

ATROPOS: Sister! Your elbow! Do your work without striking me.

LACHESIS: I can't help it—this thread is s-o-o l-o-o-ong! Never have I had to reach so far.

CLOTHO: Long and gray and dirty! All those years a slave!

LACHESIS: So it is! *(To Atropos)* Cut it, dear sister. *(Atropos cuts it—click!)* And now this one; cut this. It's a blue one—blue for bravery: blue and short.

ATROPOS: So easy to see! *(Click)*

LACHESIS: You almost cut that purple one, Atropos.

ATROPOS: This one? Purple for a king?

LACHESIS: Yes; watch what you're doing, dear. It's the life of Admetus, King of Thessaly.

APOLLO *(Aside)*: Aie!

LACHESIS: I've marked it clearly. He's to die at sunset.

APOLLO *(To the audience)*: No! No!

LACHESIS: He's the favorite of Apollo, as was his father before him, and all that tiresome house of Thessaly. The queen Alcestis will be a widow tonight.

APOLLO *(To the audience)*: Alcestis! Alcestis! No!

LACHESIS: There'll be howling in Thessaly. There'll be rolling on the ground and tearing of garments . . . Not now dear; there's an hour yet.

APOLLO *(Aside)*: To work! To work, Apollo the Crooked! *(He starts the motions of running furiously while remaining in one place, but stops suddenly and addresses the audience)* Is there anyone here who does not know that old story—the reason why King Admetus and his queen Alcestis are dear to me? *(He sits on the ground and continues talking with raised forefinger)* Was it ten years ago? I am little concerned with time. I am the god of the sun; it is always light where I am. Perhaps ten years ago. My father and the father of us all was filled up with anger against me. What had I done? *(He moves his finger back and forth)* Do not ask that now; let it be forgotten . . . He laid upon me a punishment. He ordered that I should descend to earth and live for a year among men—I, as a man among men, as a servant. Half hidden, known and not known, I chose to be a herdsman of King Admetus of Thessaly. I lived the life of a man, as close to them as I am to you now, as close to the just and to the unjust. Each day the King gave orders to the other herdsmen and myself; each day the Queen gave thought to what went well or ill with us and our families. I came to love King Admetus and Queen Alcestis and through them I came to love all men. And now Admetus must die. *(Rising)* No! I have laid my plans. I shall prevent it. To work. To work, Apollo the Crooked. *(He again starts the motions of running furiously while remaining in one place. He complains noisily)* Oh, my back! Aie, aie. They beat me, but worst of all they've made me late. I'll be beaten again.

LACHESIS: Who's the sniveler?

APOLLO: Don't stop me now. I haven't a moment to talk. I'm late already. Besides, my errand's a terrible secret. I can't say a word.

ATROPOS: Throw your yarn around him, Lachesis. What's the fool doing with a secret? It's we who have all the secrets.

(The threads in the laps of the Sisters are invisible to the audience. Lachesis now rises and swings her hands three times in wide circles above her head as though she were about to fling a lasso, then hurls the noose across the stage. Apollo makes the gesture of being caught. With each strong pull by Lachesis, Apollo is dragged nearer to her. During the following speeches Lachesis lifts her end of the strands high in the air, alternately pulling Apollo up, almost strangling him, and flinging him again to the ground.)

APOLLO: Ladies, beautiful ladies, let me go. If I'm late all Olympus will be in an uproar. Aphrodite will be mad with fear—but oh, already I've said too much. My orders were to come immediately, and to say nothing— especially not to women. The thing's of no interest to men. Dear ladies, let me go.

ATROPOS: Pull on your yarn, sister.

APOLLO: You're choking me. You're squeezing me to death.

LACHESIS *(Forcefully)*: Stop your whining and tell your secret at once.

APOLLO: I can't. I dare not.

ATROPOS: Pull harder, sister. Boy, speak or strangle. *(She makes the gesture of choking him)*

APOLLO: Ow! Ow!—Wait! I'll tell the half of it, if you let me go.

ATROPOS: Tell the whole or we'll hang you up in the air in that noose.

APOLLO: I'll tell, I'll tell. But—*(He looks about him fearfully)*—promise me! Swear by the Styx that you'll not tell anyone, and swear by Lethe that you'll forget it.

LACHESIS: We have only one oath—by Acheron. And we never swear it—least of all to a sniveling slave. Tell us what you know, or you'll be by all three rivers in a minute.

APOLLO: I tremble at what I am about to say. I . . . ssh . . . I carry . . . here . . . in these bottles . . . Oh, ladies, let me go. Let me go.

CLOTHO AND ATROPOS: Pull, sister.

APOLLO: No! No! I'll tell you. I am carrying the wine for . . . for Aphrodite. Once every ten days she renews her beauty . . . by . . . drinking this.

ATROPOS: Liar! Fool! She has nectar and ambrosia, as they all have.

APOLLO (*Confidentially*): But is she not the fairest? . . . It is the love gift of Hephaistos; from the vineyards of Dionysos; from grapes ripened under the eye of Apollo—of Apollo who tells no lies.

SISTERS (*Confidentially to one another in blissful anticipation*): Sisters!

ATROPOS (*Like sugar*): Pass the bottles up, dear boy.

APOLLO (*In terror*): Not that! Ladies! It is enough that I have told you the secret! Not that!

ATROPOS: Surely, Lachesis, you can find on your lap the thread of this worthless slave—a yellow one destined for a long life?

APOLLO (*Falling on his knees*): Spare me!

ATROPOS (*To Lachesis*): Look, that's it—the sallow one, with the tangle in it of dishonesty, and the stiffness of obstinacy, and the ravel-ravel of stupidity. Pass it over to me, dear.

APOLLO (*His forehead touching the floor*): Oh, that I had never been born!

LACHESIS (*To Atropos*): This is it. (*With a sigh*) I'd planned to give him five score.

APOLLO (*Rising and extending the bottles, sobbing*): Here, take them! I'll be killed anyway. Aphrodite will kill me. My life's over.

ATROPOS (*Strongly, as the Sisters take the bottles*): Not one more word out of you. Put your hand on your mouth. We're tired of listening to you.

(*Apollo, released of the noose, flings himself facedown upon the ground, his shoulders heaving. The Sisters put the flagons to their lips. They drink and moan with pleasure.*)

SISTERS: Sisters!

LACHESIS: Sister, how do I look?

ATROPOS: Oh, I could eat you. And I?

CLOTHO: Sister, how do I look?

LACHESIS: Beautiful! Beautiful! And I?

ATROPOS: And not a mirror on all the mountain, or a bit of still water, to tell us which of us is the fairest.

LACHESIS (*Dreamily, passing her hand over her face*): I feel like . . . I feel as I did when Kronos followed me about, trying to catch me in a dark corner.

ATROPOS: Poseidon was beside himself—dashing across the plains trying to engulf me.

CLOTHO: My own father—who can blame him?—began to forget himself.

ATROPOS (*Whispering*): This is not such a worthless fellow, after all. And he's not bad-looking. (*To Clotho*) Ask him what he sees.

LACHESIS: Ask him which of us is the fairest.

CLOTHO: Boy! Boy! You bay meek. I mean, you . . . you may thpeak. Thpeak to him, Lakethith; I've lotht my tongue.

LACHESIS: Boy, look at us well! You may tell us which is the fairest.

(*Apollo has remained facedownward on the ground. He now rises and gazes at the Sisters. He acts as if blinded: he cowers and uncovers his eyes, gazing first at one and then at another.*)

APOLLO: What have I done? This splendor! What have I done? You—and you—and you! Kill me if you will, but I cannot say which one is the fairest. *(Falling on his knees)* Oh, ladies—if so much beauty has not made you cruel, let me now go and hide myself. Aphrodite will hear of this. Let me escape to Crete and take up my old work.

ATROPOS: What was your former work, dear boy?

APOLLO: I helped my father in the marketplace; I was a teller of stories and riddles.

(The Sisters are transfixed. Then almost with a scream:)

SISTERS: What's that? What's that you said?

APOLLO: A teller of stories and riddles. Do the beautiful ladies enjoy riddles?

SISTERS *(Rocking from side to side and slapping one another)*: Sisters, do we enjoy riddles?

ATROPOS: Oh, he would only know the old ones. Puh! The blind horse . . . the big toe . . .

LACHESIS: The cloud . . . the eyelashes of Hera . . .

CLOTHO *(Harping on one string)*: What is it that first goes on four legs . . . ?

ATROPOS: The porpoise . . . Etna . . .

APOLLO: Everyone knows those! I have some new ones—

SISTERS *(Again, a scream)*: New ones!

APOLLO *(Slowly)*: What is it that is necessary to—*(He pauses. The Sisters are riveted)*

LACHESIS: Go on, boy, go on. What is it that is necessary to—

APOLLO: But—I only play for forfeits. See! If I lose . . .

CLOTHO: If you looth, you mutht tell uth which one ith the faireth.

APOLLO: No! No! I dare not!

LACHESIS *(Sharply)*: Yes!

APOLLO: And if I win?

ATROPOS: Win? Idiot! Stupid! Slave! No one has ever won from us.

APOLLO: But if I win?

LACHESIS: He doesn't know who we are!

APOLLO: But if I win?

CLOTHO: The fool talkth of winning!

APOLLO: If I win, you must grant me one wish. One wish, any wish.

LACHESIS: Yes, yes. Oh, what a tedious fellow! Go on with your riddle. What is it that is necessary to—

APOLLO: Swear by Acheron!

CLOTHO AND LACHESIS: We swear! By Acheron! By Acheron!

APOLLO *(To Atropos)*: You, too.

ATROPOS *(After a moment's brooding resistance, loudly)*: By Acheron!

APOLLO: Then: ready?

LACHESIS: Wait! One moment. *(Leaning toward Atropos, confidentially)* The sun is near setting. Do not forget the thread of Ad—You know, the thread of Ad—

ATROPOS: What? What Ad? What are you whispering about, silly?

LACHESIS *(Somewhat louder)*: Not to forget the thread of Admetus, King of Thessaly. At sundown. Have you lost your shears, Atropos?

ATROPOS: Oh, stop your buzzing and fussing and tend to your own business. Of course I haven't lost my shears. Go on with your riddle, boy!

APOLLO: So! I'll give you as much time as it takes to recite the names of the Muses and their mother.

LACHESIS: Hm! Nine and one. Well, begin!

APOLLO: What is it that is necessary to every life—and that can save only one?

(The Sisters rock back and forth with closed eyes, mumbling the words of the riddle.

Suddenly Apollo starts singing his invocation to the Muses:)

Mnemosyne, mother of the nine;
Polyhymnia, incense of the gods—

LACHESIS *(Shrieks)*: Don't sing! Unfair! How can we think?

CLOTHO: Stop your ears, sister.

ATROPOS: Unfair! *(Murmuring)* What is it that can save every life—*(They put their fingers in their ears)*

APOLLO:

> Erato, voice of love;
> Euterpe, help me now.
>
> Calliope, thief of our souls;
> Urania, clothed of the stars;
> Clio of the backward glances;
> Euterpe, help me now.
>
> Terpsichore of the beautiful ankles;
> Thalia of long laughter;
> Melpomene, dreaded and welcome;
> Euterpe, help me now.

(Then in a loud voice) Forfeit! Forfeit!

(Clotho and Atropos bury their faces in Lachesis's neck, moaning.)

LACHESIS *(In a dying voice)*: What is the answer?

APOLLO *(Flinging away his hat, triumphantly)*: Myself! Apollo the sun.

SISTERS: Apollo! You?

LACHESIS *(Savagely)*: Pah! What life can you save?

APOLLO: My forfeit! One wish! One life! That life of Admetus, King of Thessaly.

(A horrified clamor arises from the Sisters.)

SISTERS: Fraud! Impossible! Not to be thought of!

APOLLO: By Acheron.

SISTERS: Against all law. Zeus will judge. Fraud.

APOLLO *(Warning)*: By Acheron.

SISTERS: Zeus! We will go to Zeus about it. He will decide.

APOLLO: Zeus swears by Acheron and keeps his oath.

(Sudden silence.)

ATROPOS *(Decisive but ominous)*: You will have your wish—the life of King Admetus. But—

APOLLO *(Triumphantly)*: I shall have the life of Admetus!

SISTERS: But—

APOLLO: I shall have the life of Admetus! What is your *but?*

ATROPOS: Someone else must die in his stead.

APOLLO *(Lightly)*: Oh—choose some slave. Some gray and greasy thread on your lap, divine Lachesis.

LACHESIS *(Outraged)*: What? You ask me to take a life?

ATROPOS: You ask us to murder?

CLOTHO: Apollo thinks that we are criminals?

APOLLO *(Beginning to be fearful)*: Then, great sisters, how is this to be done?

LACHESIS: Me—an assassin? *(She spreads her arms wide and says solemnly)* Over my left hand is Chance; over my right hand is Necessity.

APOLLO: Then, gracious sisters, how will this be done?

LACHESIS: Someone must *give* his life for Admetus—of free choice and will. Over such deaths we have no control. Neither Chance nor Necessity rules the free offering of the will. Someone must choose to die in the place of Admetus, King of Thessaly.

APOLLO *(Covering his face with his hands)*: No! No! I see it all! *(With a loud cry)* Alcestis! Alcestis! *(And he runs stumbling from the scene)*

END OF PLAY

TWO

Bernice

(Pride)

CHARACTERS

MR. MALLISON, Mr. Walbeck's lawyer, fifty-nine
BERNICE MAYHEW, Mr. Walbeck's maid, fifty
THE DRIVER
MR. WALBECK, forty-seven

SETTING

Drawing room of a house in Chicago, 1911.

Door into the hall at the back. All we need see are an elaborate, but not weighty, table in the center and two chairs. At the front of the stage are some andirons and a poker, indicating a fireplace.

Mallison, fifty-nine, all a lawyer, now very nervous, is standing before the table holding an open watch in his hand. By the door is Bernice, colored, fifty, in a maid's uniform.

MALLISON: Remind me . . . remind me, please . . . your name?

BERNICE *(Unimpressed)*: Bernice.

MALLISON: Thank you. —Now Mr. Burgess, your employer, may be a little bit . . . moody. You do whatever he wants. Have you enough help to run the house?

BERNICE: I did what you told me. There's Jason for the heavy work and the furnace. This Mr. Burgess—will he be alone in this house?

MALLISON: Alone? Oh! Most probably. At all events, you are in charge. Get whatever help you need. I am Mr. Burgess's lawyer, but he will be getting another lawyer soon. All your bills will be paid, I'm sure . . . You have some dinner waiting for him now?

BERNICE *(Slowly)*: Why do you talk so funny about this Mr. Burgess? Is he coming from the crazy house or something?

MALLISON *(Outraged)*: No, indeed!! I don't know where you got such an idea. All that's expected of you is . . . uh . . . good meals and a well-run house.

BERNICE: You talk very funny, Mr. Mallison.

MALLISON *(After swallowing with dignity and glaring at her)*: Mrs. Willard recommended you as an experienced cook and housekeeper, Bernice. My duty ends there.

BERNICE: I don't have to take any jobs unless I likes them, Mr. Mallison. I never agrees to work any place more than three days. Mrs. Willard don't like it, but that's my terms—if I likes it, I stays.

MALLISON: Well, I hope you like it here. You're getting very well paid and you can ask for any further help you need—within reason. There's an automobile stopping before the door now. I think you'd better go to the door.

(Bernice doesn't move. Arms akimbo she looks musingly at Mallison.)

BERNICE: I seen people like you before . . . You're up to something.

(The front door bell rings.)

MALLISON: I don't like your tone. You've been engaged to work here—for three days, anyway. You can begin by answering that door bell.

(Bernice goes out. Mallison straightens his clothes, goes to the table and picks up his briefcase, then stands waiting with pursed lips. Sounds of altercation from the hall.)

DRIVER'S VOICE: All right! The price is twenty dollars. But if I'd know'd it was a night like this—

(Enter the Driver, a livery stable chauffeur, Irish, slightly drunk. He is carrying a small rattan suitcase, which he puts down by the door. He is followed by Walbeck, forty-seven, prematurely gray; he speaks softly, but gives an impression of controlled power. Bernice enters behind them.)

WALBECK *(To Mallison, in a low voice)*: I understood that the fare was paid in advance?

MALLISON: The twenty dollars was paid in advance.

DRIVER: Anybody'd charge twice to drive on a night like this. First it was rain and snow—

MALLISON: The livery stable was given twenty dollars—
(To Bernice) You can prepare the dinner!

(Exit Bernice.)

DRIVER: Then it turned to ice. The worst night I've ever seen, to go to Joliet and pick up a I-don't-know-what. The car falling off the road every minute. To go to Joliet and pick up a criminal of some sort—

WALBECK *(Gesture of empty pockets)*: I have no money.

MALLISON *(To the driver)*: I will give you five dollars, but I shall report you to the livery stable.

DRIVER *(Taking the bill)*: What do I care? Thirty-five miles each way and half the time you couldn't see the road five yards in front of you; and the other half sliding into the ditch. All right, tell 'em and see what I tell 'em.

MALLISON: You have your five dollars. If you go now, I'll say nothing to your superiors—But go!

DRIVER *(Starting for the door, then turning on Walbeck)*: And who do you think you are, Mr. Bur-gessss! Keeping your mouth so shut! You a murderer or I-don't-know-what; and too big and mighty to talk to anybody. —Oh, you had to *think*, did you? So you had to think? Well, you've got enough to think about for the rest of your goddamned life.

(He goes out.)

MALLISON *(Stiffly)*: Good evening, Mr. Walbeck.

(The front door is heard closing with a slam.)

WALBECK *(Always softly, but impersonally)*: What is this name of . . . Burgess?

MALLISON: We assumed, Mr. Walbeck, that you would prefer us to engage the household staff and . . . make certain other arrangements under . . . another name. Since you did not reply to our letters on this matter, we selected the name of Burgess.

WALBECK: I see. —Is . . . my wife here?

MALLISON *(Astonished)*: You did not get Mrs. Walbeck's letters?

WALBECK: I did not open any letters.

MALLISON: And *our* letters, Mr. Walbeck?

WALBECK: I haven't opened any letters for six months.

MALLISON *(Controlling his outrage, primly)*: Mrs. Walbeck left a week ago—with the children—for California. She has filed a petition for divorce. In her letters she probably explained it to you at length. She did not wish to make this move earlier . . . She wished it to be known that she stood by you through . . . your ordeal. When she heard that your sentence had been reduced and that you would be returning this week, she—

WALBECK *(Coolly)*: There's no need to say anything more, Mr. Mallison.

MALLISON: A woman has been engaged to attend to your needs. Her name is Bernice. A wardrobe—that is, a wardrobe of clothes—you will find upstairs. Your measurements were obtained by your former tailor from the authorities at the . . . institution from which you have come. —Here are the keys of the house. Here are the statements from your bank. A checkbook. Here *(He places a long envelope on the table)* are five hundred dollars which I have drawn for your immediate needs.

WALBECK: Thank you. Good night.

MALLISON: Mr. Walbeck, hitherto the firm of Bremerton, Bremerton, Mallison and Mallison has been happy to serve as your legal representatives. From now on we trust that you will find other counsel. We relinquish— here *(He lays down another document)* our power of attorney. And in this envelope you will find all the documents and information that our successors will require. I wish you good night.

WALBECK *(Stonily)*: Good night.

(Mallison turns at the door.)

MALLISON: You read no letters?

WALBECK *(His eyes on the ground)*: No.

MALLISON: That reminds me. Your daughter Lavinia wished to leave a letter for you. Her mother forbade her to do so. However, I . . . I was prepared to take the responsibility. Your daughter gave me this letter to give to you.

(He gives an envelope to Walbeck, who puts it in his breast pocket. His silence and level glance complete Mallison's discomfiture.)

Good night, sir.

(Exit Mallison. Walbeck stands motionless gazing fixedly before him. Suddenly, in a rage, he overturns the table before him; but immediately recovers his self-control. Enter Bernice.)

BERNICE: Dinner's served, sir.

WALBECK: I won't have any dinner.

BERNICE: Yes, Mr. Burgess.

WALBECK: What?

BERNICE: I said, "Yes, Mr. Burgess." I'll just set that table to rights.

WALBECK *(Quickly)*: I'll do it.

(He does.)

BERNICE *(Watchfully but unsentimentally)*: I've got a real good steak in there. I'm the best cook in Chicago, Mr. Burgess. There's lots of people that knows that.

WALBECK: Is there any liquor in the house?

BERNICE: Oh, yes. There's everything.

WALBECK: Rye. Rye straight. —You eat the steak.

BERNICE: Thank you, Mr. Burgess.

(She starts out, then turns.)

Now, you don't want to eat that steak, Mr. Burgess, but I've got some tomato soup there that's the best tomato soup you ever ate. You aren't going to waste my time by refusing to eat that soup.

WALBECK *(Looking at her; impersonally)*: What is your name?

BERNICE: My name's Bernice Mayhew. People calls me Bernice.

WALBECK: Bernice, I don't want to eat in that dining room. You can bring me the rye and some of that soup in here.

BERNICE: Yes, Mr. Burgess.

WALBECK: My name is Walbeck.

BERNICE: What's that?

WALBECK: My name: Wal-beck, Walbeck.

BERNICE: Yes, Mr. Walbeck.

WALBECK: And pour yourself some rye.

BERNICE: I don't touch it, Mr. Walbeck. Ten years ago I made my life over. I changed my name and I changed everything about myself. I thank you, but I don't touch liquor.

(She goes out. Walbeck, standing straight, his eyes on the ground, puts his hand in his pocket and draws out his daughter's letter. After a moment's hesitation, he opens it. He holds it suspended in his hand a moment. Then he tears the letter and envelope, each two ways, and throws the fragments into the fire (invisible to us), between the andirons.

Bernice returns, pushing a small service table. She gives him the rye, then unfurls a tablecloth and starts laying the table. Walbeck drinks half the rye in one swallow.)

WALBECK: Were you here when my wife was here?

BERNICE: No, sir. Nobody's been here today but that lawyer-man. I came here this morning and all day Jason and I have been cleaning the house.

WALBECK: Do you know where I come from?

BERNICE *(Quietly, lowered eyes)*: Yes, I do.

WALBECK: Did that lawyer tell you?

BERNICE: No . . . I knew . . . I been there myself . . . So I knew. I'll get your soup.

(She goes out. Suddenly Walbeck goes to the fireplace. Falling on his knees, he tries without burning his fingers to rake out the fragments of the letter. Apparently it is too late.

Bernice enters with a covered soup tureen. Watchfully, but with no show of surprise, she tries to take in what he is doing. Walbeck rises, dusting off his knees.)

You want me to build up that fire, Mr. Walbeck?

WALBECK: No, it's all right as it is.

(He seats himself at the table.)

BERNICE *(Eyeing the fireplace speculatively)*: There's some toast there, too.

WALBECK: You say you changed your name?

BERNICE: Yes. My born name was Sarah Temple. When I came out of prison I was Bernice Mayhew. Of course, I had some other names too. I was married twice. But Bernice Mayhew was the name I gave myself. *(Without emphasis; her eyes on the distance)* I was in because I killed somebody.

WALBECK *(The soup spoon at his mouth, speaks in her tone)*: I was in because I cheated two or three hundred people out of money.

BERNICE *(Musingly)*: Well, everybody's done something.

(Pause. Walbeck eats.)

WALBECK: You say you changed everything about yourself?

BERNICE: Yes. Everything was changed, anyway. I was in a disgrace—nobody can be in a bigger disgrace than I was. And some people were avoiding me and some people were laughing at me and some people were being kind to me, like I was a dog that came to the back door. And some people were saying: cheer up, Sarah, you've paid your price. There's lots of things to live for. You're young yet. —You're sure you wouldn't like a piece of that steak, Mr. Walbeck, rare or any way you'd like it?

WALBECK: No. I'm going downtown soon. If I get hungry, later, I'll pick up something to eat down there.

BERNICE *(After a short pause, while she continues to gaze into the distance)*: Did anybody come to meet you when you came out of the door of the place you was at?

WALBECK: No.

BERNICE: That's what I mean. I don't blame them. I wouldn't want to go 'round with a person who's very much in a disgrace—like with a person who's killed somebody. I wouldn't choose 'em.

WALBECK: Or with a person who's stolen a lot of people's life savings.

BERNICE: I only mentioned that to show a big part of the change: you're alone.

WALBECK: Did that lawyer who was here, or the agency, know that you'd been in prison?

BERNICE: Oh, no. It was Sarah Temple who did that. She's dead. When I changed my name she became dead. You see the first part of my life I lived in Kansas City. Then I came to Chicago. Bernice Mayhew has never been to Kansas City. She don't even know what it looks like.

WALBECK (*Impersonally, without looking at her*): If you've been on your feet all day cleaning the house, I think you'd better sit down, Bernice.

BERNICE: Well, thank you, I will sit down.

WALBECK: Would you advise me to kill off George Walbeck?

BERNICE (*Seeming more and more remote, in her musings*): Not so much for your sake as for other people's sake. It's not good for other people to have to do with persons who are in a disgrace; it brings out the worst in them. I don't like to see that.

WALBECK (*Slowly, his eyes on the distance*): I guess you're right. I'd better do that.

BERNICE: It's like what happens about poor people. You're a thousand times richer than I am, but I'm richer than millions of people. What good does it do to think about them? I only need one real meal a day; the rest is just stuffing. But I don't notice as how I give up my other two meals. I'm always right there at mealtimes. When I went hungry, most times I didn't let people know about it; and when I'm in a disgrace, why should I make them uncomfortable?

WALBECK: Before you became Bernice Mayhew, did you have any children?

BERNICE: Yes, I did . . . Their mother's dead, of course. But I guess somebody's reminding them every day that their mother was a murderer.—That's bad enough, but it's not as bad as knowing their mother's alive. —Have you noticed that we gradually forgive them that's dead? If I was alive they'd be thinking about me, in one way or another: hating me or maybe trying to stand up for me. There are a lot of ideas young people could go through about a thing like that.

WALBECK (*As though to himself*): Yes.

(*The telephone rings in the hall. Walbeck rises uneasily.*)

Who could that be? Answer it, will you, Bernice? Don't say that I'm here.

(*Bernice goes into the hall. Her voice can be heard shouting as though she were unaccustomed to the telephone.*)

BERNICE: It's me talking—Bernice.

Yes. Who are you, talking?

Who? Oh.

I can't understand much.

A letter? I hear you, a letter.

Yes, miss. What? I can't hear good. The machine don't work good.

All right, you come. I'm here.

Bernice. Yes, you come. I'm here.

(*Bernice returns to the stage.*)

She says she's your daughter.

WALBECK: So-o-o! She didn't go to California with her mother.

BERNICE: She says she sent you a letter. In the letter she asked you to telephone her . . . that she could come and see you. She was asking over and over again if you was here, but I made out that the machine didn't work good. She says she'll be here soon.

(Bernice has been clearing the table, putting the objects on the wheeled service table, which she starts pushing to the door.)

WALBECK: I can't see her tonight. —What do you suppose she wants?

BERNICE *(At the door with lowered eyes)*: I think I can figger that out: about what half the daughters in the world would want. She wants to make a home for you. And to give up her life for you.

(She goes out with the service table.)

WALBECK *(Softly)*: Good God—

(Bernice returns and stands at the door.)

She's seventeen! How could she get such an idea! Her mother must have told her what she thought of me— told her every day for eight years what she thought of me—

BERNICE *(Always without looking at him, broodingly)*: Yes.

(Slight pause.)

Mr. Walbeck, you ought to know that women don't believe what women say. Least of all their mothers. They'll believe any old fool thing a man says.

WALBECK: She's seventeen! How did she do it? How did she get away from her mother? She must have run away at the railway station. She probably has very little money.

BERNICE *("Seeing" it; staring before her)*: She's got some rings, hasn't she? She'll be selling them. She'll be going to the stores hunting for a job.

WALBECK *(Staring at her)*: Yes. —But her mother will have come back to look for her. Or will have telephoned the police to look for her.

BERNICE: Maybe not. Maybe not at all . . . It's terrible when young girls are brave.

WALBECK *(In a sort of terror. For the first time loudly)*: Bernice! —What shall I do?

BERNICE *(A quick glance of somber anger)*: It ain't right to ask advices. It ain't right, Mr. Walbeck.

WALBECK: See here, Bernice! Do this for me.

BERNICE: Do what, for you?

WALBECK: Do what you'd do, if it were your own daughter.

BERNICE *(Sudden flood of tormented emotion)*: How do I know if I did right?—What I did about my own daughter? Maybe my daughter'd be having a good big life living with me. Maybe she's just having one of them silly lives, living with silly people and saying jab-ber-jabber silly things all day. *(Gazing before her)* I hate people who don't know that lots of people is hungry and that lots of people has done bad things. If my daughter was with me, we'd talk . . . I got so many things I've *learned* that I could tell to a girl like that . . . And we'd go downtown and we'd shop for her clothes together . . . and talk . . . I've got a weak heart; I shouldn't get excited. *(She looks at the floor a minute)* No, Mr. Walbeck, don't ask me to throw your daughter back into the trashy lives that most people live.

WALBECK: Bernice: when she comes, give her her choice. I'll go upstairs.

BERNICE: Young people can't make choices. They don't know what they're choosing.

WALBECK *(With increasing almost choked urgency)*: Then tell her . . . she and I'll go away together. Somewhere. We'll start a new life.

(Bernice is silent a moment. Then her mood changes. For the first time she brings a long deep gaze toward him.)

BERNICE: No! —These are just fancies. We're a stone around their necks now! If we were with them we'd be a bigger stone. Sometimes I think death come into the world so we wouldn't *be* a stone around young people's necks. Besides you and I—we're alone. We did what we did because we were that kind of person—the kind that chooses to think they're smarter and better than other people . . . And people that think that way end up alone. We're not *company* for anybody.

(Pause. Walbeck's mood also changes.)

WALBECK *(His mind made up)*: Then tell her that the doctors told me that I had only a few months to live . . . that I've gone off so as not to be a weight on anybody . . . on her, for instance. *(He pulls the envelope from his pocket)* If she's not followed her mother to California, she'll be needing some money. Give her this envelope. *(His tormented urgency returns)* And tell her . . . Tell her . . .

BERNICE *(Somberly but largely)*: I knows what else to tell her, Mr. Walbeck. You go upstairs and hide youself. You's almost dead. You's dyin'.

(Walbeck goes out. Bernice sits in a chair facing the audience, waiting, her eyes on the distance.)

END OF PLAY

THREE

The Wreck on the Five-Twenty-Five

(Sloth)

CHARACTERS

MRS. HAWKINS, forty
MINNIE, her daughter, almost sixteen
MR. FORBES, a neighbor
MR. HERBERT HAWKINS, Mrs. Hawkins's husband

SETTING

Today. The Hawkins home.

Six o'clock in the evening. Mrs. Hawkins, forty, and her daughter Minnie, almost sixteen, are sewing and knitting. At the back is a door into the hall and beside it a table on which is a telephone.

MRS. HAWKINS: Irish stew doesn't seem right for Sunday dinner, somehow. *(Pause)* And your father doesn't really like roast or veal. *(Pause)* Thank Heaven, he's not crazy about steak.

(Another pause while she takes some pins from her mouth.)

I must say it's downright strange—his not being here. He hasn't telephoned for years, like that—that he'd take a later train.

MINNIE: Did he say what was keeping him?

MRS. HAWKINS: No . . . something at the office, I suppose. *(She changes pins again)* He never really did like chicken, either.

MINNIE: He ate pork last week without saying anything. You might try pork chops, Mama; I don't really mind them.

MRS. HAWKINS: He doesn't ever say anything. He eats what's there.—Oh, Minnie, men never realize that there's only a limited number of things to eat.

MINNIE: What did he say on the telephone exactly?

MRS. HAWKINS: "I'll try to catch the six-thirty."

(Both look at their wristwatches.)

MINNIE: But, Mama, Papa's not cranky about what he eats. He's always saying what a good cook you are.

MRS. HAWKINS: Men!

(She has put down her sewing and is gazing before her.)

They think they want a lot of change—variety and change, variety and change. But they don't really. Deep down, they don't.

MINNIE: Don't *what?*

MRS. HAWKINS: You know for a while he read all those Wild Western magazines: cowboys and horses and silly Indians . . . two or three a week. Then, suddenly, he stopped all that. It's as though he thought he were in a kind of jail or prison. —Keep an eye on that window, Minnie. He may be coming down the street any minute.

(Minnie rises and, turning, peers through a window, back right.)

MINNIE: No. —There's Mr. Wilkerson, though. He came back on the five-twenty-five, anyway. Sometimes Papa stops at the tobacco shop and comes down Spruce Street.

(She moves to the left and looks through another window.)

MRS. HAWKINS: Do you feel as though you were in a jail, Minnie?

MINNIE: *What?!*

MRS. HAWKINS: As though life were a jail?

MINNIE *(Returning to her chair)*: No, of course not. —Mama, you're talking awfully funny tonight.

MRS. HAWKINS: I'm not myself. *(Laughs lightly)* I guess I'm not myself because of your father's phone call—his taking a later train, like that, for the first time in so many years.

MINNIE *(With a little giggle)*: I don't know what the five-twenty-five will have done without him.

MRS. HAWKINS *(Not sharply)*: And all those hoodlums he plays cards with every afternoon.

MINNIE: And all the jokes they make.

(Mrs. Hawkins has been looking straight before her—through a window—over the audience's heads, intently.)

MRS. HAWKINS: There's Mrs. Cochran cooking her dinner.

(They both gaze absorbedly at Mrs. Cochran a moment.)

Well, I'm not going to start dinner until your father puts foot in this house.

MINNIE *(Still gazing through the window; slowly)*: There's Mr. Cochran at the door . . . They're arguing about something.

MRS. HAWKINS: Well, that shows that he got in on the five-twenty-five, all right.

MINNIE: Don't people look foolish when you see them, like that—and you can't hear what they're saying? Like ants or something. Somehow, you feel it's not right to look at them when they don't know it.

(They return to their work.)

MRS. HAWKINS: Yes, those men on the train will have missed those awful jokes your father makes. *(Minnie giggles)* I declare, Minnie, every year your father makes worse jokes. It's growing on him.

MINNIE: I don't think they're awful, but, I don't understand *all* of them. Do you? Like what he said to the minister Sunday. I was so embarrassed I didn't want to tell you.

MRS. HAWKINS: I don't want to hear it—not tonight.
 (Her gaze returns to the window) I can't understand why Mrs. Cochran is acting so strangely. And Mr. Cochran has been coming in and out of the kitchen.

MINNIE: And they seem to keep looking at us all the time.

(After a moment's gazing, they return to their work.)

MRS. HAWKINS: Well, you might as well tell me what your father said to the minister.

MINNIE: I . . . I don't want to tell you, if it makes you nervous.

MRS. HAWKINS: I've lived with his jokes for twenty years. I guess I can stand one more.

MINNIE: Mr. Brown had preached a sermon about the atom bomb . . . and about how terrible it would be . . . and at the church door Papa said to him: "Fine sermon, Joe. I enjoyed it. But have you ever thought of this, Joe"— he said—"suppose the atom bomb didn't fall, what would we do then? Have you ever thought of that?" Mr. Brown looked terribly put out.

MRS. HAWKINS *(Puts down her sewing)*: He said that!! I declare, he's getting worse. I don't know where he gets such ideas. People will be beginning to think he's *bitter*. Your father isn't bitter. I know he's not bitter.

MINNIE: No, Mama. People like it. People stop me on the street and tell me what a wonderful sense of humor he has. Like . . . like . . . *(She gives up the attempt and says merely)* Oh, nothing.

MRS. HAWKINS: Go on. Say what you were going to say.

MINNIE: What did he mean by saying: "There we sit for twenty years playing cards on the five-twenty-five, hoping that something big and terrible and wonderful will happen—like a wreck, for instance?"

MRS. HAWKINS *(More distress than indignation)*: I say to you seriously, Minnie, it's just *self-indulgence*. We do everything we know how to make him happy. He loves his home, you know he does. He likes his work—he's proud of what he does at the office.

(She rises and looks down the street through the window at the back. Moved) Oh, it's not *us* he's impatient at: it's the whole world. He simply wishes the whole world were different—that's the trouble with him.

MINNIE: Why, Mama, Papa doesn't complain about anything.

MRS. HAWKINS: Well, I wish he would complain once in a while.

(She returns to her chair) For Sunday I'll see if I can't get an extra good bit of veal.

(They sit in silence a moment. The telephone rings.)

Answer that, will you, dear?—No, I'll answer it.

(Minnie returns to her work. Mrs. Hawkins has a special voice for answering the telephone, slow and measured.)

This is Mrs. Hawkins speaking. Oh, yes, Mr. Cochran. What's that? I don't hear you.

(A shade of anxiety) Are you *sure*? You must be mistaken.

MINNIE: Mama, what is it? *(Mrs. Hawkins listens in silence)* Mama! Mama!! —What's he saying? Is it about Papa?

MRS. HAWKINS: Will you hold the line one minute, Mr. Cochran? I wish to speak to my daughter. *(She puts her hand over the mouthpiece)* No, Minnie. It's not about your father at all.

MINNIE *(Rising)*: Then what *is* it?

MRS. HAWKINS *(In a low, distinct and firm voice)*: Now you do what I tell you. Sit down and go on knitting. Don't look up at me and don't show any surprise.

MINNIE *(A groan of protest)*: Mama!

MRS. HAWKINS: There's nothing to be alarmed about—but I want you to *obey* me.

    (She speaks into the telephone) Yes, Mr. Cochran . . . No . . . Mr. Hawkins telephoned that he was taking a later train tonight. I'm expecting him on the six-thirty.

    You do what you think best.

    I'm not sure that's necessary but . . . you do what you think best.

    We'll be right here.

(She hangs up and stands thinking a moment.)

MINNIE: Mama, I'm almost sixteen. *Tell* me what it's about.

MRS. HAWKINS *(Returns to her chair; bending over her work, she speaks as guardedly as possible)*: Minnie, there's probably nothing to be alarmed about. Don't show any surprise at what I'm about to say to you. Mr. Cochran says that there's been somebody out on the lawn watching us—for ten minutes or more. A man. He's been standing in the shadow of the garage, just looking at us.

MINNIE *(Lowered head)*: Is *that* all!

MRS. HAWKINS: Well, Mr. Cochran doesn't like it. He's . . . he says he's going to telephone the police.

MINNIE: The police!!

MRS. HAWKINS: Your father'll be home any minute, anyway. *(Slight pause)* I guess it's just some . . . some *moody* person on an evening walk. Maybe Mr. Cochran's done right to call the police, though. He says that we shouldn't pull the curtains or anything like that—but just act as though nothing has happened. —Now, I don't want you to get frightened.

MINNIE: I'm not, Mama. I'm just . . . interested. Most nights *nothing* happens.

MRS. HAWKINS *(Sharply)*: I should hope not!

(Slight pause.)

MINNIE: Mama, all evening I *did* have the feeling that I was being watched . . . and *that* man was being watched by Mrs. Cochran; and *(Slight giggle)* Mrs. Cochran was being watched by us.

MRS. HAWKINS: We'll know what it's all about in a few minutes.

(Silence.)

MINNIE: But Mama, what would the man be looking at? —Just us two sewing.

MRS. HAWKINS: I think you'd better go in the kitchen. Go slowly—and don't look out the window.

MINNIE *(Without raising her head)*: No! I'm going to stay right here. But I'd like to know *why* a man would do that—would just stand and look. Is he . . . a crazy man?

MRS. HAWKINS: No, I don't think so.

MINNIE: Well, say *something* about him.

MRS. HAWKINS: Minnie, the world is full of people who think that everybody's happy except themselves. They think their lives should be more exciting.

MINNIE: Does that man think that our lives are exciting, Mama?

MRS. HAWKINS: Our lives are just as exciting as they ought to be, Minnie.

MINNIE *(With a little giggle)*: Well, they are tonight.

MRS. HAWKINS: They are all the time; and don't you forget it.

(The front door bell rings.)

Now, who can that be at the front door? I'll go, Minnie. *(Weighing the dangers)* No, *you* go. —No, I'll go.

(She goes into the hall. The jovial voice of Mr. Forbes is heard.)

MR. FORBES'S VOICE: Good evening, Mrs. Hawkins. Is Herb home?

MRS. HAWKINS'S VOICE: No, he hasn't come home yet, Mr. Forbes. He telephoned that he'd take a later train.

(Enter Mr. Forbes, followed by Mrs. Hawkins.)

MR. FORBES: Yes, I know. The old five-twenty-five wasn't the same without him. Darn near went off the rails.
   (To Minnie) Good evening, young lady.

MINNIE *(Head bent; tiny voice)*: Good evening, Mr. Forbes.

MR. FORBES: Well, I thought I'd drop in and see Herb for a minute. About how maybe he'd be wanting a new car—now that he's come into all that money.

MRS. HAWKINS: Come into *what* money, Mr. Forbes?

MR. FORBES: Why, sure, he telephoned you about it?

MRS. HAWKINS: He didn't say anything about any money.

MR. FORBES *(Laughing loudly)*: Well, maybe I've gone and put my foot in it again. So he didn't tell you anything about it yet? Haw-haw-haw. *(Confidentially)* If he's got to pay taxes on it we figgered out he'd get about eighteen thousand dollars. —Well, you tell him I called, and tell him that I'll give him nine hundred dollars on that Chevrolet of his—maybe a little more after I've had a look at it.

MRS. HAWKINS: I'll tell him. —Mr. Forbes, I'm sorry I can't ask you to sit down, but my daughter's had a cold for days now and I wouldn't want you to take it home to your girls.

MR. FORBES: I'm sorry to hear that. —Well, as you say, I'd better not carry it with me.

(He goes to the door, then turns and says confidentially) Do you know what Herb said when he heard that he'd got that money? Haw-haw-haw. I've always said Herb Hawkins has more sense of humor than anybody I know. Why, he said, "All window glass is the same." Haw-haw. "All window glass is the same." Herb! You can't beat him.

MRS. HAWKINS: "All window glass is the same." What did he mean by that?

MR. FORBES: You know: that thing he's always saying. About life. He said it at Rotary in his speech. You know how crazy people look when you see them through a window—arguing and carrying on—and you can't hear a word they say? He says that's the way things look to him. Wars and politics . . . and everything in life.

(Mrs. Hawkins is silent and unamused.)

Well, I'd better be going. Tell Herb there's real good glass—*unbreakable*—on the car I'm going to sell him. Good night, miss; good night, Mrs. Hawkins.

(He goes out. Mrs. Hawkins does not accompany him to the front door. She stands a moment looking before her. Then she says, from deep thought:)

MRS. HAWKINS: That's your father who's been standing out by the garage.

MINNIE: Why would he do that?

MRS. HAWKINS: Looking in. —I should have known it.

MINNIE *(Amazed but not alarmed)*: Look! All over the lawn!

MRS. HAWKINS: The police have come. Those are their flashlights.

MINNIE: All over the place! I can hear them talking . . . *(Pause)* . . . Papa's angry . . . Papa's *very* angry.

(They listen.)

Now they're driving away.

MRS. HAWKINS: I should have known it.

(She returns to her seat. Sound of the front door opening and closing noisily.)

That's your father. Don't mention anything unless he mentions it first.

(They bend over their work. From the hall sounds of Hawkins singing the first phrase of "Valencia." Enter Hawkins, a commuter. His manner is of loud, forced geniality.)

HAWKINS: Well—HOW are the ladies?

(He kisses each lightly on the cheek.)

MRS. HAWKINS: I didn't start getting dinner until I knew when you'd get here.

HAWKINS *(Largely)*: Well, *don't* start it. I'm taking you two ladies out to dinner. —There's no hurry, though. We'll go to Michaelson's after the crowd's thinned out.
    (Starting for the hall on his way to the kitchen) Want a drink, anybody?

MRS. HAWKINS: No. The ice is ready for you on the shelf.

(He goes out. From the kitchen he can be heard singing "Valencia." He returns, glass in hand.)

What kept you, Herbert?

HAWKINS: Nothing. Nothing. I decided to take another train.

(He walks back and forth, holding his glass at the level of his face.)

I decided to take another train. *(He leans teasingly a moment over his wife's shoulder, conspiratorially)* I thought maybe things might look different through the windows of another train. You know: all those towns I've never been in? Kenniston—Laidlaw—East Laidlaw—Bennsville. Let's go to Bennsville some day. Damn it, I don't know why people should go to Paris and Rome and Cairo when they could go to Bennsville. Bennsville! Oh, Bennsville—

MRS. HAWKINS: Have you been drinking, Herbert?

HAWKINS: This is the first swallow I've had since last night. Oh, Bennsville . . . breathes there a man with soul so dead—

(Minnie's eyes have followed her father as he walks about with smiling appreciation.)

MINNIE: I know a girl who lives in Bennsville.

HAWKINS: They're happy there, aren't they? No, not exactly happy, but they live it up to the full. In Bennsville they kick the hell out of life.

MINNIE: Her name's Eloise Brinton.

HAWKINS: Well, Bennsville and East Laidlaw don't look different through the windows of another train. It's not by looking through a train window that you can get at the *heart* of Bennsville.

(Pause.)

There all we fellows sit every night on the five-twenty-five playing cards and hoping against hope that there'll be that wonderful, beautiful—

MINNIE *(Laughing delightedly)*: Wreck!!

MRS. HAWKINS: Herbert! I won't have you talking that way!

HAWKINS: A wreck, so that we can crawl out of the smoking, burning cars . . . and get into one of those houses. Do you know what you see from the windows of the train? Those people—those cars—that you see on the streets of Bennsville—they're just dummies. *Cardboard.*

They've been put up there to deceive you. What really goes on in Bennsville—inside those houses—*that's* what's interesting. People with six arms and legs. People that can talk like Shakespeare. Children, Minnie, that can beat Einstein. Fabulous things.

MINNIE: Papa, *I* don't mind, but you make Mama nervous when you talk like that.

HAWKINS: Behind those walls. But it isn't only behind those walls that strange things go on. Right on that train, right in those cars. The damndest things. Fred Cochran and Phil Forbes—

MRS. HAWKINS: Mr. Forbes was here to see you.

HAWKINS: Fred Cochran and Phil Forbes—we've played cards together for twenty years. We're so expert at hiding things from one another—we're so cram-filled with things we can't say to one another that only a wreck could crack us open.

MINNIE (*Indicating her mother, reproachfully*): Papa!

MRS. HAWKINS: Herbert Hawkins, why did you stand out in the dark there, looking at us through the window?

HAWKINS: Well, I'll tell you . . . I got a lot of money today. But more than that I got a message. A message from beyond the grave. From the dead. There was this old lady—I used to do her income tax for her—old lady. She'd keep me on a while—God, how she wanted someone to talk to . . . I'd say anything that came into my head . . . I want another drink.

(*He goes into the kitchen. Again we hear him singing "Valencia."*)

MINNIE (*Whispering*): Eighteen thousand dollars!

MRS. HAWKINS: We've just got to let him talk himself out.

MINNIE: But Mama, why did he go and stand out on the lawn?

MRS. HAWKINS: Shh!

(*Hawkins returns.*)

HAWKINS: I told her a lot of things. I told her—

MINNIE: I know! You told her that everything looked as though it were seen through glass.

HAWKINS: Yes, I did. *(Pause)* You don't hear the words, or if you hear the words, they don't fit what you see. And one day she said to me: "Mr. Hawkins, you say that all the time: why don't you do it?" "Do what?" I said. "Really stand outside and look through some windows."

(Pause.)

I knew she meant my own . . . Well, to tell the truth, I was afraid to. I preferred to talk about it.

(He paces back and forth.)

She died. Today some lawyer called me up and said she's left me twenty thousand dollars.

MRS. HAWKINS: Herbert!

HAWKINS *(His eyes on the distance)*: "To Herbert Hawkins, in gratitude for many thoughtfulnesses and in appreciation of his sense of humor." From beyond the grave . . . It was an order. I took the four o'clock home . . . It took me a whole hour to get up the courage to go and stand *(He points) out there.*

MINNIE: But Papa, you didn't *see* anything! Just us sewing!

(Hawkins stares before him, then, changing his mood, says briskly:)

HAWKINS: What are we going to have for Sunday dinner?

MINNIE: I know!

HAWKINS *(Pinching her ear)*: Buffalo steak?

MINNIE: No.

HAWKINS: I had to live for a week once on rattlesnake stew.

MINNIE: Papa, you're awful.

MRS. HAWKINS *(Putting down her sewing; in an even voice)*: Were you planning to go away, Herbert?

HAWKINS: What?

MRS. HAWKINS: *(For the first time, looking at him)*: You were thinking of going away.

HAWKINS *(Looks into his glass a moment)*: Far away.

(Then again putting his face over her shoulder teasingly, but in a serious voice) There is no "away." . . . There's only "here." —Get your hats; we're going out to dinner. —I've decided to move to "here." To take up residence, as they say. I'll move in tonight. I don't bring much baggage. —Get your hats.

MRS. HAWKINS *(Rising)*: Herbert, we don't wear hats any more. That was in your mother's time. —Minnie, run upstairs and get my blue shawl.

HAWKINS: I'll go and get one more drop out in the kitchen.

MRS. HAWKINS: Herbert, I don't like your old lady.

HAWKINS *(Turning at the door in surprise)*: Why, what's the matter with her?

MRS. HAWKINS: I can understand that she was in need of someone to talk to. —What business had she trying to make you look at Minnie and me *through windows*? As though we were strangers.

(She crosses and puts her sewing on the telephone table.)

People who've known one another as long as you and I have are not supposed to *see* one another. The pictures we have of one another are inside. —Herbert, last year one day I went to the city to have lunch with your sister. And as I was walking along the street, who do you think I saw coming toward me? From quite a ways off? *You!* My heart stopped beating and I *prayed*—I prayed that you wouldn't see me. And you passed by without seeing me. I didn't want you to see me in those silly clothes we wear when we go to the city—and in that silly hat—with that silly look we put on our face when we're in public places. The person that other people see.

HAWKINS *(With lowered eyes)*: You saw *me*—with that silly look.

MRS. HAWKINS: Oh, no. I didn't look long enough for that. I was too busy hiding myself.—I don't know why Minnie's so long trying to find my shawl.

(She goes out. The telephone rings.)

HAWKINS: Yes, this is Herbert Hawkins.—Nat Fischer? Oh, hello, Nat . . . Oh! . . . All right. Sure, I see your point of view . . . Eleven o'clock. Yes, I'll be there. Eleven o'clock.

(He hangs up. Mrs. Hawkins returns wearing a shawl.)

MRS. HAWKINS: Was that call for me?

HAWKINS: No. It was for me all right. —I might as well tell you now what it was about.

(He stares at the floor.)

MRS. HAWKINS: Well?

HAWKINS: A few minutes ago the police tried to arrest me for standing on my own lawn. Well, I got them over that. But they found a revolver on me—without a license. So I've got to show up at court tomorrow, eleven o'clock.

MRS. HAWKINS *(Short pause; thoughtfully)*: Oh . . . a revolver.

HAWKINS *(Looking at the floor)*: Yes . . . I thought that maybe it was best . . . that I go away . . . a long way.

MRS. HAWKINS *(Looking up with the beginning of a smile)*: To Bennsville?

HAWKINS: Yes.

MRS. HAWKINS: Where life's so exciting.

   (Suddenly briskly) Well, you get the license for that revolver, Herbert, so that you can prevent people looking in at us through the window, when they have no business to. —Turn out the lights when you come.

END OF PLAY

FOUR

A Ringing of Doorbells

(Envy)

CHARACTERS

MRS. BEATTIE, sixty-five, crippled with arthritis
MRS. MCCULLUM, her housekeeper
MRS. KINKAID, a caller, forty-five
DAPHNE, Mrs. Kinkaid's daughter, eighteen

SETTING

The front room of Mrs. Beattie's small house in Mount Hope,
Florida, circa 1939.

*Mrs. Beattie, sixty-five, crippled with arthritis, ill, of a bad color,
but proud, stoical and every inch the "General's Widow," wheels
herself carefully into the room in her invalid's chair. She comes
to a halt beside her worktable and starts to spread out the material for her knitting. A ball of yarn falls to the ground. She eyes
it resentfully. Presently, and with great precautions, she gets out*

of her chair, stoops over and retrieves the wool. She has just regained her seat in the chair when Mrs. McCullum, her housekeeper, can be heard offstage.

MRS. MCCULLUM: Mrs. Beattie, Mrs. Beattie! *(She puts her head in the door)* I have the most extraordinary thing to tell you. I mean it's perfectly terrible. I'll put the groceries in the kitchen. *(She enters from the back, her hands full of parcels and herself breathless with excitement)* —And they'll be here any minute! *(She comes to the front of the stage and peers through a window toward the right)* They'll be coming down that street in a minute.

MRS. BEATTIE: Now, do catch your breath, Mrs. McCullum, and tell me calmly what you have to say.

MRS. MCCULLUM: I recognized them at once—both the mother and daughter. You won't *believe* what I have to tell you.

MRS. BEATTIE *(Calmly)*: I think you'd better sit down.

MRS. MCCULLUM: But they'll be here any minute.

MRS. BEATTIE: Who'll be here?

MRS. MCCULLUM: These dreadful people . . . I know you won't want to see them. I'll just send them away.

MRS. BEATTIE: Did you get my medicine?

MRS. MCCULLUM: Yes, I did. —Here's the bottle. And here's the change. —There I was sitting in Mr. Goheny's drug-store—and *they* came in. —The medicine was two-forty; you gave me a ten-dollar bill. Here's . . . seven . . . sixty . . . The mother asked Mr. Goheny where Willow Street was . . . and asked him if Mrs. Beattie was in town!! And she asked him if Mrs. Brigham lived in Mount Hope, too. —You see, *that's* what she does; she goes to people's houses. —People that have been in the army. *High up* in the army.

MRS. BEATTIE: Did you cash my check?

MRS. MCCULLUM *(Fumbles in her handbag; brings out an envelope, which she gives to Mrs. Beattie)*: Yes, I did. Here it is. Mr. Spottswood sends his regards and hopes that you are feeling better. —Oh, Mrs. Beattie, they're just common adventuresses. *Don't* see them.

MRS. BEATTIE (*She verifies the contents of the envelope; then says with decision*): Mrs. McCullum, I don't like fluster. Now, you go over there and sit by the piano; and you don't say a word until I've counted to five. —Then you tell me what this is all about—starting from the beginning.

(*Mrs. McCullum goes to the front of the stage and sits by an—invisible—piano, containing herself. Mrs. Beattie, calmly adjusting her knitting and starting a row, slowly counts to five.*)

One . . . two . . . breathe tranquilly, Mrs. McCullum . . . three . . . four . . . Where did you *first* see or know about this mother and daughter?

MRS. MCCULLUM: I do want to apologize, Mrs. Beattie, for being so excited, *but (Again peering through the window)* I wanted you—

MRS. BEATTIE: Yes, Mrs. McCullum. You first met them—?

MRS. MCCULLUM: When I was working for Mrs. Ferguson in Winter Park two years ago, they came to the door. She said that her husband had been in the army under General Ferguson . . . in Panama . . . no, in Hawaii . . . and what good friends they'd been. They don't beg. I mean they don't *seem* to beg. She says that the daughter has a beautiful voice and that she hasn't the money to train this girl's beautiful voice. And the girl gets up to sing and she faints.

MRS. BEATTIE: What?

MRS. MCCULLUM: Mrs. Beattie, the girl gets up as though she's about to sing, but she doesn't sing. She crumples up and falls on the floor. And the mother tells a whole story about how they're starving, and Mrs. Ferguson gave her two hundred dollars. But that's not all. The next day Mrs. Ogilvie called Mrs. Ferguson on the telephone and said that these two adventuresses had called at her house and the girl had fainted and she gave them one hundred dollars.

MRS. BEATTIE *(Knitting impassively)*: Thank you. Did Mrs. Ferguson and Mrs. Ogilvie remember the names of these people?

MRS. MCCULLUM: No . . . but this mother seemed to know *all about* General Ferguson and General Ogilvie . . . They go everywhere and get money.

MRS. BEATTIE: Now be quiet and let me think a minute!

(Pause.)

Do you remember their name?

MRS. MCCULLUM *(Peering out the window)*: No, I'm sorry I don't. But Mrs. Ferguson looked it up in the army register and it was there.

MRS. BEATTIE: How old is the girl?

MRS. MCCULLUM: Well, that's the funny part about it. I think she must be all of eighteen, *now*, but her mother dresses her up as though she were much younger—so that she'll be more pathetic when she faints.

MRS. BEATTIE: Does the mother look like a lady?

MRS. MCCULLUM: Yes . . . pretty much.

MRS. BEATTIE *(Her eyes on Mrs. McCullum with a sort of sardonic brooding)*: Think of how full their lives must be! —Full . . . occupied!

MRS. MCCULLUM *(With a start)*: What? What's that you said, Mrs. Beattie? *Occupied!* —But what they're doing is immoral.

MRS. BEATTIE: I'd exchange places with them *like that*!

MRS. MCCULLUM: You're in one of those moods when I don't begin to understand a word you *say*! Anyway, you're not going to see them, are you?

MRS. BEATTIE *(Calmly)*: Of course, I'm going to see them. —Mrs. McCullum, will you kindly get the hot water bottle for my knees?

MRS. MCCULLUM: I'll do that right now. But they'll be *here* in a minute. Won't you let me wheel you into your bedroom and bring you the bottle there?

MRS. BEATTIE: In the first place, I don't like to be wheeled anywhere. And whether they come at once or later, I'd like the hot water bottle now.

MRS. MCCULLUM *(Starting)*: Yes, Mrs. Beattie.

MRS. BEATTIE: One minute: tell me about the girl. She has lots of spirit. —Is this daughter pretty?

MRS. MCCULLUM: Yes. —Yes, she is . . . and that reminds me: will you excuse, Mrs. Beattie, if I make a suggestion?

MRS. BEATTIE: Yes, indeed, what is it?

MRS. MCCULLUM: Excuse me . . . but I think I should prepare you. The daughter—it struck me at once—resembles, very much resembles, that . . . dear photograph on the piano. I mean I couldn't help noticing it. Will you let me take the photograph into your bedroom?

MRS. BEATTIE *(Impassive, only her eyes concentrated)*: I see no need to change anything in this room, Mrs. McCullum.

MRS. MCCULLUM: I'll get the hot water bottle.

(She goes out. Again Mrs. Beattie painfully descends from the chair. She moves to the piano and gazes long at the photograph. Then she moves farther forward on the stage and turns her head down the street. She sees the couple. She stares at them fixedly and somberly. Mrs. McCullum enters with a hot water bottle.)

MRS. MCCULLUM: Mrs. Beattie! You're up!

(Mrs. Beattie indicates with a gesture the couple up the street. Mrs. McCullum rushes to her side.)

Yes! That's they. She has that sort of list in her hand she studies all the time. —Oh, let me send them away. They're just swindlers—common swindlers.

MRS. BEATTIE: Look!—She's studying her notes. —Yes, the girl—there is a resemblance . . . Isn't it strange . . . *(Broodingly, with a touch of bitterness)* Young . . . and beautiful . . . occupied . . .

MRS. MCCULLUM: And wicked!

MRS. BEATTIE *(Dismissing this)*: Oh! . . . Alive . . . *(Starting to hobble off)* Alive and together . . . Bring them in here. Be very polite to them. Tell them I'm lying down. We'll make them wait a bit . . . If they don't have calling cards, get their names very carefully and bring them in to me . . . I'm going to receive them without my wheelchair.

MRS. MCCULLUM: Mrs. Beattie!

MRS. BEATTIE: And while they're waiting for me I'm going to ask you to bring some tea in to them.

MRS. MCCULLUM *(Looking out the window)*: Oh! They're almost here!

MRS. BEATTIE: Alive and together—that's the point.

(She goes out.)

MRS. MCCULLUM *(Picking up her parcels and pushing the empty chair)*: Why, Mrs. Beattie, you're better every day. You know you are. [*(She is out)*]

(The doorbell rings.)

(Offstage) Mrs. Beattie? Yes. Will you come in, please? Who shall I say is calling?

(Enter Mrs. Kinkaid and Daphne. Mrs. Kinkaid is about forty-five, simply and tastefully dressed. She was once very pretty, but is now pinched, tense and unhappy. Daphne is eighteen, dressed for sixteen; she is cool, arrogant and sullen. Mrs. Kinkaid selects a calling card from her handbag.)

MRS. KINKAID *(Giving the card, without effusiveness)*: Will you say Mrs. Kinkaid, the widow of Major George

Kinkaid, a friend of General Beattie! And our daughter
Daphne.

MRS. MCCULLUM: Mrs. Kin . . . kaid. Will you sit down,
please. Mrs. Beattie is resting. I'll ask if she can see you.

MRS. KINKAID: Thank you.

MRS. MCCULLUM: There are some magazines here, if you
wish to look at them.

MRS. KINKAID: Thank you.

*(Mrs. McCullum goes out. The visitors sit very straight,
scarcely turning their heads. Their eyes begin to appraise
the room. When they speak, they move their lips as little as
possible.)*

DAPHNE *(After a considerable pause, contemptuously)*: Just
junk.

MRS. KINKAID: The cabinet's very good.

(They both gaze at it appraisingly.)

When you fall, fall *that* side.

DAPHNE: We won't get fifty dollars.

MRS. KINKAID: And do that sigh—that sort of groan you
did in Orlando. You've been forgetting to do that lately.
Daphne! You've forgotten to take your wristwatch off.
Really, you're getting awfully careless lately.

*(Daphne removes her wristwatch and puts it in her hand-
bag. She rises stealthily and goes tiptoe to the back and listens. Mrs. Kinkaid has taken a piece of notepaper from her
handbag, but watches Daphne's movements anxiously. As
Daphne continues to listen, Mrs. Kinkaid applies herself
to the notes in her hand, murmuring the words as though for
memorization.)*

Manila, 1912 to 1913 with General Beattie and General
Holabird . . . 1907 to 1911 . . . Do you remember Mrs.

Holabird in West Palm Beach . . . The Presidio, 1910 . . .
Oh, dear . . .

DAPHNE *(Returning to her chair, cool)*: Something's going to
go wrong today.

MRS. KINKAID *(Deeply alarmed)*: What do you mean,
Daphne?

DAPHNE: I can always tell.

MRS. KINKAID: No. No . . . How can you tell?

DAPHNE: There's going to be all hell let loose. Like that
time in Sarasota.

MRS. KINKAID *(Rising, passionately)*: Then let's go. Let's
go at once. If it's going to be like that, I can't stand it,
I really can't.

DAPHNE: Sit down! Stop making a fool of yourself.

MRS. KINKAID: This is the last time. I cannot go on with this
any longer.

DAPHNE *(Harshly)*: Cork it, will you!

(Mrs. Kinkaid sits down and sobs tonelessly into her hand-kerchief.)

Of *course*, we've got to take risks. If we didn't take risks
where'd we be? Do you want me to go back selling
stockings? . . . I like risks . . . and if there's going to be
trouble, I *like* it. I like talking back to these old witches
. . . Pull yourself together and learn your stuff. *(Pause)*
Do *you* want to go back to that reception job in that
hospital!?!

MRS. KINKAID *(Low, but intense)*: Yes, I do, Daphne. Anything but this.

DAPHNE: Seventy a week! *(She again fixes her eyes on the
cabinet)* Yes, that's not bad. It could go with the table at
Mrs. O'Hallohan's. And the rugs at the Krantzes.

MRS. KINKAID: West Point, twelve. West Point, twelve.
—Daphne, if you do see there may be trouble, give me
the signal. You get so furious you forget to give me the
signals. —Schofield Barracks. General Wilkins . . . 1909.

DAPHNE: *(Eyebrows raised; she means she hears Mrs. McCullum coming)*: Hickey!

(Enter Mrs. McCullum carrying a tea tray.)

MRS. MCCULLUM: Mrs. Beattie says she'll be happy to see you. She asked me to bring you some tea while you're waiting.

MRS. KINKAID: That's *very* kind, indeed. Isn't that kind of Mrs. Beattie, Daphne?

MRS. MCCULLUM: The marmalade's from our own oranges.

MRS. KINKAID: Imagine that? —I hope Mrs. Beattie is well. Mrs. Farnsborough spoke of her as . . . as convalescent.

MRS. MCCULLUM: Thank you, Mrs. Beattie's pretty well.

(Silence.)

Now, I think you have everything.

MRS. KINKAID: Indeed, yes. Thank you very much.

(Mrs. McCullum goes out. Mrs. Kinkaid looks at her daughter's face anxiously.)

DAPHNE *(Looking out into space, scarcely moving her lips)*: Trouble!

MRS. KINKAID *(Almost trembling; pouring the tea)*: The last time!

DAPHNE: Nonsense. Just do what you have to do and get it over.

MRS. KINKAID: You're very difficult, Daphne. You're cruel. —Well, there are only six more addresses in Florida . . . and that's *all*.

DAPHNE *(Blandly)*: California's as full of them as blackberries.

MRS. KINKAID: We are *not* going to California.

(Daphne goes over to take her cup. She kisses her mother.)

DAPHNE: Poor dear mother! *(Whispering)* You forget so easily: our house . . . our car . . . my wedding . . .

MRS. KINKAID *(Clasping her face)*: Oh, I wish you were married, Daphne, and *this* were all over.

DAPHNE: Well, find me the *man*, dear. Do I ever meet any men?

MRS. KINKAID: Charles is such a nice young man.

DAPHNE *(Suddenly darkly irritated)*: Are you *crazy?* Who's *he?* —Go back and study your notes. We've got to play our cards well today.

(Mrs. Kinkaid's eyes have fallen on the photograph on the piano.)

MRS. KINKAID: Daphne! Do you see what I see?

DAPHNE: What?

MRS. KINKAID: That photograph. Dear—

DAPHNE: What?

MRS. KINKAID: . . . The resemblance. It—it looks just like you.

DAPHNE *(A casual glance)*: No, it doesn't.

MRS. KINKAID: It's amazing. *(Reopening her handbag)* I know who it is, too.

(Reading some notes from a reference book) "A daughter: Lydia Westerveldt, born 1912, died 1930." She's beautiful. She hasn't your eyes, dear . . . but the shape and the hair: it's amazing.

(Daphne rises, stands before the photograph and gazes at it intently.)

DAPHNE: Lydia . . . general's daughter . . .

"Miss Beattie, may I have the next dance?" . . .

"I'm so sorry, Lieutenant, but I've promised the next dance to Colonel Randolph."

"My daughter's away at finishing school. I don't know when she'll be back. She's staying with friends all over New England."

(Turning to her mother, sharply) She has a wedding ring on.

MRS. KINKAID: Do come and sit down, dear.

DAPHNE *(To the photograph)*: Of course, I don't like her. She had everything she wanted. She didn't know what it was to know *nobody*, to have to spend all your time among common vulgar people, to skimp—

MRS. KINKAID: Daphne!

DAPHNE: . . . and she didn't have to see her own mother insulted *(Whirling about to face her mother)* like *you* were by Mrs. Smith.

MRS. KINKAID: Dear, I wasn't *insulted*—

DAPHNE *(Back at the photograph)*: And you never knew what it was to be treated *just ghastly* by men, because you were poor; you didn't know anything. *(She spits at the picture)* There! There!

MRS. KINKAID *(Has risen; keeping her voice)*: Daphne, you stop that right now, and drink your tea. Sometimes I don't know what comes over you . . .

(Daphne returns, grand and somber, to her chair.)

I never taught you to say things like that.

DAPHNE *(Airily)*: I don't like the way she looks at me.
(Rendered pleasurably light-headed by her outburst) I feel better. I'm glad I talked to her. . . . Mother-mousie, we're going to be very successful today. I feel it in my bones . . . and tonight we're going to a movie, and *you know which one. (She hears a noise in the hall)* Hickey!

(Both compose themselves for the entrance of Mrs. Beattie. Mrs. Beattie enters alone, walking with the greatest difficulty, but putting on a cordial smile.)

MRS. BEATTIE: Mrs. Kinkaid, good afternoon. I am Mrs. Beattie. Don't get up, please.

MRS. KINKAID *(Rising)*: Good afternoon, Mrs. Beattie. This is my daughter, Daphne.

MRS. BEATTIE *(Stopping and looking at her hard)*: Good afternoon, Miss Kinkaid. Please sit down, both of you.

MRS. KINKAID: We want to thank you . . . for sending the tea. So kind.

MRS. BEATTIE *(Sitting down)*: Mrs. McCullum tells me you knew my husband.

MRS. KINKAID: Mrs. Beattie . . . My husband, Major George Kinkaid, was in the Philippines at the same time as General Beattie. He was a lieutenant at that time—it was 1912 and 1913—and probably had very little opportunity to meet the General, but he knew very well a number of the members of your husband's staff—General Ferguson—then Colonel Ferguson; and Colonel Fosdick.

(Mrs. Beattie nods.)

I was not there at the time. I was very ill for a number of years and the doctors thought it inadvisable that I should make the trip to the Far East.

MRS. BEATTIE: Were you ever in the Far East?

MRS. KINKAID: No, I wasn't.

MRS. BEATTIE *(To Daphne)*: And where were you born, Miss Kinkaid?

DAPHNE *(Slight pause)*: In Philadelphia.

MRS. BEATTIE *(Turning back to Mrs. Kinkaid)*: I assume that there is something that you wish to see me about?

MRS. KINKAID *(She makes a pause, and clutching her hand-bag begins to speak with earnest candor)*: There is, Mrs. Beattie—I am faced with a problem and I have called on you in the hope that you will give me some advice. My daughter, Daphne *(Mrs. Beattie turns her eyes on Daphne)* is endowed with a most unusual singing voice. Qualified musicians have told me that she has indeed an extraordinary voice. And in addition to that voice, a deeply musical nature. Professor Boncianiani of New York, who is recognized as one of the leading teachers, has predicted a great career for her. Perhaps, if you wish—a little later—I shall ask Daphne to sing for you. My problem is this—where will I find the means to cultivate her voice? So far I have been barely able to afford a certain amount of instruction . . . naturally, in a very modest way.

(She pauses.)

MRS. BEATTIE: I see. You draw a pension, of course—

MRS. KINKAID: No, Mrs. Beattie, I do not. *(She takes a handkerchief from her handbag)* I do not. My husband's career in the army began most promisingly. I have here letters from his superior officers expressing the highest opinion of his work. But my husband had . . . a weakness. *(She touches the handkerchief to her nose)* I find this very hard to say . . . he was intemperate . . .

MRS. BEATTIE: I beg your pardon?

MRS. KINKAID: Somehow . . . alone in the Far East . . . he took to drinking. And on one occasion . . . under the influence of alcohol . . . he forgot himself . . . He was, I believe, impertinent to a superior officer . . .

MRS. BEATTIE: To whom?

MRS. KINKAID: To General Foley.

(Pause. Mrs. Kinkaid dries her eyes.)

MRS. BEATTIE: How have you made your living, Mrs. Kinkaid?

MRS. KINKAID: For a while I assisted in a small dress shop in Miami Beach. Then I was a receptionist in a hotel.

MRS. BEATTIE: And now?

MRS. KINKAID: I have not come to you with any problem about our livelihood, Mrs. Beattie. I hope to be able to sustain ourselves; it is Daphne's career—her God-given voice—that I feel to be my responsibility. —I would like you to hear Daphne sing. She is able to accompany herself.

(She looks inquiringly at Mrs. Beattie who remains silent.)

Daphne, do that French song.

(Daphne has felt Mrs. Beattie's weighted glance.)

DAPHNE: Mother, I don't feel like singing. I think we
should thank Mrs. Beattie for the tea and go.

MRS. KINKAID: Do make an effort, Daphne. Mrs. Beattie
has been so kind.

*(Daphne turns and looks at Mrs. Beattie who meets her
gaze.)*

DAPHNE *(Under her breath)*: Mrs. Beattie has not asked me
to sing.

MRS. BEATTIE: I should very much like to hear you sing,
Miss Kinkaid.

DAPHNE *(Rising)*: Very well, I will.

MRS. BEATTIE *(Distinctly)*: It will not be necessary to faint.

MRS. KINKAID *(Bridling)*: To faint!?

MRS. BEATTIE: It will not be necessary to faint. I have
understood the problem. —Sit down, Miss Kinkaid.
(Turning to Mrs. Kinkaid, with decision) How much of
what you have told me is true?

MRS. KINKAID *(Rising; with indignation)*: I do not know
what you mean. I have never been spoken to in such a
way. Come with me, Daphne.
  (To Mrs. Beattie) Every word I have said is *true*.

*(Mrs. Beattie remains impassive, her eyes on Daphne, who
has not moved from where she stopped on her way to the
piano.)*

MRS. BEATTIE: I shall not telephone the police unless you
force me to.

MRS. KINKAID *(About at the door)*: The police! We have
done nothing that concerns the police.

MRS. BEATTIE: They could ask you to give an account of the money you have received. —Have you an unusual voice, Miss Kinkaid?

DAPHNE *(Beginning with low contempt)*: Oh, you can talk. You don't know what other people's lives are like. Our lives are just awful. You've got everything you want and you've always had everything you want. You don't know what it is for me to see my mother treated just like dirt by people she shouldn't even have to speak to.

MRS. KINKAID: Daphne! You know I've never complained—

DAPHNE: And everybody else has *cars* . . . and when they eat they eat things fit to eat. You don't know what it is to see your own mother—

(Mrs. McCullum has come to the door.)

MRS. MCCULLUM: Mrs. Beattie, you remember what the doctor said . . . You're not to have any excitement. I must ask these ladies to go.

MRS. BEATTIE *(Raising her hand)*: I wish to hear what they have to say.

MRS. KINKAID *(Comes forward as if there had been no interruption)*: Daphne has not expressed our intention correctly. Daphne is a very imaginative child and is given to exaggeration. I have never made any complaint about our lives, as far as I am concerned; but you cannot know what it is, Mrs. Beattie, to bring up a refined and sensitive girl like Daphne . . . without money and without . . . any social situation. The only girls and young men we have any opportunity to meet are coarse, and vulgar . . . often unspeakably vulgar. Daphne's place is among ladies and gentlemen. I have spent sleepless nights—many sleepless nights—trying to find some way to better our situation.

DAPHNE *(Now going to the door)*: Come, Mother, she doesn't know what we're talking about. She was born ignorant . . . and her daughter went from one dance to another dance . . . and her children would have the same thing. And what right did you have to a life like that? None at all. You were born into the right cradle. That's all you did to earn it.

MRS. BEATTIE: *(Firmly but not sharply to Daphne)*: Have you a remarkable voice?

DAPHNE: No.

MRS. KINKAID: Daphne!

[*(Mrs. Beattie and Daphne look at one another. Mrs. Kinkaid and Mrs. McCullum are frozen where they stand. Mrs. Beattie glances at Mrs. Kinkaid and then toward the antique cabinet on which stand the telephone and a writing kit with a pen holder and a checkbook. She moves carefully to the cabinet and pauses as if coming to an important decision.)*]

MRS. BEATTIE: [Alive and together . . . that's the point.]

[*(Mrs. Beattie picks up the pen and checkbook and turns back to face Daphne and Mrs. Kinkaid, as the lights fade.)*]

END OF PLAY

*This play became available through the research and editing of F. J. O'Neil of manuscripts in the Thornton Wilder Collection at Yale University. *

In June 1957, Thornton Wilder wrote in his journal that *In Shakespeare and the Bible* and *A Ringing of Doorbells* were plays he could "terminate any day, but which will never be finished."[1]

The author's manuscript of *A Ringing of Doorbells* ended abruptly with this exchange:

MRS. BEATTIE *(Firmly but not sharply to Daphne)*: Have you a remarkable voice?

DAPHNE: No.

MRS. KINKAID: Daphne!
MRS. BEATTIE:

Just how "terminated" is the play? The answer would appear to be: all but Mrs. Beattie's last line. After dinner one evening at his home in Hamden, Connecticut, Thornton Wilder read aloud to me a nearly complete draft of this play and spoke of his plan to bring the story to a logical, but unconventional, conclusion. Mrs. Beattie, as envious of the Kinkaids as they are of her, wants to help them in spite of their attempt to trick her. A fair solution then to the missing last line seemed to be a reprise of Mrs. Beattie's earlier line: "Alive and together . . . that's the point," as her summing up at the point of decision. The stage directions that I added are consistent with what appears to be Wilder's intention. Combining the antique cabinet and the telephone, both already established in the text, with a writing kit and checkbook, allows a moment of suspense as Mrs. Beattie moves toward the desk, and then a final tableau as she turns back to face the Kinkaids, checkbook in hand.

F. J. O'Neil
April 1997

---

[1] *The Journals of Thornton Wilder 1939–1961*, entry 749, page 266, selected and edited by Donald Gallup, Yale University Press, 1985.

FIVE

In Shakespeare and the Bible

(Wrath)

CHARACTERS

MARGET, a maid
JOHN LUBBOCK, a young attorney, twenty-seven, Katy
    Buckingham's fiancé
MRS. MOWBREY, Katy Buckingham's aunt, late fifties
KATY BUCKINGHAM, twenty-one

SETTING

An oversumptuous parlor, New York, 1898.

*All we need see are three chairs, a low sofa and a taboret. Two
steps descend from the hall at the back into the room. A Swedish
maid, Marget, introduces John Lubbock, twenty-seven, self-
assured; face and bearing under absolute control.*

LUBBOCK: Mrs. Mowbrey wrote me, asking me to call. My
    name is Lubbock.

MARGET: Yes, sir. Mrs. Mowbrey is expecting you. She will be down in a moment, sir. She says I'm to bring you some port. I'll go and get it.

(Exit Marget.
Lubbock, hands in his pockets, whistling under his breath, strolls about examining closely, one by one, the pictures hanging on the wall invisible to us.
Marget returns bearing a small tray on which are two decanters and two goblets. She puts them on the taboret.)

There's port in this one, sir, and sherry in this. Mrs. Mowbrey says you're to help yourself.
LUBBOCK: Thank you. *(Still examining the pictures)* These are relatives and ancestors of Mrs. Mowbrey?
MARGET: Oh, yes. Mrs. Mowbrey comes of a very fine family. I've heard her say that that is her father. As you can see, a clergyman.
LUBBOCK *(Casually)*: She lives alone here?
MARGET: Oh, yes. She's a widow, poor lady. And very much alone. Would you believe it, if I said that no one's come to the house to call for the whole time I've been here, except her lawyer man. And, oh yes, the minister of her church.
LUBBOCK: For several months.
MARGET: Oh, I've been here about a year. But today we're going to have two callers—you, sir, and a young lady that's coming later. Yes, and I mustn't forget: when the doorbell rings for the young lady, I'm to take out the decanters before I open the door. Now I mustn't forget that. And then I'm to bring in the tea. Now, you'll help yourself, won't you?

(Marget goes out.
Lubbock, thoughtfully, pours himself a considerable amount of sherry and, sipping it, returns to his examination of the room and the pictures.)

Enter Mrs. Mowbrey, late fifties, handsome, florid, powdered. She wears a black satin dress covered with bugles and jet. She addresses Lubbock from the hall before descending into the room.)

MRS. MOWBREY: Mr. Lubbock, I am Mrs. Mowbrey.

LUBBOCK: Good afternoon, ma'am.

MRS. MOWBREY: You don't know who I am?

LUBBOCK: No, ma'am. I got your letter asking me to call.

MRS. MOWBREY *(Coming forward)*: Won't you sit down?

(They sit, Mrs. Mowbrey behind the taboret.)

Mr. Lubbock, I had two reasons for asking you to call today. In the first place, I wish to engage a lawyer. I thought we might take a look at one another and see if we could work together. *(She pauses. He bows his head slightly and impersonally)* I mean a lawyer to handle my affairs in general and to advise me. *(Same business)* My second reason for asking to see you is that I am your fiancée's aunt.

LUBBOCK *(Amazed)*: Miss Buckingham's aunt! She never told me she had an aunt.

MRS. MOWBREY: No, Mr. Lubbock, she wouldn't. I am the black sheep of the family. My name is not mentioned in that house. —Will you pour me some port, please. I am glad to see that you have helped yourself ... Thank you ... Yes, I am your future mother-in-law's sister. *(He is standing up, holding his glass—waiting)* Our lives took different directions. *(He sits down)*

But before we get into the legal matter, let's get to know one another a little better. —Tell me, I haven't seen my niece for fifteen years. Is she a pretty girl?

LUBBOCK: Yes—very.

MRS. MOWBREY: We're a good-looking family.

LUBBOCK *(Indicating the pictures on the wall)*: And a distinguished one. Miss Buckingham would be very interested in seeing these family portraits.

MRS. MOWBREY: Yes. *(She sips her wine, then says dryly, without a smile)* It's not hard to find family portraits, Mr. Lubbock. There are places on Twelfth Street, simply full of them. Bishops and generals—whatever you want.

LUBBOCK *(Continuing to look at them, also without a smile)*: Very fine collection, I should say.

(She takes another sip of wine.)

MRS. MOWBREY: Mr. Lubbock, I've made some inquiries about you. You are twenty-seven years old.

LUBBOCK: Yes, I am.

MRS. MOWBREY: You took your time finding yourself, didn't you? All that unpleasantness down in Philadelphia. What happened exactly? Well, we won't go into it. Then you gave yourself a good shaking. You pulled yourself together. Law school—very good. People are still wondering where you got all that spending money. It wasn't horse racing. It wasn't cards. No one could figure it out. Apparently it was something you were doing up in Harlem. —Certainly, your parents couldn't afford to give you anything. In fact, you were very generous to them. You bought them a house on Staten Island. You were a very good son to them and I think you'll make a very good family man.

LUBBOCK *(With a slight bow and a touch of dry irony)*: You are very well informed, ma'am.

MRS. MOWBREY: Yes, I am. *(She takes another sip of wine)* On Saturday nights you often went to 321 West Street— "The Palace," you boys called it. Nice girls, every one of them, especially Dolores.

LUBBOCK *(Mastering violence; rises)*: I don't like this conversation, ma'am. I shall ask you to let me take my leave.

MRS. MOWBREY *(Raising her voice)*: You and I have met before, Mr. Lubbock. You knew me under another name. I owned The Palace.

LUBBOCK: Mrs. Higgins!!

MRS. MOWBREY: My hair is no longer blond. *(She rises and crosses the room)* You may leave any moment you wish, but I never believed you were a hypocrite.

LUBBOCK *(After returning her fixed gaze wrathfully; then sitting down again)*: What do you *want?*

MRS. MOWBREY: Yes, I owned The Palace and several other establishments—refined, very refined in every way. I've sold them. I've retired. I see no one—no one—whom I knew in those days. Except today I am seeing yourself. Naturally, I am never going to mention these matters again. I am going to forget them, and I hope that you will forget them, too. But it would be very valuable to me to have a lawyer who knew them and who was in a position to forget them. —I'll have a little more port, if you'll be so good.

(Lubbock takes the glass from her hand in silence, fills it at the taboret and carries it to her. She murmurs: "Thank you." He returns and stands by the taboret, talking to her across the length of the stage.)

LUBBOCK: I don't believe you asked me here to engage me as your lawyer. There's something else on your mind. Will you say it and then let me take my leave?

MRS. MOWBREY: You were always like that, Jack.

LUBBOCK *(Loud)*: I will ask you not to call me Jack.

MRS. MOWBREY *(Bowing her head slightly)*: That was always your way, Mr. Lubbock. Suspicious. Quick to fight. Imagining that everybody was trying to take advantage of you.

LUBBOCK: What do you want? I don't know what you're talking about. *(He starts with fuming lowered head for the door)* Good afternoon.

MRS. MOWBREY: Mr. Lubbock, I will tell you what I want. *(He pauses with his back to her)* I am a rich woman and I intend to get richer. And I am a lonely woman, and I don't think that that is necessary. I want to live. And when you and Katy are married, I want you to help me. *(He is "caught" and half turns)* I want company. I want to entertain. I also want to help people. I want—so to speak—to adopt some. Not *young* children, of course, but young men and women who want bringing out in some way or other. I have a gift for that kind of thing. —Even in my former work I was able to do all sorts of things for my girls. —Did you ever hear anyone say that Mrs. Higgins was mean—unkind—to the girls in her place? *(He refuses to answer; the port is going to her head. She strikes her bosom emotionally)* I'm kind to a *fault.* I love to see young people *happy.* Dozens of those girls—I helped them get married. I encouraged them to find good homes. *Against my own interest.* — Your friend, Dolores: married a policeman. Happy as a lark. *(She puts a delicate lace handkerchief to her eyes and then to her nose)* —Will you consent to be my lawyer?

LUBBOCK *(Scorn and finality)*: My firm doesn't allow us to serve family connections.

MRS. MOWBREY: Oh, I don't want to have anything to do with that wretched firm: Wilbraham, Clayton, what's-its-name? All you do for me will be on your own time. I shall start giving you three thousand a year for your advice. Then—

LUBBOCK: I beg your pardon. It's entirely out of the question.

MRS. MOWBREY *(After a slight pause; in a less emotional voice)*: Yes, yes. I know that you are always ready with your no! no! You haven't yet heard what I can do for you. And I don't mean in the sense of money. There is something you are greatly in need of . . . *(Pause)* . . . John Lubbock. One can see that you are a lawyer—and a very good one, I suspect. —So, you looked about you and you selected my niece?

LUBBOCK: Oh, much more than that. I'm very much in love with your niece. You should know her. Katy's an extra-ordinary girl.

MRS. MOWBREY: Is she? There's nothing very extraordinary about her mother? What's extraordinary about Katy?

LUBBOCK: Why, she's . . . I feel that I'm the luckiest man in the world.

MRS. MOWBREY: Come now, Mr. Lubbock. You don't have to talk like that to me.

LUBBOCK *(Earnestly)*: I assure you, I mean it.

MRS. MOWBREY *(A touch of contempt)*: Very clever, is she? Reads a lot of books and all that kind of thing?

LUBBOCK: *No-o. (With a slight laugh)* But she asks a lot of questions.

MRS. MOWBREY *(Pleased)*: Does she? So do I, Mr. Lubbock, as you have noticed. *(She rises and starts toward her former seat by the decanter of port)* She asks lots of questions. I like that. —I asked her to call this afternoon.

LUBBOCK *(Startled and uneasy)*: You did? Did you tell her that I would be here?

MRS. MOWBREY: No. I thought I would surprise her.

LUBBOCK: Katy doesn't like surprises. *(Preparing to leave, with hand outstretched)* I think that at your first meeting with—after so long a time—you should see her alone. Perhaps I can call on you at another time.

MRS. MOWBREY *(Still standing)*: What *are* you so nervous about? It's not time for her to come yet, and besides I have this law matter to discuss with you.

LUBBOCK: Thank you. —I'll ask if I can call some other time.

MRS. MOWBREY: Anyway, perhaps she won't come. She'll have shown my letter to her mother and her mother will have forbidden her to come. Would Katy disobey her mother?

LUBBOCK: Yes.

MRS. MOWBREY *(Eyeing him)*: Has Katy chosen to marry you against her mother's wishes?

LUBBOCK: Yes. Very much so.

MRS. MOWBREY: I see. Tears? Scenes? Slamming of doors?

LUBBOCK: Yes, I think so.

MRS. MOWBREY *(Leaning toward him confidentially, lifted*

finger): Katy is like *me*, Mr. Lubbock. I can feel it with every word you say.

(Still uneasy, Lubbock has been taking a few steps around the room; he looks up at the ceiling and weighs this thoughtfully:)

LUBBOCK: If you told her you were her aunt . . . Yes, I think she will come. Katy likes to know . . . where she stands; what it's all about, and that kind of thing.

MRS. MOWBREY: I see. A lawyer's wife. As you suggested a few moments ago: she's inquisitive?

LUBBOCK *(With a nervous laugh)*: Yes, she is.

MRS. MOWBREY: And you think I'm inquisitive, too—don't you?

LUBBOCK: Yes, I do.

MRS. MOWBREY: Well, let me tell you something, Mr. Lubbock. Everybody says we women are inquisitive. Most of us are. We have to be. I wouldn't give a cent for a woman who wasn't. And why? *(The wine has gone to her head. She emphasizes what she is about to say by tapping with jeweled rings on the taboret)* Because a good deal is asked of us for which we are not prepared. Women have to keep their wits about them to survive at all, Mr. Lubbock. *(She leans back in her chair)* When I was married I didn't hesitate to read every scrap of paper my husband left lying around the house. But *(She leans forward)* as I said, I have some business to discuss with you before Katy comes. —Do you always walk about that way?

LUBBOCK *(Surprised)*: People tell me I do. I do in court. If it makes you uneasy—

MRS. MOWBREY: I would like to ask another thing. When you are married—and as a wedding present I shall give Katy a very large check, I assure you—I want you both to give me the opportunity to meet some of your friends, young people in whom I could take an interest. New York must be full of them. But most of all I want to see *you two*. I want you to feel that this house is your second home. *(Very emotional)* I will do everything for you. I have no one else in the world. I will do everything for you. *(Again she puts her handkerchief to her face)*

Now I've talked a good deal. Have you anything to say to all this?

LUBBOCK *(After rising and taking a few steps about)*: Mrs. Mowbrey, I like people who talk frankly, as you do, and who go straight to the point. And I'm going to be frank with you. There's one big hitch in what you propose.

MRS. MOWBREY: Hitch?

LUBBOCK: Katy. *(He looks directly at her and repeats)* Katy. Naturally, she wouldn't have anything to say about my professional life. —And I want to thank you for the confidence you express in my ability to be of service to you. *(He looks up at the ceiling in thought)* But about those other points: I don't know. I tell you frankly, Mrs. Mowbrey, I'm in love with Katy. I'm knocked off my feet by Katy. But I feel that I don't know her. How can I put it? I'm . . . I'm even afraid of Katy.

MRS. MOWBREY *(Almost outraged)*: What? A man like you, afraid of a mere girl!

LUBBOCK *(Short laugh)*: Well, perhaps that's going too far; but I swear to you I still can't imagine what it will be like to be married to Katy.

(His manner changes and he goes to her briskly as though to shake her hand) Really, I think it's best that I say good night now. Katy will want to see you alone. So I'll thank you very much and say good-bye. And ask if I may call on you at some other time.

MRS. MOWBREY: Nonsense! What possible harm could there be —?

(The doorbell rings.)

There! That's the doorbell. That's Katy. It's too late to go now. Do calm down, Mr. Lubbock.

(Enter Marget.)

MARGET: That's the front door bell, Mrs. Mowbrey. Shall I take out the tray?

MRS. MOWBREY: Yes, Marget. And be quick about it.

(Marget scutters out with the tray.)

Really, I don't understand you, Mr. Lubbock. This is not like you at all. There's nothing to get nervous about. The young girls of today are perfect geese—don't I know them! Pah!

(Marget at the door.)

MARGET: Miss Buckingham to see you, ma'am.

(Katy, twenty-one, very pretty, stands a moment at the top step and looks all about the room.)

MRS. MOWBREY *(Throwing her arms wide, without rising)*: Ah, *there* you are, dear.

KATY *(Taking a few steps forward, her eyes on Lubbock)*: Aunt Julia, I'm very glad to see you.

MRS. MOWBREY *(Apparently expecting to be kissed)*: This *is* a joy!

(Katy, approaching her, looks at her smiling, and suddenly drops her reticule which she has opened. Thus avoiding an embrace, she leans over and takes some time picking the objects up. Lubbock and Marget come to her assistance.)

KATY: Oh, how awkward of me! I'm so sorry. I'm always doing things like this. Thank you. There's my key . . . and my card case. Thank you.

MRS. MOWBREY: Marget, we're ready for tea now. I'm sure you'll want some tea, dear.

(Exit Marget.)

KATY: Thank you, I would. —You're here, John?

LUBBOCK *(Uncomfortable)*: Mrs. Mowbrey wrote me and asked me to call.

MRS. MOWBREY: Yes, dear, I've wanted a lawyer so badly. Now sit down and let me look at you.

(Katy sits in the chair Mrs. Mowbrey has indicated.)

What a dear, beautiful girl you are! —And you're so like my father! You're like me and my father!

LUBBOCK *(Reluctantly)*: Yes . . . There is something there.

MRS. MOWBREY: Oh, I've lost my looks—I know that! I've been through *great* unhappiness, but the resemblance is there, there's no doubt about it.

KATY: Did you know I was coming, John?

LUBBOCK: No, no.

KATY: Is John going to be your lawyer, Aunt Julia?

MRS. MOWBREY: I hope so, dear. I certainly hope he will be. That'll bring us all closer and closer together.

KATY: Aunt Julia . . . I scarcely remember you. Why . . . why haven't we seen you more often?

MRS. MOWBREY: Mildred, dear, your mother and I . . . let's not talk about it. I'll just say this: sometimes in families, there are people who simply can't get on together. I hope your mother's happy. I wish her every good thing in the world. If she doesn't wish to see me, that doesn't change anything. I wish her every good thing in the world. You can tell her that any time you wish, Mildred. —But Mr. Lubbock tells me you wish to be called Kate?

KATY: Yes, I do.

MRS. MOWBREY: But why?

KATY *(After looking down a moment)*: That would take too long to explain, Aunt Julia.

MRS. MOWBREY: Well, you are a dear original girl, aren't you?

KATY: John, are you Aunt Julia's lawyer?

MRS. MOWBREY: He *will* be. He will be. We've just settled that. So that both my business and my pleasure—my affection, let us hope—will be close together. Oh, here's the tea.

(Enter Marget with the tea service.)

Oh, I have such plans for you. Cream and sugar—both of you?

KATY AND LUBBOCK: Thank you.

MRS. MOWBREY: You see, dear, I've lived too much alone, since my dear husband's death. That's not good. That's not right. And you are going to bring me out. —Now tell me, Katy, where are you going to live? Have you found just what you wanted?

KATY: Yes, we have. —Thank you.

MRS. MOWBREY: Splendid! Tell me, dear, don't have a moment's hesitation . . . What will it be: linen? silver?

KATY: Aunt Julia, I don't like receiving presents. I never have. I may be strange in that, but . . . I don't.

MRS. MOWBREY: Presents! But I'm your aunt—this is the family.

KATY *(Clearly)*: But we don't know one another very well yet.

(Mrs. Mowbrey is stopped short. She fumbles with her handkerchief. She begins silently to weep.)

Have you been living in New York, Aunt Julia?

MRS. MOWBREY: That was not kind, Mildred. That was not kind.

KATY *(Searching herself, softly)*: I'm sorry. I'm sorry, if . . . I think I'm supposed to be a very outspoken person, Aunt Julia, but I didn't mean to be unkind.

MRS. MOWBREY *(Still drying one eye; but in a low firm tone of instruction)*: That means you must have been *hurt* in life, in some way. I've seen it often.

KATY *(Another glance at John, slowly)*: No, I . . . don't think I have.

LUBBOCK *(Floundering, but trying to do his part)*: Katy's right, Mrs. Mowbrey. But when she does make a friend, she's a real one.

MRS. MOWBREY: *That* I believe. And so am I. And I want to prove it to you. I want you to come to feel that this is your second home. I want to be useful to you, in any way.

Do you know, Katy, that when I was a girl *I* changed my name, too? I was christened Julia; but I didn't like it. I wanted a name out of the Bible. I liked the story of Esther. I liked her courage. That's what I like— courage. Now will you tell me why you changed yours?

KATY: Well . . . I used to read Shakespeare all the time. And I liked the girls in Shakespeare. Even when I was very young . . . Every day I'd pretend I was a different one. And, you know, they . . . most of them have no fathers or mothers, or else . . . and they have to go live in foreign countries or live in a forest . . . and they even have to change their clothes and pretend they're men. They're very much thrown on their own resources. That's what they learn. There are four or five that I admired most—but I knew I wouldn't be like them. So I chose one of the lesser ones, one of the easier ones—

MRS. MOWBREY: I remember. I remember. That play. I can't remember its name—but that Kate had an awful temper. Mr. Lubbock, has our Kate got an awful temper?

(Katy stiffens.)

LUBBOCK: No, indeed, Mrs. Mowbrey.

KATY: No, I wish I did. I think people with a temper are lucky.

MRS. MOWBREY: Lucky! How could you wish a thing like that.

KATY: When things seem all wrong to me, I do something worse than have a temper. I turn all cold and stormy inside. It's as though something were dead in me.

MRS. MOWBREY: I understand every word of that. Katy, dear, we will be good friends. —Now surely there's some furniture I can lend you, some household appointments?

KATY *(Quietly)*: Thank you very much, Aunt Julia. But, of course, we mean to live very simply. And we won't be seeing anyone for the first year or two. —Will we John?

LUBBOCK *(Floundering)*: Just as you wish, Katy . . .

MRS. MOWBREY: Oh, dear! That's so unwise! My dear children, you must come and see *me*—and my friends. I have so many friends who will be delighted to meet you: artists and writers and young men in politics—so valuable for Mr. Lubbock's work. And the dear rector of my church, Mr. Jenkins.

KATY: All that's for John to decide, of course.

(Katy turns inquiringly toward him, as does Mrs. Mowbrey.)

LUBBOCK *(Belatedly he stammers)*: Oh, we . . . won't be seeing too many people . . .

MRS. MOWBREY: There's Judge Whittaker's son for example. You'll laugh till the tears run down your cheeks. *(With confidential emphasis to Katy)* Judge Whittaker can do anything in New York—*anything* you ask him . . . Old friend of mine.

(To Lubbock, rising) People with influence like that—you must know them.

(To Katy) And then I want to take you shopping, dear. Stores where they know me. They practically *give* me the things. Great Heavens, I haven't had to pay the marked [price] for anything, for years. Friends, friends everywhere. —Now I'm going to leave you two alone together. I know you have a world of things to talk about.

(Katy rises.)

If you want some more tea, just ring and ask Marget for it.

KATY *(Always quietly)*: Aunt Julia, I can see John perfectly well in my own home. I came to call on you.

MRS. MOWBREY *(Moving to the door)*: What a sweet thing to say. —No, no. I know young people in love; don't say I don't. And beginning today I want you to think of this house as your second home. Besides, I have a present for you and I must go and get it. *(She indicates a ring on her finger)* A very pretty thing, indeed.

KATY *(Following Mrs. Mowbrey toward the door; with a touch of firmer protest)*: But, Aunt Julia!—

MRS. MOWBREY: Ten minutes! I'll give you ten minutes!

(She goes out. Katy turns and with lowered eyes goes slowly to her chair. She sits and covers her face with her hands.)

KATY *(As though to herself)*: I can't understand it . . . What a dreadful, dreadful person.

LUBBOCK *(Uncomfortable)*: Come now, Katy. It's not as bad as all that . . . Of course, she's a little . . . odd; but I imagine she's been through a lot of . . . trouble of some sort.

(Katy looks at him a moment and then says with great directness:)

KATY: What has she done, John? *(He doesn't answer)* It must be something serious. Mother won't talk about her *one minute!*—Tell me! What is it?

LUBBOCK: Well . . . uh . . . she may have made some wrong step . . . early in life. Something like that.

KATY *(After weighing this thoughtfully)*: No. My mother would have forgiven that . . . It must be something much worse.

LUBBOCK: Whatever it was it's behind her. It's in the past.

KATY *(Shakes her head; she gives a shudder)*: It's there—*now*. *(Always very sincerely, this as though to herself)* I don't even know the names of things. Except what I've read about. In books. *(Brief pause)*
　　(As with an effort to say such an awful thing) Was she a . . . usurer?

LUBBOCK: What's that?—Oh, a *usurer. (With too loud a laugh)* NO, no—she wasn't that!

KATY: Was she a perjurer?

LUBBOCK: Katy, where do you get these old expressions? I don't know, but I guess she wasn't that.

KATY *(Gravely pursuing her thought)*: *Was* she . . . that other kind of bad person. That word that's in the Bible and in Shakespeare . . . *(This takes solemn courage)* . . . that begins with "double-you" . . . with "double-you aitch"—?

(This takes a minute to dawn on Lubbock. He reacts violently; with as little comic effect as possible.)

LUBBOCK: Katy!! How can you say such a thing.

KATY: I don't know how to pronounce it.

LUBBOCK: Do stop this! Put this all out of your head, *please.*

KATY: But she's my own aunt. I must have some idea to go by. Mother won't say a word. She just bursts into tears and leaves the room.

LUBBOCK: Please, Katy. —For Heaven's sake, change the subject.

KATY: I don't want to know anything that it's *unsuitable* for me to know. But I don't want to live with people hiding things from me. I don't think ignorance helps anybody. I can see perfectly well that you know the answer: Was Aunt Julia that thing that beings with "double-you"?

LUBBOCK: I'm not going to answer you, Katy. This conversation *is* unsuitable. Very unsuitable.

KATY *(Who has kept her eyes on him; calmly)*: Then she *was.*

LUBBOCK: No—I didn't say that. Anyway, how would I know a thing like that?—Probably, she was just connected with such things—at a distance.

KATY: How do you mean?

LUBBOCK: She wasn't in it herself . . . She just—sort of—stood by . . . I'm not going to stay here another moment. Where's that woman put my hat?

KATY: I see . . . She arranged them. That's in Shakespeare, too. She was a bawd.

LUBBOCK: Katy!

KATY: It's in the Bible, too: she was a . . . *(She pronounces the "aitch")* whoremonger.

(She rises.)

LUBBOCK *(Fiercely)*: Stop this right now. How can you say such ugly words?

KATY: Are there any others that aren't ugly?—Anyway, now I know.

(She quickly moves up toward the entrance.)

LUBBOCK: Where are you going?

KATY *(From the steps)*: You don't want me to stay, do you?

LUBBOCK: Think a moment, Katy. Stop and think.

KATY: Think what?

LUBBOCK: Well . . . this Bible you're quoting from . . . should have taught you to be charitable about people's mistakes. About Mary Magdalene and all that.

KATY *(Turning in deep thought)*: Yes, it should, shouldn't it?—But Mary Magdalene wasn't the second thing; she was the first. *(She returns to her chair and sits, her eyes on the floor. Again as though to herself)* I don't know anything about anything. *(She suddenly looks at him and says with accusing directness)* And you're not helping me. Tell me what I should think. Are you going to be like this always? . . . When I ask questions? . . .

LUBBOCK *(Urgently)*: No, Katy. I promise you. I'll answer anything you ask me!

KATY: When?

LUBBOCK: When we're married. —But not here! Not now! —Today, anyway, put all this out of your head.

KATY *(Reluctantly acquiescent, rises again)*: When we're married. That's like what Mother's always saying: "When you're older; when you're older." *(Turning to him with decision)* But if she *is* those things—those things that Shakespeare said—

LUBBOCK: Don't say them!

KATY: Promise me that you'll never see her again.

LUBBOCK: Now, K-a-a-ty! She's a client. In business we can't stop to take any notice of our client's morals . . .

KATY: In business they don't? I mean: thieves and criminals? Don't men meet that kind of people all the time?

LUBBOCK *(Putting his hands over his ears)*: Questions! Questions! You're going to drive me crazy.

KATY *(Looking around the room, musingly)*: And all this money came from . . . that! *(Her eyes return to him)* And when she asks us to come here to dinner?

LUBBOCK: Of *course*, we don't have to come often. But she's a lonely woman who's trying to put the mistakes of her life behind her. Be kind, Katy. Be charitable!

KATY *(Weighs this, then says simply)*: Have you ever seen her before?

LUBBOCK: Mrs. Mowbrey? *(Loud laugh of protest)* Of *course* not.

(Katy goes to the hall. From the top step she turns and says with great quiet but final significance:)

KATY: And you want me to invite her to the wedding?

(Lubbock cannot answer. His jaw is caught rigid. Katy returns into the room, drawing a ring off her finger.)

All I know is what I read in Shakespeare and the Bible. That's all I have to go by, John. Nobody else helps. You don't help me. I'm giving you back your ring.

(She puts the ring on the taboret and goes quickly, with lowered head, out of the house. The front door is heard closing. Lubbock stands rigid. Slowly he goes to the taboret and takes up the ring. Mrs. Mowbrey appears at the hall indignant.)

MRS. MOWBREY: Who went out the front door? Was that Katy?

(He puts down the ring on the taboret.)

LUBBOCK: Yes, Mrs. Mowbrey. She went home.

MRS. MOWBREY *(Coming in)*: Without saying good-bye to me! Her own aunt! Well—there's a badly brought up girl! *(Sitting down)* What did she say?

LUBBOCK: She left no message.

MRS. MOWBREY: I'm ashamed of her, Mr. Lubbock. I never heard of such behavior. The idea!
      (Seeing the ring) What's this? What's this ring?

LUBBOCK: She left it. It's her engagement ring.

MRS. MOWBREY: She broke her engagement?
      (Rising) Mr. Lubbock, listen to me! You can call yourself a very lucky man. One look at her, and I could see she wasn't the right girl for you. —Left without saying one word of good-bye! I don't know what's become of the girls these days. A niece of mine—behaving like that. *(Giving him the ring and wagging her finger in his face)* Now you must put that in a safe place—and you'll find the real right girl for you. They aren't all dead *yet*. You're going to find some splendid girl and I'm going to make a second home for you here. We're going to have fun. *You only live once,* as the Good Book says.

LUBBOCK: *You* did this! Look! *(Holding the ring toward her)* She's gone. —You with your conniving and sticking your nose into other people's business. WHY the hell did you have to put your goddamned nose into my affairs?

MRS. MOWBREY: I have never allowed profanity to be used in my presence.

LUBBOCK: Well, you'll hear it now. You—with your sentimental whining about wanting friends. *You'll* never have any friends. You don't deserve to have any friends. God, have you wrecked your chances today! —While you were wrecking mine.

(She has descended coolly into the room. Lubbock passes her toward the hall.)

You can sit here alone for ever and ever, as far as I care. Where'd that girl put my hat?

MRS. MOWBREY: Yes, Mr. Lubbock, you go and you stay away. You have just shown yourself to be the biggest fool I ever saw. It wasn't I that lost you that girl; it was yourself. And you deserve to lose her.

LUBBOCK: How do you know what happened?

MRS. MOWBREY: I will ring and Marget will get your hat.

(She pulls a bell rope. The waiting.)

Katy is my niece. Every inch my niece. She put you to the test and you were . . . *(Vituperatively) Shown up. Shown up.* Oh, you men! On your high saddles.

LUBBOCK: I tried to save *you,* anyway.

MRS. MOWBREY: I never saw anyone so stupid.

(Enter Marget.)

MARGET: Yes, Mrs. Mowbrey.

MRS. MOWBREY: Mr. Lubbock's been looking for his hat, Marget.

MARGET: Yes, ma'am.

(Marget disappears and returns with a straw hat. Lubbock takes it. Marget disappears. Lubbock lingers at the top of the stairs.)

LUBBOCK: Well—out with it. What should I have done?

MRS. MOWBREY: In the first place you should have lied, of course. Strong and loud and clear. A girl like that is not ready to learn what she wants to know. And at this stage it's not your business or mine to tell her.

LUBBOCK: She said she left me because I wasn't any help to her. Is lying any help?

MRS. MOWBREY: Of course it is. I suppose you think you were trying to tell her the truth? Young man, you're not old enough to tell the truth and it doesn't look as though you ever will be. In the first place, you should have lied, firmly, cleanly. THEN, you should have shown her that you *were* her friend. Katy did just right. Katy left you standing here, because she saw that you never would be her friend—that you haven't the faintest idea what it is to be a friend. What took place here took place in my own life. It's taking place all the time. Mr. Lubbock, people don't like to be—

(Lubbock rises, crosses the room and says aggressively and a little brutally:)

LUBBOCK: Mrs. Mowbrey, this has all been very interesting; and you've played your various cards very neatly and all that, but I want to know why you really asked me to come and see you today.

MRS. MOWBREY *(Also getting tougher)*: I am coming to that. *(She pauses)* Do you prefer to stand?

LUBBOCK *(Shortly)*: Yes, I do.

MRS. MOWBREY: There's one event in your life—in our lives—that I'd like you to explain to me. One night, at The Palace—it was in the spring of—you lost your head, or rather you lost control of yourself. You broke every bottle in my bar. You did like that with your arm. *(Her arm makes wide sweeping gestures, from right to left and left to right)* You terrorized everyone. You didn't strike anyone, but the flying glass could have blinded my girls. You weren't drunk. What happened? What made you do that?

LUBBOCK *(Furious, but coldly contained)*: I paid for it, didn't I?

MRS. MOWBREY: Oh, Mr. Lubbock. Don't talk like a child. You and I know that there are a great many things that can't be paid for. —Was it something that Dolores said to you—or that I said to you? *(Pause)* Or did that

friend of yours—what was his name? Jack Wallace or
Wallop?—did he hurt your feelings? No, it couldn't be
that; because you didn't strike *him*. The only thing you
struck was a lot of bottles and *you weren't drunk*.

*(She waits in silence; finally he says in barely controlled
impatience:)*

LUBBOCK: What of it? What of it? I lost my temper, that's all.

MRS. MOWBREY: I can understand your losing your temper
at *people*, Mr. Lubbock—we all do; but I can't understand your losing your temper at *things*.

LUBBOCK: What are you trying to get at, ma'am? Out with
it. Are you trying to tell me that you think I'm not fit to
be the husband of your niece?

MRS. MOWBREY: No, indeed. I think you're just the right
husband for her; and the more I talk to you, the more I
think you're just the right lawyer for me.

*(Lubbock is stunned by this sudden shift in Mrs. Mowbrey's
attitude.)*

Now, do you know what I have out in the sun porch?
Do you? *(He shakes his head in confusion)* A bottle of
champagne. And do you know what Lena is looking at
in the kitchen? Two great big steaks.

LUBBOCK *(Slowly recovering himself)*: I don't really like
champagne, Mrs. Mowbrey; but would you happen to
have any bourbon in the house?

MRS. MOWBREY: Bourbon! Have I bourbon? After six
o'clock that's all I touch. *(Guiding him to the door)* And
if you're a good boy I'll show you the list of my invest-
ments. There are one or two I'm worried about. Really
worried. [*(She pauses at the top step; he beside her. She
puts her hand on his arm)*] We all have disappoint-
ments in life, John—every one of us—but remember

Shakespeare said— [*(She smiles and taps him significantly on the chest with her jeweled forefinger)*] you know—

[*(She laughs and exits. He stands a moment, uncertain, then notices the straw hat still in his hand. He descends into the room, and gazes thoughtfully about. Then he places his straw hat on the taboret, turns and quickly exits in the direction Mrs. Mowbrey has taken. The Lights fade.)*]

END OF PLAY

This play became available through the research and editing of F. J. O'Neil of manuscripts in the Thornton Wilder Collection at Yale University.

The author's manuscript of *In Shakespeare and the Bible* existed in three nearly completed drafts, the latest of which had a number of rewrites, additions and corrections toward a fourth draft. Pages and sections of the earlier drafts, which were lined-through or crossed-out, have been examined but have not played a significant part in assembling this version of the play. Wilder's habit of throwing out what he emphatically rejected ("The writer's best friend is his wastepaper basket," is a motto he often articulated), but keeping around what he might refer to again and *use* again provided a richly marked road map to the play printed here.

Wilder leaves us wondering whether John will succumb to the strong impulse to grab success at any cost. For this reason I added stage directions (in brackets) at the end to give John a moment to collect his thoughts, wonder what the right path is, and then, at least for the moment, to cave in.

F. J. O'Neil
April 1997

SIX

Someone from Assisi

(Lust)

CHARACTERS

PICA, a twelve-year-old girl
MONA LUCREZIA, a crazy woman, forty
MOTHER CLARA, a sister at Saint Damian's, thirty-one
FATHER FRANCIS, a visiting priest, forty

SETTING

Poor Sisters Convent at Saint Damian's near Assisi.

The kitchen-garden behind the convent. A number of low benches surround the playing area. The actors' entrance at the back represents a door into the convent; it is framed by a trellis covered with vines. Opposite, the aisle through the audience represents a path to the village street.

A young girl, Pica, twelve, barefoot and wearing a simple smock, comes running out of the convent; she stares down the aisle through the audience and starts to shout in anger and grief.

PICA: No! No! Old Crazy—go home! You mustn't come here today. Go home! Go HOME!! We have someone specially important coming and you mustn't be here! Go home! You'll spoil everything!

(Mona Lucrezia, looking much older than her forty years, comes lurching through the audience to the stage. She is crazy. Her black, gray and white hair is uncombed. She carries a large soiled shawl. She mumbles to herself as she advances.)

MONA: Don't make such a noise, child. I must think what I'm going to say when he comes. Now, *you* go away. I must think.

PICA: No, *you* go away. —Oh, this is terrible!
    (Pica turns and rushes into the convent, calling:)
Mother Clara! Mother Clara!

MONA *(Shouting)*: It's I who have someone important coming—not you. And . . . *(Worriedly)* I must be ready. It's so hard to be ready. I must put gold on my hair . . . and perfumes, more perfumes. He'll have elephants and . . . camels.

(Mother Clara, thirty-one, enters and stands at the convent door looking thoughtfully at Mona Lucrezia. Pica passes her and comes toward the center of the stage.)

PICA: Mother, she mustn't be here today when *he* comes. Tell Old Thomas to drive her away. She'll sing and make a noise and spoil everything. —Old Crazy, *go home*! Mother Clara, we would die of shame, if *he* heard the things she says.

CLARA *(Quietly, her gaze on Mona)*: Be quiet, Pica. —Mona, do you know me? —What is her name, Pica?

PICA: I don't know. I've forgotten.

CLARA: Go and ask Old Thomas what her name is. I don't want you to call her Old Crazy. —Has she a home to go to?

PICA: Oh, Mother —she is very rich. But her family drives her out of the house all day.

(Mona has seated herself on one of the benches, her elbows on her knees. She is staring at the ground.)

CLARA: Go and find out what her name is.

(Pica runs into the convent.)

Mona, do you know me? . . . Mona, do you know me? I am Mother Clara of the Poor Sisters at Saint Damian's. Do you know me? . . . What is your name?

MONA *(Rising; impressively)*: I am who I am. —*He* is coming today. You know I am the Queen of . . .

CLARA: What? . . . Who is coming?

MONA: The King of . . .

CLARA: Yes. What king?

MONA *(Becoming confused)*: The King of Solomon. To see me. I must be ready. He is coming . . . from France. And . . .

CLARA: From France?!!

MONA: Of course, from France. I must have presents to give him. And . . . He will have lions. And . . .

CLARA: Yes. You must be ready, Mona.

(In order to induce Mona to leave the garden, Clara crosses the stage and starts walking backward through the audience.)

Come. You must go to your home and make yourself ready. Look! . . . Just look! You must comb your hair beautifully. And you must *wash your face*! —Who is it you say is coming?

MONA *(Following her; angrily)*: I *told* you—the King of Solomon . . . Of France. That is: French France. I didn't *love* him—*no*!; but he loved me. But now he has become a great person and he sends me all these messages.

(Stopping at the edge of the stage, she looks at the floor in a troubled way; softly) Did I tell you the truth? Did I love him? Did I?—Oh, he wrote such songs for me. Songs and songs.

CLARA: Come, Mona. I think you should rest, too.

MONA *(Confidentially)*: If I walk slowly he will not see that I am lame. One of the boys in the street kicked me.

CLARA: Kicked . . . !! Yes, walk slowly. Like a queen. No, no, stand up straight, Mona—like a queen. You can do it. Come. What will you say when you see the king?

MONA: I shall say . . . *(Standing straight)* Oh, King of Solomon, I shall say: Change the world!

CLARA *(Astonished)*: You will say that?

MONA: They throw stones at me. They kick me. Everywhere people hate people. My daughters—with brooms—they drive me away. I can't go home; I can only go home when the sun goes down. And I shall say: Oh, King, change the hearts of the world.

CLARA *(Returns to the stage; as Mona passes her on the way to the village)*: That is a very good thing to say. You won't forget it?

MONA *(Loudly)*: The world is *bad*.

CLARA: Yes.

MONA: Nobody is kind anymore.

CLARA: You tell your daughters that Mother Clara of Saint Damian's says that they are to let you into the house; and you will wash your face and your hair, won't you? And God bless you, dear Mona, and make you wise . . . wise and beautiful . . . for your friend.

(Mona has almost disappeared. From the convent sounds of joyous cries and laughter. Pica comes running out like an arrow.)

PICA *(Shrilly)*: He has come, Mother Clara. Father Francis is here!

(She flies back into the convent.)

MONA *(Returning a few steps)*: What did you say? . . . Wise?

CLARA: Yes . . . and beautiful. Good-bye, Mona. Remember. Good-bye.

MONA *(Mumbling)*: Wise . . . and beautiful . . . *(She goes out)*

(Francis appears at the convent door. He is forty, browned by the weather, almost blind, and with very few teeth.
 Also he is very happy. Clara, joyously, and as lightly as a young girl, runs to the center of the stage and falls on her knees.)

CLARA: Bless me, Father.

FRANCIS *(Kneels, facing her)*: God bless you, dearest Sister, with all His love. —And now you bless me, Sister.

CLARA *(Lowered eyes, laughing protest)*: Father!

FRANCIS: Say after me: God bless you, Brother Francis, and God forgive you that load of sins with which you have offended Him.

CLARA: God bless you, Brother Francis, with all His love.

FRANCIS: And . . .

CLARA *(Rippling laughter of protest)*: I cannot say that, Father.

FRANCIS: I order you by your holy obedience.

CLARA: . . . And God forgive you that load of sins— Father!—with which you have offended Him. —There!

FRANCIS: Yes.

(They both stay on their knees a moment, looking at one another, radiantly. Francis rises first and says with a touch of earnest injunction:)

I want you to say that prayer . . . that *whole* prayer . . . for me, every day.

CLARA: I will, Father. —Now sit in the sun. The meal will be ready very soon.

FRANCIS *(Sitting)*: And how is my little plant?

CLARA *(Again soft running laughter)*: Your little plant is very well, Father.

FRANCIS: Let me see . . . was it ten years ago we cut off your beautiful hair and found you a bridegroom?

CLARA: Ten years ago next month.

FRANCIS: Yes . . . Never, Sister Clara, have I seen a more beautiful wedding . . .

CLARA *(Blushing with pleasure)*: Father!

FRANCIS *(Softly)*: . . . Except, of course, my own.

CLARA: Oh, yes—*yours.* We know all about that—to the Lady Poverty.

FRANCIS: The Lady Poverty.

CLARA: Yes. —And how are *you*, dear Father?

FRANCIS: Well . . . Well . . .

CLARA: And your eyes?

FRANCIS: Oh, Sister . . . I can see the path. I can see the brothers and sisters. I can see the Crucified on the wall.

CLARA: Oh, then, I'm so happy. I'd heard that you had some difficulty.

FRANCIS *(Emphatically)*: Oh, yes, I can *see. (Confidentially)* Maybe I'm a little bit blind; but . . . I *hear* so well. I *hear* so much better.

CLARA: Do you?

FRANCIS: Everything talks all the time. The trees. And the water. And the *stones.*

CLARA *(Holding her breath)*: What, Father?

FRANCIS: The stones. The rocks. Now, when I go up there to pray, I must say to them: "Be quiet."

CLARA: "Be quiet."

FRANCIS: "Be quiet for a while." And they are quiet.

CLARA: Yes, Father.

(There is a moment while she digests this; then she begins again with animation.)

My sisters are so happy that you have come. Sister Agnes has made something for you. Now promise that you will eat all of it. It will break her heart if you don't.

FRANCIS: All?

CLARA *(Laughing)*: Oh, it is very little. We have learned that.

FRANCIS: *All?* My stomach has grown so small . . . *(Making a ring with his thumb and forefinger)* . . . That is enough.

CLARA: We understand. But this time there is a touch—a touch of saffron.

FRANCIS: Saffron!!

CLARA: The Count sent it to us from the castle, especially for you. He remembered that you liked it . . . *before* . . .

FRANCIS: Before? Before when?

CLARA: Well . . . Father . . . before . . . Before you entered the religious life.

FRANCIS *(Agitated)*: Before!!? When I was the most sinful of men! No, no, Sister Clara! Go quickly and tell Sister Agnes—no saffron! No saffron.

CLARA *(Calling sharply and clapping her hands)*: Pica! Pica!

(Pica enters at once.)

PICA: Yes, Mother.

CLARA: Tell Sister Agnes *no* saffron in Father's dish. And do not stand by the door.

PICA: Yes, Mother.

(During this interchange, Mona has returned, mumbling, through the audience.)

MONA: They throw stones at me. They kick me. Hmm. But when the king comes they will learn who I am. Hmm. They will sing another song.

CLARA *(Her eyes again thoughtfully on Mona, who has seated herself on one of the benches)*: She has lost her wits . . . She comes of a prosperous family, but they send her out of the house all day. I think the children torment her. She likes to come and sit here, rain or shine. —Father—she thinks she is the Queen of Sheba! And that King Solomon is coming to visit her!

FRANCIS *(Delighted)*: She thinks she is . . . ! How rich she is. How happy she must be!

CLARA (*Pointing to her own forehead*): Yes—but she is touched.

FRANCIS: Touched? . . . Oh, touched. —Is she able to receive the blessed sacrament?

CLARA: No. I think not. They tell me that in church she cries out and says unsuitable things. No, she is not allowed in the church.

FRANCIS: What is her name?

CLARA: Everyone here seems to have forgotten it. They simply call her Old Crazy. We call her Mona.

FRANCIS (*Taking a few steps toward Mona*): Mona! . . . Yes, your king is coming.

MONA (*Violently*): Go away from me! I know all about your nasty filthy wicked ways!

CLARA (*Authoritatively*): Now, Mona, you must be quiet or we will send you away—with a broom, too. You know our Thomas. Our Thomas knows how to make you move.

FRANCIS (*Quiets Clara with a gesture; his eyes on Mona in reflection*): Who can measure the suffering—the waste—in the world? And every being born into the world—except One—has added to it. You and I have made it more and more.

(*He turns to Clara and adds with eager face*) Let us go to the church now and fall on our knees. Let us ask forgiveness.

CLARA: Father, we shall go to the church later. Now you have come here to take the noon meal with my dear sisters.

FRANCIS (*With a sigh, as of a pleasure postponed*): Yes . . . yes.

CLARA (*Resuming the animated tone*): You received my letter? We can't give thanks enough! More and more are coming all the time. Sometimes I'm at my wit's end to find room and food for all these girls and women who are coming to join us. Oh, but I won't trouble you with *those* things—beds and food. We always find a way.

FRANCIS: Yes. Yes. No one would believe how we always find more beds and food.

CLARA: And their happiness! From morning to night. —You will hear them sing. They have been learning some new music to sing to you.

FRANCIS *(Rising, stuttering with eagerness)*: Sister C-C-Clara, let us go into the chapel and thank God.

CLARA: We will. We will. But *now*, dear Father, just for a moment, let us sit in the sun and rest ourselves.

FRANCIS *(Again resigned)*: ... Yes ... Very well.

CLARA: Father, there is something I've long wanted to ask you. Can we talk for a moment of childish things? —Father, you *will* eat the noonday meal at our table today? You will?

FRANCIS: Sister! Sister! Can't I have it out here? *Where* I eat it is of no importance. I shall see the sisters later when I preach to them.

CLARA: Father, you hurt them.

FRANCIS: *Hurt* them?! I hurt them?

CLARA: They cannot understand it. You let Brother Avisio and Brother Juniper eat with us.

FRANCIS: Yes ... yes ...

CLARA: But you have never sat down with us at our table ... Why is that? *(Lowering her voice)* My sisters are beginning to believe that you think that women are of a *lower order* in God's love.

FRANCIS: Sister Clara!!

CLARA: They have heard that you share your meal with ... wolves and birds, but never with *them*. —Can the Father Francis whom we love—this once—sit down with us women?

FRANCIS *(Agitated slightly but compliant)*: Yes ... oh, yes ... I will.

CLARA *(Urgently)*: It is so important, Father. I work among these good women and girls. They have left everything. They have God in Heaven but they have very little on earth.

(He nods repeatedly.)

Thank you! Now there's another childish thing I want to ask you. Brother Avisio told me a short time ago that you were christened John. Is that true?

FRANCIS: Yes. Yes. John.

CLARA: You chose the name Francis?

FRANCIS: My friends gave it to me. But that's long ago.

MONA *(From under the hood of her shawl, as though brooding to herself)*: Francis the Frenchman . . . They all called him that. That's what I called him, too.

(After Francis and Clara have looked at Mona a moment:)

FRANCIS: Long ago—when I was a young man. Before I found something better, I was never tired of hearing all those songs and stories that came down from France . . . about knights in armor who went about the world killing dragons and tyrants. A growing boy must have something to admire—to make his heart swell. I talked about those stories to everyone I knew. I dressed myself in foreign dress. I made songs, too—many of them. And . . . but . . .

CLARA: Why do you stop, Father?

FRANCIS: And I heard that each of these knights had a lady. *(He looks at her with pain and appeal)* I looked everywhere. I . . . I . . . looked everywhere.

CLARA: Do not talk of it, if it distresses you.

FRANCIS *(Low and urgently)*: . . . May God forgive me that load of sin with which I offended him!

CLARA: Yes.

FRANCIS: I went through a troubled time . . . *(Suddenly he looks at her happily)* And then I found my lady.

CLARA *(Laughing)*: Yes, we know, Father.

FRANCIS: Poverty! And I married her!

CLARA: Yes.

FRANCIS: And ever since, I go about the world singing her praises.

CLARA: Yes.

FRANCIS *(Eagerly)*: Before I knew her I was a coward. Yes. I was afraid of everything: of going into the forests at night; I was afraid of hunger and of cold. I was afraid to knock at the doors of nobles and great people. But *now*—with *her* beside me—I go everywhere. I do not trouble when I go into the Pope's presence, even. I am not afraid when twenty new brothers arrive at our house: where shall I put them? How shall I feed them? *She* shows me. *(Clara nods in complete agreement)* But how can one say how beautiful she is! And . . . and *(Lowering his voice)* how severe. Sometimes I almost offend her. And then I know that her eyes are *turned away* from me! . . .

(Suddenly raising his hands) No saffron! No saffron! —But most of the time we live together in great happiness.

(He crosses the stage, groping in his memory for an old song.)

. . . That song . . . that old song I wrote for her:

> When in the darkness of the night
> I see no lantern and no star,
> My lady's eyes will bring me light.
> When in pathless woods I stray
> My feet have stumbled in despair
> My lady's eyes will show the way.

MONA:

> When prison chains do fetter me—

FRANCIS *(A loud cry of recognition)*: Mona Lucrezia!!
MONA *(Harshly)*: Shame on you! To sing that song in the ears of a holy woman! *That* is Mother Clara of Saint Damian's. Cover your ears, Mother Clara.

(Advancing on Francis) What do you know of Francis the Frenchman? *I* know him. He wrote that song for me.

When prison chains do fetter me
And it is written I must die
My lady's eyes will set me free.

Yes, we all knew that he searched for his lady. We all knew that—the mayor's wife and Ninina Dono . . . and I . . .

FRANCIS: Mona Lucrezia.

(*Trembling, to Clara*) Leave me alone with her.

MONA: Mother Clara, they say that he goes all over the world now; that he sees the Pope and says good morning, good morning; that he's gone to Palestine to convert the Grand Turk himself—

CLARA: Do not be long, Father. The meal is almost ready.

(*She hurries out.*)

MONA (*Calling after her*): He said my body was of marble and snow—no, he said that my body was of fire and snow.

(*She starts leaving the stage through the audience.*)

He'll convert the Grand Turk. The Devil will help him. He converted the mayor's wife and me—the Devil helping him.

(*Francis, shaken and speechless, stands looking after her. Pica has entered stealthily from the convent. Francis appears not to hear her.*)

PICA: Father Francis, we did everything we could to prevent that crazy woman from coming here today. Mother Clara says that you are going to sit at table with the sisters—for the first time. You must sit quite still during the reading because Sister John of the Nails is going to draw a picture of you that we can have on the wall. When people draw you, you have to sit very still, because when you move, they can't see what to draw—

(Sounds of shouting from the street.)

MONA *(Offstage)*: Go away from me! Peter, put down that stone! Aiiiiiiee!
PICA: Oh, Father Francis! She's coming back again. They've been throwing stones at her.

(She goes down the aisle.)

Don't . . . come . . . back. We'll beat you!
FRANCIS: Come here and be quiet!

(Mona lurches back, shouting toward the street. One side of her face is covered with blood. She is struck again and sinks on one knee at the edge of the stage.)

MONA: Pigs—all of you. Lock your mothers up and there'll be no more of you.
FRANCIS: Come and sit down here, Mona Lucrezia.
MONA *(To Francis)*: Don't strike me—*you*! Go away from me.
FRANCIS *(Authoritatively to Pica)*: Get a bowl of water and a clean cloth. Put some leaves and stems of the hazel into it. And be quick.

(Pica stands gaping.)

Be quick! Be quick!

(Pica runs off.)

MONA *(Harshly to Francis)*: You kicked me!
FRANCIS: No, Mona Lucrezia.
MONA: You did.

FRANCIS: Come over here and sit down. You are among friends now.

MONA *(Sitting down)*: There are no friends. I don't want any friends. I had some.

(She stares at Francis, somberly) Who are you? What's your name?

FRANCIS: I was christened John.

MONA: John! —Do you know who John was?

FRANCIS *(In a small voice)*: Yes.

MONA: You stand there—idle as a log—and *do* nothing. If all the men in the world named John would join themselves together and be worthy of their name, the world would not be like *that*.

FRANCIS: Don't put your hand on your wound, Lucrezia. We'll wash it in a moment.

MONA *(Harshly)*: Don't talk to me!

(Silence.)

(Then broodingly to herself) The king will look for me. "Where is my queen?" I'll hide where he can't find me. —And I had something to tell him.

(Clara enters swiftly with water and a cloth. She kneels before Mona.)

CLARA: Hold your face up, Mona Lucrezia.

MONA: Don't touch me! You are a holy woman. I will do it myself. Or let that log do it—that worthless John.

(As though overcoming a powerful repulsion, Francis applies the wet cloth to Mona's forehead.)

MONA *(Striking him)*: That hurts.

FRANCIS: Yes, it will hurt for a minute. Sit quiet. Sit quiet.

MONA *(With a sob, but submitting)*: That hurts.

(At a signal from Francis, Clara leaves.)

FRANCIS: There, that's better. Now your hands . . .

MONA *(With closed eyes)*: They wash the dead. They washed us when we were born.

(Silence.)

FRANCIS: Now your face again.

MONA: No! Don't touch me again. I don't like to be touched. *(She takes the cloth)*

    (Grumbling as though to herself) On an important day like this! . . . And you one of those great good-for-nothing monks, filling your big belly with meals at other people's tables. *(Directly at him, fiercely)* God must weep!

FRANCIS: Yes.

MONA: Francis the Frenchman became a monk. I knew him. I never said to him what I should have said. It was clear in my mind, like writing on the wall; but I never said it. Whatever Francis the Frenchman wanted to do, oh, he did it. His will was like . . . ! It was that that made us break our vows. I had never deceived my husband. I told him I was afraid of God. What do you suppose he said? I told him I was afraid of losing God's love.

(She stares at him.)

He said: all love is one!

FRANCIS: No-o!

MONA: He said that he would make me the lady of his life and that he would do anything that I ordered him to do . . . I should have ordered him to do . . . that though that was like writing on the wall. Even then, though I was a girl, I knew that the world was a valley without rain . . . a city without food. I knew . . . I felt . . . he could . . . *(She becomes confused)*

FRANCIS *(Low)*: What would you have said, Lucrezia?

MONA *(Rising)*: I shall be your lady. And I command you: OWN NOTHING. No one will listen to you, if you have a roof over your head. No one will listen to you if you know where you will eat tomorrow. It is fear that has driven love out of the world and only a man without fear can bring it back.

(She glares at him a moment, then sinks back on the bench.)

But I never said it!

FRANCIS: Lucrezia, do you know me? I am Francis.

MONA *(Without interest)*: No, you are some other Francis. I am going now.

FRANCIS *(Calling)*: Pica! Pica!

MONA *(Starting to the town)*: I'm tired . . . but I'm afraid of the butcher's dog . . . and the mayor's—

FRANCIS: Pica!

(Pica rushes in.)

I am taking Mona Lucrezia to her home. *(He indicates with his eyes)* I will need you to show me the way.

PICA: Father Francis, the sisters are ready to sit down at the table. You will break their hearts.

MONA *(Starting)*: I had a stick. The boys are always taking away my stick.

(Stopping.)

Someone was coming to town today . . .

PICA *(Spitefully)*: Yes! Father Francis himself. And you've spoiled everything!

FRANCIS *(To Pica)*: Hsh! —I cannot see the path. Give me your hand.

MONA *(Turning)*: Those dogs—the butcher's Rufus. Brother John, haven't you got a stick?

PICA *(Giggling)*: She doesn't even know that dogs don't bite Father Francis!

MONA *(Stopping and peering at Francis)*: Haven't you got a stick?

FRANCIS: No, Mona Lucrezia. I have nothing.

(They go out.)

END OF PLAY

SEVEN

Cement Hands

(Avarice)

CHARACTERS

EDWARD BLAKE, a lawyer, fifty
PAUL, a waiter, fifty-five
DIANA COLVIN, Blake's niece, twenty-one
ROGER OSTERMAN, Diana's fiancé, twenty-seven

SETTING

Corner in the public rooms of a distinguished New York hotel.

A screen has been placed at the back (that is, at the actors' entrance) to shut this corner off from the hotel guests. A table in the center of the stage with a large RESERVED *sign on it. Various chairs. At the end of the stage farthest from the entrance is a low bench; above it we are to assume some large windows looking onto Fifth Avenue.*

Enter Edward Blake, a lawyer, fifty. He is followed by Paul, a waiter, fifty-five.

BLAKE *(Rubbing his hands)*: Paul, we have work to do.

PAUL: Yes, Mr. Blake.

BLAKE: There will be three for tea. I arranged with Mr. Gruber that this corner would be screened off for us; and I specially asked that you would wait on us. As I say, we have some work to do. *(Smilingly giving him an envelope)* There's a hundred dollars, Paul, for whatever strain you may be put to.

PAUL: Thank you, sir. —Did you say "strain," Mr. Blake?

BLAKE: I'm going to ask you to do some rather strange things. Are you a good actor, Paul?

PAUL: Well—I often tell the young waiters that our work is pretty much an actor's job.

BLAKE: I'm sure you're a very good one. Now the guests today are my niece, Diana Colvin. —You know Miss Colvin, don't you?

PAUL *(With pleasure)*: Oh, yes, Mr. Blake. Everyone knows Miss Colvin.

BLAKE: And her fiancé—that's a secret still—Mr. Osterman?

PAUL: Which Mr. Osterman, sir?

BLAKE: Roger—Roger Osterman. You know him?

PAUL: Oh, yes, sir.

BLAKE: Now it's not clear which of us is host. But it's clear to *me* which of us is host. Roger Osterman has invited us to tea. He will pay the bill.

PAUL: Yes, sir.

BLAKE: There may be some difficulty about it—some distress; some squirming; some maneuvering—protesting. But he will pay the bill.

(A slight pause while he looks hard and quizzically at Paul, who returns his gaze with knowing raised eyebrows.)

Now at about 5:20 you're going to bring Mr. Osterman a registered letter. The messenger will be waiting in the hall for Mr. Osterman's signature. Roger Osterman will ask to borrow half a dollar of me. I won't have half a dollar. He will then turn and ask to borrow half a dollar of you. And you won't hear him.

PAUL: I beg your pardon, sir?

BLAKE: He'll ask to borrow half a dollar of you, but you won't hear him. You'll be sneezing or something. Your face will be buried in your handkerchief. Have you a cold, Paul?

PAUL: No, sir. We're not allowed to serve when we have colds.

BLAKE: Well, you're growing deaf. It's too bad. But . . . you . . . *won't* . . . *hear* him.

PAUL *(Worriedly)*: Yes, sir.

BLAKE: You'll say *(Raising his voice)* "Yes, Mr. Osterman, I'll get some hot tea, at once." This appeal to you for money may happen several times.

PAUL *(Abashed)*: Very well, Mr. Blake, if you wish it.

BLAKE: Now, Paul, I'm telling you why I'm doing this. You're an intelligent man and an old friend. My niece is going to marry Roger Osterman. I'm delighted that my niece is going to marry him. He's a very nice fellow— and what else is there about him, Paul?

PAUL: Why, sir—it is understood that he is very rich.

BLAKE: Exactly. But the Ostermans are not only fine people and very rich people—they have oddities about them, too, haven't they?—A certain oddity?

(Blake slowly executes the following pantomime: he puts his hands into his trouser pockets and brings them out, open, empty and "frozen.")

PAUL *(Reluctantly)*: I know what you mean, sir.

BLAKE: Have you a daughter, Paul, or a niece?

PAUL: Yes, sir. I have two daughters and three nieces.

BLAKE: Then you know: we older men have a responsibility to these girls. I have to show my niece what her fiancé is like. I have to show her this odd thing—this one little unfortunate thing about the Ostermans.

PAUL: I see, Mr. Blake.

BLAKE: I'm not only her uncle; I'm her guardian; and her lawyer. I'm all she's got. And I must show her—here she comes now—and for that I need your help.

(Enter Diana Colvin, twenty-one, in furs. The finest girl in the world.)

DIANA: Here you are, Uncle Edward. —Good afternoon, Paul.

PAUL: Good afternoon, Miss Colvin.

BLAKE: Will you wait for tea, Diana?

DIANA *(Crossing the stage to the bench)*: Yes.

(Paul goes out.)

BLAKE: Aren't you going to kiss me?

DIANA: No!! I'm furious at you. I'm so furious I could cry. You've humiliated me. I'm so ashamed I don't know what to do. Uncle Edward, how could you do such a thing?

BLAKE *(Calmly)*: What, dear?

DIANA: I've just heard that—*(She rises and strides about, groping for a handkerchief in her bag)*—you're asking the Osterman family how much allowance Roger will give me when we're married. And you're making some sort of difficulty about it. Uncle Edward! The twentieth century! And as though I were some poor little goose-girl he'd discovered in the country. Oh, I could die. I swear to you, I could die.

BLAKE: *(Still calmly)*: Sit down, Diana.

(Silence. She walks about, dabs her eyes and finally sits down.)

Diana, I'm not an idiot. I don't do things like this by whim and fancy.

DIANA: Perfectly absurd. Why, all those silly society columnists keep telling their readers every morning that I'm one of the richest girls in the country. Is it true? *(He shrugs)* I'll never need a cent of the Ostermans' money. I'll never take a cent, not a cent.

BLAKE: What?

DIANA: I won't have to.

BLAKE: What kind of marriage is that?

(He rises. She looks at him a little intimidated.)

Well, you'll be making an enormous mistake and it will cost you a lot of suffering.

DIANA: What do you mean?

BLAKE: Marriage is a wonderful thing, Diana. But it's relatively new. Twelve, maybe fifteen thousand years old. It brings with it some ancient precivilization elements. Hence, difficult to manage. It's still trying to understand itself.

DIANA *(Shifting in her seat, groaning)*: Really, Uncle Edward!

BLAKE: It hangs on a delicate balance between things of earth and things of heaven.

DIANA: Oh, Lord, how long?

BLAKE: Until a hundred years ago a wife *had* no money of her own. All of it, if she had any, became her husband's. Think that over a minute. Billions and billions of marriages where the wife had not one cent that she didn't have to *ask* for. You see: it's important to us men, us males, us husbands that we supply material things to our wives. I'm sorry to say it but we like to think that we own you. First we dazzle you with our strength, then we hit you over the head and drag you into our cave. We buy you. We dress you. We feed you. We put jewels on you. We take you to the opera. I warn you now—most seriously—don't you start thinking that you want to be independent of your husband as a provider. You may be as rich as all hell, Diana, but you've got to give Roger the impression every day that you thank him—thank him humbly, that you aren't in the gutter.

DIANA *(Short pause; curtly)*: I don't believe you.

BLAKE: Especially Roger. *(Leaning forward; emphatic whisper)* You are marrying into a very strange tribe. *(They gaze into one another's eyes)* Roger is the finest young man in the world. I'm very happy that you're going to marry him. I think that you will long be happy—but you'll only be happy if you know beforehand exactly what you're getting into.

DIANA: What *are* you talking about?

(She rises and crosses the stage.)

I want some tea.

BLAKE: No, we don't have tea until he comes. *He* is giving us tea. Please sit down. What am I talking about? Diana, you've been out with Roger to lunch and dinner many times, haven't you? You've gotten in and out of taxis with him. You've arrived at railroad stations and had porters carry your bags, haven't you?

DIANA: Yes.

BLAKE: Have you ever noticed anything odd about his behavior in such cases?

DIANA: What do you mean?

(He gazes levelly into her eyes. She begins to blush slightly. Silence.)

BLAKE: Then you have?

DIANA *(Uncandidly)*: What do you mean?

BLAKE: Say it!

(Pause.)

DIANA *(Suddenly)*: I love him.

BLAKE: I know. But say what's on your mind.

DIANA: It's a little fault.

BLAKE: How little?

DIANA: I can gradually correct him of it.

BLAKE: That's what his mother thought when she married his father . . . After you leave a restaurant do you go back and leave a dollar or two for the waiter, when Roger's not looking? Do you hear taxi drivers shouting indecencies after him as he walks away? Have you seen him waste time and energy to avoid a very small expenditure?

DIANA *(Rising, with her handbag and gloves, as though about to leave)*: I don't want to talk about this any more. It's tiresome; and more than that it's in bad taste. Who was it but *you* who taught me never to talk about money, never to mention money. And now we're talking about money in the grubbiest way of all—about *tipping*. And you've been talking to the Osterman family about an allowance for me. I feel soiled. I'm going for a walk. I'll come back in twenty minutes.

BLAKE: Good. That's the way you should feel. But there's one more thing you ought to know. Paul will help us.

(He goes to the entrance at the back, apparently catches Paul's eye, and returns.)

DIANA: You're not going to drag Paul into this?

BLAKE: Who better?—Now if *you* sit at ease, it will put *him* at ease.

(Enter Paul.)

PAUL: Were you ready to order tea, Mr. Blake?

BLAKE: No, we're waiting for Mr. Osterman. You haven't seen him, have you?

PAUL: No, I haven't.

BLAKE: Paul, I was talking with Miss Colvin about that little matter you and I were discussing. You gave me permission to ask you a few questions about the professional life in the hotel here.

PAUL: If I can be of any help, sir.

BLAKE: The whole staff of waiters is accustomed to a certain lack of . . . generosity on the part of the Osterman family. Is that true?

PAUL *(Deprecatingly)*: It doesn't matter, Mr. Blake. We know that they give such large sums to the public in general . . .

BLAKE: Is this true of any other families?

PAUL: Well . . . uh . . . there's the Wilbrahams. *(Blake nods)* And the Farringtons. That is, Mr. Wentworth and Mr. Conrad Farrington. With Mr. Ludovic Farrington it's the other way 'round.

BLAKE: Oh, so every now and then these families produce a regular spendthrift?

PAUL: Yes, sir.

BLAKE: I see. Now, have the waiters a sort of nickname for these less generous types?

PAUL *(Reluctantly)*: Oh . . . the younger waiters . . . I wouldn't like to repeat it.

BLAKE: You know how serious I am about this. I wish you would, Paul.

PAUL: Well . . . they call them "cement hands."

DIANA *(Appalled)*: WHAT?

BLAKE *(Clearly)*: Cement hands. —What you mean is that they can give away thousands and millions but they cannot put their fingers into their pockets for . . . a quarter or a dime? And, Paul, is it true that in many cases the wives of the Ostermans and Wilbrahams and Farringtons return to the table after a dinner or supper and leave a little something—to correct the injustice?

PAUL: Yes, Mr. Blake. —Mrs. . . . but I won't mention any names . . . sometimes sends me something in an envelope the next day.

BLAKE: Yes.

PAUL: Perhaps I should tell you a detail. In these last years, the gentlemen merely *sign* the waiter's check. And they add a present for the waiters in writing.

BLAKE: *That* they can do. Well?

PAUL: Pretty well. What they cannot do—

BLAKE:—is to put their hands in their pockets. Thank you. And have you noticed that one of these hosts . . . as the moment approaches to . . . *(He puts his hands gropingly in his pockets)* . . . he becomes uncomfortable in his chair . . . his forehead gets moist? . . .

PAUL: Yes, sir.

BLAKE: He is unable to continue conversation with his friends? Some of them even start to quarrel with you?

PAUL: I'm sorry to say so.

BLAKE *(Shakes Paul's hand)*: Thank you for helping me, Paul.

PAUL: Thank you, sir.

(Paul goes out. Diana sits crushed, her eyes on the ground. Then she speaks earnestly:)

DIANA: Why is it, Uncle Edward? Explain it to me! How can such a wonderful and generous young man be so mean in little things?

BLAKE: Your future mother-in-law was my wife's best friend. Katherine Osterman has given her husband four children. She runs two big houses—a staff of twenty at least. Yet every expenditure she makes is on account—it goes through her husband's office—sign for everything—write checks for everything. You would not believe the extent to which she has no money of her own—in her own hand. Her husband adores her. He can't be absent from her for a day. He would give her hundreds of thousands in her hands but she *must ask for it*. He wants that picture: that everything comes from him. Why, she has to go to the most childish subterfuges to get a little cash—she buys dresses and returns them, so as to have a hundred dollars in bills. She doesn't want to do anything underhand, but she wants to do something personal—small and friendly and personal. She can give a million to blind children, but she can't give a hundred to her maid's daughter.

(Diana, weeping, blows her nose.)

Now you say you have your own money. Yes, but I want to be sure that you have an allowance *from Roger* that you don't have to account to him for. Money to be human with—not as housekeeper or as a beautifully dressed Osterman or as an important philanthropist— but as an imaginative human being; and I want that money to come from your husband. It will puzzle him and bewilder him and distress him. But maybe he will come to understand the principle of the thing.

DIANA *(Miserably)*: How do you explain it, Uncle Edward?

BLAKE: I don't know. I want you to study it right here today. Is it a sickness?

DIANA *(Shocked)*: Uncle Edward!

BLAKE: Is it a defect in character?

DIANA: Roger has no faults.

BLAKE: Whatever it is, it's deep—deep in the irrational. For Roger it's as hard to part with twenty-five cents as it is for some people to climb to the top of a skyscraper, or to eat frogs, or to be shut up with a cat. Whatever it is—it proceeds from a *fear*, and whatever it is, it represents an incorrect relation to—

DIANA: To what?

BLAKE *(Groping)*: To . . .

(Paul appears at the entrance.)

PAUL: Mr. Osterman has just come into the hall, Mr. Blake.

BLAKE: Thank you, Paul.

(Paul goes out.)

DIANA: Incorrect relation to what?

BLAKE: To material things—and to circumstance, to life— to everything.

(Enter Roger Osterman, twenty-seven, in a rush. The finest young fellow in the world.)

ROGER: Diana! Joy and angel of my life. *(He kisses her)* Uncle Edward. —Ten minutes past five. I've got to make a phone call. To Mother. I'll be back in a minute. Mother and I are setting up a fund. I'll tell you all about it. Uncle Edward, what are you feeding us?

BLAKE: We haven't ordered yet. We were waiting for our host.

ROGER *(All this quickly)*: Am I your host? Very well. You've forgotten that you invited us to tea. Didn't he, Diana?

BLAKE: You distinctly said—

ROGER: *You* distinctly said—really, Diana, we can't let him run away from his responsibilities like that. Uncle Edward, we accept with pleasure your kind invitation—

BLAKE: You called me and told me to convey your invitation to Diana. Diana, thank Roger for his kind invitation.

DIANA *(Rising, with a touch of exasperation)*: Gentlemen, gentlemen! Do be quiet. The fact is *I* planned this party and you're both my guests. So do your telephoning, Roger, and hurry back.

ROGER: You're an angel, Diana. Tea with rum in it, Uncle Edward.

DIANA: Come here, you poor, poor boy. *(She looks gravely into his eyes and gives him a kiss)*

ROGER *(Laughing)*: Why am I a poor, poor boy?

DIANA: Well, you are.

(She gives him a light push and he goes out laughing.)

BLAKE: We must act quickly now. I've arranged for some things to happen during this hour. You're going to spill some tea on your dress—no, some chocolate from a chocolate éclair.

DIANA: What?!

BLAKE: And you'll have to go to the ladies' room to clean it up. And you're going to need fifty cents. Open your purse. Give me all the change you have—under a five dollar bill.

DIANA: Why?

BLAKE: Because you'll have to borrow the fifty-cent piece from *him*. —Give me your change.

DIANA: Uncle Edward, you're a devil. *(But she opens her handbag and purse)*

BLAKE *(Counting under his breath)*: Three quarters. Fifty-cent piece. Dimes. No dollar bills.

DIANA *(Crossing the room, in distress)*: Uncle, I don't believe in putting people to tests.

BLAKE: Simply a demonstration—

DIANA: I don't need a demonstration. I suffer enough as it is.

BLAKE: But have you forgotten: we're trying to learn something. Is it a sickness or is it a—

DIANA: Don't say it!

BLAKE: And I want you to notice something else: every subject that comes up in conversation . . .

(He starts laughing.)

DIANA *(Suspicious and annoyed)*: What?

BLAKE: To call your attention to it, I'll *(He drops his purse)* drop something. Every subject that comes up in the conversation will have some sort of connection with money.

DIANA *(Angrily drops her handbag)*: But that's all you and I have been talking about—until I'm about to go crazy.

BLAKE: Yes . . . yes, it's contagious.

DIANA *(With weight)*: Uncle Edward, are you trying to break up my engagement?

BLAKE *(With equal sincerity, but quietly)*: No! I'm trying to ratify it . . . to *save* it.

DIANA: How?

BLAKE *(Emphatic whisper)*: With . . . understanding.

(Enter Paul.)

Oh, there you are, Paul. Tea for three and a decanter of rum. And a chocolate éclair for Miss Colvin.

DIANA: But I hate chocolate éclairs!

(Blake looks at her rebukingly.)

Oh, all right.

BLAKE: And, Paul, when we've finished tea, you'll place the check beside Mr. Osterman.

(Diana purposefully drops her lipstick.)

PAUL *(Picking up the lipstick)*: Yes, sir.

DIANA: Thank you, Paul.

(Paul goes out. Diana leans toward Blake and says confidentially:)

Now you must play fair. If you cheat, I'll stop the whole thing.

(Enter Roger.)

ROGER: All is settled. It's really very exciting. Mother and I setting up a fund where there's a particular particular need.

DIANA: What is it, Roger?

ROGER *(Laughs; then)*: Guess where Mother and I are going tomorrow?

DIANA: Where?

ROGER: To the poorhouse!

(Blake pushes and drops the ashtray from the table.)

DIANA *(Covering her ears)*: Uncle Edward, do be careful!

ROGER: In fact, we're going to three. Mother's already been to thirty—in England and France and Austria—I've been to ten. We're doing something about them. We're making them attractive. Lots of people come to the ends of their lives without pensions, without social security. We're taking the curse off destitution.

BLAKE: And you're taking the curse off superfluity.

(Diana looks at Blake hard and drops her gloves.)

ROGER: We're beginning in a small way. Mother's giving two million and Uncle Henry and I are each giving one. We're not building new homes yet—we're improving the conditions of those that are there. Everywhere we go we ask a thousand questions of superintendents, and of the old men and women . . . And do you know what these elderly people want most? *(He looks at them expectantly)*

DIANA *(Dropping a shoe)*: Money.

ROGER *(Admiringly)*: How did you know?!

(Diana shrugs her shoulders.)

You see, in a sense, they have everything: shelter, clothes, food, companionship. We've scarcely found one who wishes to leave the institution. But they all want the one thing for which there is no provision.

(Paul enters with a tray: tea; rum; éclair; the service check, which he places on the table beside Roger; and a letter.)

PAUL: A letter has come for you, Mr. Osterman, by special messenger. Will you sign for it, Mr. Osterman?

ROGER: For me? But no one else knows that I'm here.

BLAKE: By special messenger, Paul?

PAUL: Yes, Mr. Blake.

BLAKE: And is the messenger waiting?

    (Intimately) Roger . . . the messenger's waiting in the hall . . .

ROGER: What?

BLAKE: Fifty cents . . . for the messenger.

ROGER *(A study)*: But I don't think this is for me.

(He looks at it.)

DIANA *(Taking it from him)*: "Roger Osterman, Georgian Room, etc." Yes, I think it's for you.

(Roger makes some vague gestures toward his pockets.)

ROGER: Uncle Edward . . . lend me a quarter, will you?

BLAKE *(Slowly searching his pockets)*: A quarter . . . twenty-five cents . . . Haven't got it.

ROGER: Paul, give the boy a quarter, will you?

PAUL *(Deaf as a post)*: Hot water? Yes, Mr. Osterman—

ROGER *(Loud)*: No . . . a QUARTER, Paul . . . give the boy a quarter . . .

PAUL: It's right here, Mr. Osterman.

ROGER *(Has torn the letter open; to Blake)*: It's from *you.* You say you'll be here. Well, if the messenger boy is from your own office, you can give him a quarter.

BLAKE *(Smiting his forehead; gives quarter to Paul)*: That's right . . . Paul . . . I'll see you . . .

ROGER *(Dabbing his forehead with his handkerchief)*: My, it's hot in here.

DIANA: Roger—you were saying that these old people wanted money. They have everything provided, but they still want money.

ROGER: Yes, I suppose it's to give presents to their nephews and nieces . . . to one another . . . They have everything except that . . .
(He starts laughing; then leans forward confidentially and says) You know, I think one of the reasons Mother became so interested in all this was . . . *(Then he stops, laughs again, and says)* Anyway, she's interested.

DIANA: What were you going to say?

ROGER *(Reluctantly)*: Well . . . she's always had the same kind of trouble. *(The other two stare at him)* Do you know that Mother once pawned a diamond ring?

BLAKE: *Your mother* went to a pawnshop?

ROGER: No. She sent her maid. Even today she doesn't know that I know. —I was at boarding school, and I'd begun a collection of autographs. More than anything in the world I wanted for my birthday a certain letter of Abraham Lincoln that had come on the market. I couldn't sleep nights I wanted it so bad. But Father thought it was unsuitable that a fifteen year old should get so worked up about a thing like that. —So Mother pawned her ring.

(Diana rises and crosses the room. She is flushed and serious.)

DIANA: I don't think we should be talking about such things—but—let me ask one thing, Roger. Your mother has always had a great deal of money of her own?

ROGER *(Laughing)*: Yes. But, of course, Father keeps it for her. More than that: he's doubled and tripled it.

BLAKE: Of course. It passes through his hands.

ROGER: Yes.

BLAKE *(Looking at Diana)*: He sees all the checks. Like the old people in the poorhouse, your mother has *everything* except money?

ROGER *(Laughing)*: Exactly!—The other thing the old people are interested in is food—

DIANA *(Looking down at her dress)*: Oh! I've spilled some of that tea and rum on my dress. I must go to the ladies' room and have the spot taken out. Uncle Edward, lend me half a dollar for the attendant.

BLAKE *(Ransacking his pockets)*: Half a dollar! Half a dollar! —I told you I hadn't a cent.

ROGER: In institutions—like prisons and poorhouses—you never have any choice—

DIANA: Roger, lend me half a dollar.

ROGER (*Taking out his purse, as he talks*): That was the awful part about prep school—all the food—(*He hands Diana a ten-dollar bill and goes on talking*)—was, so to speak, assigned to you. You never had the least voice in what it would be.

DIANA: But I don't want ten dollars. I want fifty cents.

ROGER: What for?

DIANA: To give the attendant in the ladies' room.

ROGER: Fifty cents?
    (*Rising and inspecting her dress*) I don't see any stain.
    (*To Blake*) Borrow it from Paul.

BLAKE: Paul's deaf. Roger, put your hands in your pockets and see if you haven't got fifty cents.

DIANA (*Almost hysterically*): It's all right. The stain's gone away. Forget it, please. Forgive me. I've made a lot of fuss about nothing.

ROGER (*Again touching his forehead with his handkerchief*): Awfully warm in here. We ought to have gone to the club. These places are getting to be regular traps. Why did we come here?

DIANA: What do you mean: traps?

ROGER: You're interrupted all the time—these tiresome demands on you. I love to give, but I don't like to be held up (*Gesture of putting a revolver to someone's head*) held up every minute. (*A touch of too much excitement*) I'd like to give everything I've got. I don't care how I live; but I don't like to be forced to give anything. It's not *my* fault that I have money.

DIANA: You're right, Roger.

(*She sees Paul's service check on the table. She flicks it with her finger and it falls on the floor as near the center of the stage as possible.*)

I don't think of a tip as an expression of thanks. It's just a transaction—a mechanical business convention. Take our waiter, Paul. My thanks is in my smile, so to speak. The money on the table has nothing to do with it.

ROGER: Well, whatever it is, it's a mess.

BLAKE: Once upon a time there was a very poor shepherd. It was in Romania, I think.

DIANA: Uncle!

BLAKE: Every morning this shepherd led his sheep out to a field where there was a great big oak tree.

DIANA: Really, Uncle!

BLAKE: And one day—under that oak tree—he found a large gold piece. The next day he found another. For weeks, for months, for years—every day—he found another gold piece. He bought more sheep. He bought beautiful embroidered shirts.

(Diana is suddenly overcome with uncontrollable hysterical laughing. She crosses the room, her handkerchief to her mouth, and sits on the bench by the windows. Blake waits a moment until she has controlled herself.)

No one else in the village seemed to be finding any gold pieces.

(Diana sputters a moment. Blake lowers his voice mysteriously.)

The shepherd's problem was: *Where do they come from?* And *why* are they given to *him?* Are they, maybe . . . supernatural?

ROGER *(Sharply)*: What?

(Blake points to the ceiling.)

I don't understand a word of this. Uncle Edward, do get on with it. I've never been able to understand these . . . allegories.

BLAKE: But why to *him?* Was he more intelligent—or more virtuous than the other young men?

(Pause.)

Now when you find a gold piece every morning, you get used to it. You get to need them. And you are constantly haunted by the fear that the gold pieces will no longer appear under the oak tree. What—oh, what—can he do to insure that those blessed gold pieces will continue to arrive every morning?

(Blake's voice turns slightly calculatedly superstitious; he half closes his eyes, shrewdly. His blade-like hand describes an either-or decision or bargain.)

Obviously, he'd better *give*. In return, so to speak. He gave his town a fine hospital. He gave a beautiful altar to the church. *(He changes his voice to the simple and direct)* Of course, he gave. But this shepherd was a fine human being, and it was the other question that troubled him most—frightened him, I mean: Why have I been *chosen?*

DIANA *(Sober; her eyes on the floor)*: I see that: he became frightened.

ROGER *(Looking at Diana, in surprise—laughing)*: *You* understand what he's talking about?

DIANA: Frightened, because . . . if the gold pieces stopped coming, he'd not only be poor . . . he'd be much more than poor. He'd be exposed. He'd be the man who was formerly fortunate, formerly—what did you say?—intelligent, formerly virtuous and—

BLAKE *(Pointing to the ceiling)*: Formerly favored, loved.

DIANA: Far worse than poor.

BLAKE: So he was in the terrible situation of having to GIVE all the time and of having to SAVE all the time.

DIANA: Yes . . . Yes. —Roger, I have to go.

(She rises.)

Now, who's going to pay the bill?—Roger, you do it, just to show that you like to.

ROGER *(With charming spontaneity)*: Of course, I will. Where is it?

DIANA *(Pointing)*: Right there on the floor.

ROGER *(Picking it up)*: I'll *sign* for it.—Where's Paul? There he is!

DIANA *(Putting on lipstick and watching him in her mirror)*: Surely, it's not large enough to sign for. There's something small about signing for a three or four dollar charge.

ROGER *(Looking from one to the other)*: *I* don't think so.

BLAKE: Diana's right.

ROGER *(Taking a ten-dollar bill from his purse and laying it on the bill)*: Diana, some day you must explain to me *slowly* what Uncle Edward's been talking about.

(Enter Paul. Roger indicates the money with his head. Paul makes change quickly.)

Paul, we're leaving.

    (To Diana) And you must make your Uncle Edward promise not to get tied up in any long rambling stories he can't get out of.

DIANA *(To Paul)*: Thank you, Paul.

BLAKE: Thank you, Paul.

ROGER: Thank you, very much, Paul.

PAUL *(As he goes out, leaving the bill and change on the table)*: You're very welcome.

ROGER *(While he talks, is feverishly figuring out his change)*: Because I must be very stupid . . . I can't . . . *(His hand among the coins of change, he turns and says)* Because I must say there are lots of better things to talk about than what we've been . . . *(He stops while he studies the change before him)* In fact, in our family we make it a rule never to talk about money at all . . .

(Pause.)

I don't think you realize, Diana, that my life is enough of a hell as it is: the only way I can cope with it is to *never* talk about it . . . what am I doing here? . . .

DIANA *(Going toward him; soothingly)*: What's the matter, dear? Just leave him a quarter.

ROGER *(His face lighting up)*: Would that be all right? *(She nods)* Diana, you're an angel. *(Triumphantly)* I'm going to leave him fifty cents, just to show him I love you.

DIANA: No. I'm not an angel. I'm a very *human* being. I'll need to be fed. And clothed. And—

ROGER *(Bewitched; kissing her gravely)*: I'll see you have everything.

DIANA: I can look forward to everything?

ROGER: Yes.

DIANA: Like those old ladies in the poorhouse, I can look forward to—

ROGER: *My* giving you everything.

(Diana hurries out ever so lightly, blowing her nose. Paul appears at the door. Blake and Roger go out. Paul, alone, picks up the tip. No expression on his face. Diana appears quickly.)

DIANA: I dropped a glove.
  (She drops a dollar bill on the table) Goodbye, Paul.

PAUL: Goodbye, Miss Colvin.

(They go out.)

END OF PLAY

The Seven Ages of Man

Infancy

A COMEDY

CHARACTERS

PATROLMAN AVONZINO
MISS MILLIE WILCHICK, a nursemaid
TOMMY, a baby in her care
MRS. BOKER
MOE, her baby boy

SETTING

Central Park in New York City. The 1920s.

One or more large park benches. Some low stools at the edges of the stage indicate bushes.

Enter Patrolman Avonzino, a policeman from the Keystone comic movies with a waterfall mustache, thick black eyebrows and a large silver star. Swinging his billy club jauntily, he shades his eyes and peers down the paths for trouble. Reassured, he extracts a small memorandum book from an inner pocket of his jacket and reads:

AVONZINO: "Wednesday, April 26 . . ." Right. "Centra' Park, Patrol Section Eleven, West, Middle." Right! "Lieutenant T. T. Avonzino." Correct. Like Tomaso Tancredo Avonzino. "Eight to twelve; two to six. Special Orders: Suspect—mad dog, black with white spots. Suspect—old gentleman, silk hat, pinches nurses." *(Reflects)* Pinch babies okay; pinch nurses, nuisance. *(Puts the book away, strolls, then takes it out again for further instructions)* Probable weather: late morning, percipitation—percipitation like rain. *(Strolls)* Seven to eight-thirty, no nuisances. Millionaires on horses; horses on millionaires. Young gents running in underwear; old gents running in underwear. *(Reflects)* Running in underwear, okay; *walking* in underwear, nuisance. Eight-thirty to nine-thirty, everybody late for working, rush-rush, no time for nuisances. Nine-thirty to twelve, babies. One thousand babies with ladies. Nuisances plenty: old gents poisoning pigeons; ladies stealing baby carriages. Nuisances in bushes: young gents and young girls taking liberties. *(Hotly)* Why can't they do their nuisances at home? That's what homes are for: to do your nuisances in. *(He shields his eyes and peers toward the actors' entrance at the back of the stage; emotionally)* Here she comes! Miss'a Wilchick! *Baby!*—prize baby of Centra' Park. *(He extracts a handbook from another pocket of his jacket)* "Policeman's Guide. Lesson Six: Heart Attacks and Convulsions." No. No. "Lesson Sixteen: Frostbite." No! "Lesson Eleven: . . ." Ha! "An officer exchanges no personal remarks wid de public." Crazy! *(In dreamy ecstasy)* Oh, personal re-marks. It's personal remarks dat make-a de world go round; dat make-a de birds sing. *(Indignantly)* Nobody, *nobody* wid flesh and blood can live widout'a personal re-marks. Ha! She comes! . . . *(He steals off by the aisle through the audience)*

*(Enter from the back Miss Millie Wilchick, pushing
Tommy's baby carriage. Tommy, now invisible in the carriage, is to be played by a full-grown man. Millie brings the
carriage to rest by a bench. She peers up the various paths in
search of Officer Avonzino. Disappointed, she prepares to
make herself comfortable. From the foot of the carriage she
brings out a box of chocolates, another of marshmallows,
and a novel. Before sitting down she talks into the carriage.)*

MILLIE: . . . lil sweet lovums. Miss Millie's lil lover, aren't
you? Yes, you are. I could squeeze lil Tommy to death,
yes. I could. Kiss-kiss-kiss, yes, I could. *(Again peering
down the paths)* Don't know where Mr. Policerman is!
Big handsome Officer Avonzino. He take care of Miss
Millie and lil lover-boy Tommy . . . Hmm . . . Maybe he
come by and by. *(She sits on the bench and selects a
candy)* . . . Peppermint . . . strawb'ry? . . . Well, and a
marshmallow. *(She opens the novel at the first page and
reads with great deliberation)* "Doris was not strictly
beautiful, but when she passed, men's heads turned to
gaze at her with pleasure. Doris was not strictly beautiful, but . . ." *(A squeal of joy)* Oh, they don't write
like that any more!! Oh, I'm going to enjoy this book.
Let's see how it ends. First, there must be one of those
chawclut cream centers. *(She turns to the last page of the
novel)* "He drew her to him, pressing his lips on hers.
'Forever,' he said. Doris closed her eyes. 'Forever,' she
said. The end." *(Delighted cry)* They *don't* write like
that any more. "For e . . . e . . . ever." Could I say "forever," if his lips . . . "e-e-v" . . . were pressed on mine?
(She closes her eyes and experiments) . . . e . . . ver . . . for
. . . e . . . Yes, I guess it could be done. *(She starts dream-
ing)* Oh, I *know* I could write a novel. *(She dreams)*

*(Slowly Tommy's hands can be seen gripping the side of
his carriage. With great effort he pulls himself up until his
head appears. He is wearing a lace-trimmed cap.)*

TOMMY: Fur . . . evvah . . . Do-rus . . . nah . . . strigly boo-toody . . . *(Fretfully)* I can't say it . . . boody-fill . . . Why don't they *teach* me to say it? I want to LEARN and they won't teach me. Do-rua nah stackly . . . boody . . . Fur evvah . . . *(Near to wailing)* Time's going by. I'm getting owe-uld. And nobody is showing me *anything*. I wanta make a house. I wanta make a house. I wanta make a bay-beee. Nobody show-ow-ow-s me how-ta.

MILLIE *(Waking up)*: Tommy! What are you crying about? Has 'a got a little stummyache? Has 'a got a foot caught? No. *(Leaning over him, suddenly severe)* Has Tommy wet his bed?!! No. No. Then's what's a matter?

TOMMY: Wanta make a house!

MILLIE: Wants to be petted, yes.

TOMMY *(Violently)*: Wanta make a baybeee!

MILLIE: Miss Millie's lil lover wants a little attention.

TOMMY *(Fortissimo)*: Chawclut. Chawclut. Wanta eat what you're eating. Wanta eat what you smell of . . . chawclut.

MILLIE: Now don't you climb up. You'll fall out. It's terrible the way you're growing.

TOMMY: Put me on the ground. I wanta learn to walk. I wanta walk. I wanta walk. I wanta find things to *eat*.

MILLIE *(Sternly)*: Now Miss Millie's going to spank you. Crying for nothing. You ought to be ashamed of yourself. *(She stands joggling the baby carriage with one hand and holding the opened novel with the other)* "This little pig went to *mar-ket*." There! "This little pig . . ." Shh-shh-shh! "Doris was not strictly beautiful, but . . ." Oh, I read that. "This little pig stayed at home." *(She looks into the carriage with great relief)* God be praised in His glory, babies get tired soon . . . Asleep. *(She walks across the stage; then suddenly stops)* I don't know what I'm going to do. My life is hell. Here I am, a good-looking girl almost thirty and *nothing ever happens*. Everybody's living, except me. Everybody's happy, except ME!! *(She returns, sobbing blindly to the baby carriage)* Those silly novels—I hate them—just gab-gab-gab. Now I'm crying so I can't see which is pineapple. *(She chances to look in the direction of the aisle through the audience)* Oh, my God, there comes Officer Avonzino. *(She clasps her hands in fervent prayer)* Oh, my God, help a girl! If you ever helped a girl, help her now! *(She rapidly hides novel and candy under Tommy's blankets, and takes out another book. She arranges herself at one end of the bench and pretends to fall into a reverie)*

(Enter Patrolman Avonzino through the audience. He steals behind Millie and puts his hands over her eyes. The following passage is very rapid.)

AVONZINO: You've got one guessing coming to you! *Who* is in Centra' Park? Maybe who?

MILLIE: Oh, I don't know. I really don't.

AVONZINO: You've got two guessings. Maybe the mayor of Newa-York, maybe him, you think? Now you got one guessing. Maybe T. T. Avonzino—like somebody you know, somebody you seen before.

MILLIE: Oh! Officer Avonzino!!

(He leaps on the bench beside her. She is kept busy removing his hands from her knees.)

AVONZINO: Somebody you know. Somebody you seen before.

MILLIE: Officer, you must behave. You really must behave.

AVONZINO: Action! I believe is a action! Personal remarks and da action.

(Tommy has raised himself and is staring enormous-eyed and with great disapproval at these goings-on.)

TOMMY *(Loudly)*: Ya! Ya! Ya! Ya! Ya!

(Officer Avonzino is thunderstruck. He jumps up as though caught out of order by his superior. He stands behind the bench adjusting his tie and coat and star.)

MILLIE: Why, what's the matter, Mr. Avonzino?

AVONZINO *(Low and terse)*: *Him.* Looka at him. Looka at him, *looking.*

TOMMY: Ya. Ya. Ya.

MILLIE: Go to sleep, Tommy. Just nice policerman. Tommy's friend. Go to sleep.

TOMMY *(One last warning, emphatically)*: Ya! *(He disappears)*

MILLIE: But, Officer, he's just a *baby.* He doesn't understand one little thing.

AVONZINO *(Blazing, but under his breath)*: Oh no, oh no, oh no, oh no—he got *thoughts.* Turn-a de carriage around. I no wanta see that face.

MILLIE *(Turning the carriage)*: I'm surprised at you. He's just a dear little baby. A dear little . . . animal.

AVONZINO: Miss Wilchick, I see one thousand babies a day. They got *ideas.*

MILLIE *(Laughing girlishly)*: Why, Mr. Avonzino, you're like the author of this book I've been reading. —Dr. Kennick. He says babies are regular geniuses in their first fourteen months. He says: you know why babies sleep all the time? Because they're learning all the time, they get tired by learning. Geniuses, he says, imagine!

AVONZINO: *What* he say?

MILLIE: They learn more than they'll ever learn again. And faster. Like hands and feet; and to focus your eyes. And like walking and talking. He says their brains are exploding with power.

AVONZINO: What he say?

MILLIE: Well—after about a year they stop being geniuses. Dr. Kennick says the reason why we aren't geniuses is that we weren't brought up right: we were stopped.

AVONZINO: That's a right. He gotta the right idea. Miss Wilchick, I see one thousand babies a day. And what I say is: stop 'em. That's your business, Miss Wilchick; that's my business. There's too many ingeniouses in Centra' Park right now: stop 'em. *(Tommy begins to howl. Avonzino points at him with his billy club)* What did I tell you? They all understand English. North'a Eighth Street they all understand English.

MILLIE *(Leaning over Tommy's carriage)*: There, there. Nice policeman don't mean *one* word of it.

AVONZINO *(Looking at the actors' entrance; they are both shouting to be heard)*: Here comes another brains. I go now.

MILLIE: Oh, that must be Mrs. Boker—I'm so sorry this happened, Mr. Avonzino.

AVONZINO: I see you later, maybe—when you get permission from the professor—permission in writing, Miss Wilchick. *(He goes out through the audience)*

(Enter Mrs. Boker pushing Moe's carriage. Moe starts crying in sympathy with Tommy. Both women shout.)

MRS. BOKER: What's the matter with Tommy—good morning—on such a fine day?

MILLIE *(Leaning over Tommy)*: What's a matter?

TOMMY: CHAWCLUT!! STRAWB'RY!! I'm hungree.

MILLIE: Really, I don't know what ails the child.

MRS. BOKER *(Leaning over Moe's carriage; beginning loud but gradually lowering her voice as both babies cease howling)*: ...K...L...M...N...O...P...Q...R...S... T...Have you ever noticed, Miss Wilchick, that babies get quiet when you say the alphabet to them? ...W... X...Y...A...B...C...D...I don't understand it. Moe is mad about the alphabet. Same way with the multiplication table. *(To Moe, who is now silent)* Three times five are fifteen. Three times six are eighteen. When my husband has to keep Moe quiet: the multiplication table! Never fails! My husband calls him Isaac Newton. —Seven times five are thirty-five. Eight times five are forty. Never fails.

MILLIE *(Intimidated)*: Really?

MRS. BOKER *(Pointing to the silent carriages)*: Well, look for yourself! Isn't silence grand? *(She sits on a bench and starts taking food out of Moe's carriage)* Now, dear, have some potato chips. Or pretzels. What do you like?

MILLIE: Well, you have some of my marshmallows and candy.

MRS. BOKER: Marshmallows! Oh, I know I shouldn't! —Have you noticed that being around babies makes you think of eating all the time? I don't know why that is. *(Pushing Millie in raucous enjoyment of the joke)* Like, being with babies makes us like babies. And you know what *they* think about!!

MILLIE *(Convulsed)*: Oh, Mrs. Boker, what will you say next! —How is Moe, Mrs. Boker?

MRS. BOKER *(Her mouth full)*: How *is* he!! Sometimes I wish he'd be sick for *one* day—just to give me a present. *(Lowering her voice)* I don't have to tell you what life with a baby is: *(Looking around circumspectly)* It's *war—one long war.* —Excuse me, I can't talk while he's listening. *(She rises and wheels Moe's carriage to a distance; returning, she continues in a lowered voice)* My husband believes that Moe understands every word we say.

MILLIE: Mrs. Boker!

MRS. BOKER: I don't know what to believe, but one thing I do know: that baby lies on the floor and listens to every word we say. At first my husband took to spelling out words, you know—but Albert Einstein, there—in two weeks he got them all. He would *look* at my husband, *look* at him with those big eyes! And then my husband took to talking in Yiddish—see what I mean?—but no! In two weeks Albert Einstein got Yiddish.

MILLIE: But, Mrs. Boker!! It's just a baby! He don't understand *one word.*

MRS. BOKER: *You* know that. *I* know that. But *(Pointing to the carriage)* does *he* know that? It's driving my husband crazy. "Turn it in and get a dog," he says. "I didn't ask for no prodigy," he says. "All I wanted was a baby—" *(Lowering her voice)* Of course, most of the time my

husband worships Moe . . . only . . . only we don't know
what to do with him, as you might say.

MILLIE: Oh, you imagine it, Mrs. Boker!

MRS. BOKER: Listen to me! —Have some of these pretzels;
they'll be good after those sweets. Listen to me,
Junior's at the crawling stage. He does fifty miles a day.
My husband calls him Christopher Columbus. —My
husband's stepped on him five times.

MILLIE: Mrs. Boker! You've got a playpen, haven't you?

MRS. BOKER: PLAYPEN!! He's broke two, hasn't he? We
can't afford to buy no lion's cage, Miss Wilchick—
besides, Macy's don't sell them. Now listen to me:
Christopher Columbus follows us wherever we go,
see? When I get supper—there he is! He could make a
gefilte fish tomorrow. That child—mad about the bath-
room! Know what I mean? My husband says he has a
"something" mind—you know: d. i. r. t. y.

MILLIE: Mrs. Boker.

MRS. BOKER: Sometimes I wish I had a girl—only it'd be
just my luck to get one of those Joans of Arcs. *(Moe
starts to howl)* There he goes! Like I said: understands
every word we say. Now watch this: *(She leans over
Moe's carriage, holding a handkerchief before her mouth)*
You mustn't let them smell what you've been eating, *or
else*—Listen, Moe, like I was telling you: New York
City is divided into five boroughs. There's the Bronx,
Moe, and Brooklyn and Queens— *(Moe quiets almost
at once)* See how it works?—Richmond and Manhattan. —It's crazy, I know, but what can I do about
that?—Yes, Manhattan; the largest, like I told you, is
Manhattan. Yes, Manhattan. *(She looks in the carriage.
Silence)* Isn't it a blessing that they get tired so soon?
He's exhausted by the boroughs already.

MILLIE: But he doesn't understand a word of it!!

MRS. BOKER: What has understanding got to do with it,
Miss Wilchick? I don't understand the telephone, but I
telephone.

(Tommy has raised his head and is listening big-eyed.)

TOMMY: N'Yak Citee divi fife burrs. Manha . . . Manha . . . Manha . . . *(He starts crying with frustration)* I can't *say* it. I can't *say* it.

MRS. BOKER: Now yours is getting excited.

TOMMY: I can't talk and nobody'll teach me. I can't talk . . .

MRS. BOKER *(Loud)*: Go over and put him to sleep.

MILLIE *(Loud)*: But I don't know the boroughs. Please, Mrs. Boker, just once, you show me.

MRS. BOKER: I'll try something else. Watch this! Listen, Tommy, are you listening? "I pledge legions to my flag and to the republic in which it stands." You were a girl scout, weren't you? "Something something invisible with liberty and justice for all." *(Tommy has fallen silent)* "I pledge legions to my flag . . ."

MILLIE *(Awed)*: Will anything work?

MRS. BOKER *(Lowering her voice)*: They don't like those lullabies and "This little pig went to market." See, they like it *serious*. There's nothing in the world so serious like a baby. —Well, now we got a little quiet again.

MILLIE: Mrs. Boker, can I ask you a question about Moe? . . . Take one of these; it's pineapple inside . . . Is Moe, like they say, housebroken?

MRS. BOKER: Moe?! Gracious sakes! Moe makes a great show of it. I guess there isn't a thing in the world that interests Moe like going to his potty. *(She laughs)* When he wants to make us a present: *off* he goes! When he's angry at us . . . oh, no! He plays it like these violinists play their violin . . . which reminds me! . . . *(Looking about her speculatively)* Do you suppose . . . I could just . . . slip behind these bushes a minute? . . . is that police officer around?

MILLIE: Well-ah . . . Officer Avonzino is awfully particular about nuisances, what he calls nuisances. Maybe you could go over to the avenue there—there's a branch library . . .

MRS. BOKER: Will you be an angel and watch Moe for me? If he starts to cry, give him the days of the week and the months of the year. He *loves* them. —Now where's this library?

MILLIE: Why, the Museum of National History's right over there.

MRS. BOKER *(Scream of pleasure)*: Museum of Natural History!! How could I have forgotten that! Just full of animals. Of *course*! I won't be a minute, dear! . . .

(They exchange good-byes. Mrs. Boker goes out. Millie eyes Moe's carriage apprehensively, then seats herself and resumes her novel at the last page.)

MILLIE: "Roger came into the room. His fine strong face still bore the marks of the suffering he had experienced." Oh! I imagine his wife died. Isn't that wonderful! He's *free*! "He drew her to him, pressing his lips on hers. 'Forever,' he said." Oh! "For-ever." *(In a moment, she is asleep)*

(Tommy pulls himself up and stares at Moe's carriage.)

TOMMY: Moe! . . . Moe!

MOE *(Surging up furiously)*: Don't make noises at me! Don't look at me! Don't do anything. *(Telephone business, swiftly)* Hello, g'bye! *(He disappears)*

TOMMY: Moe! . . . Moe! . . . Talk to me something! . . . Moe, why are you thatway at me?

MOE *(Surging up again, glaring)*: My daddy says I'm stupid. He says, "Stupid, come here!" He says, "All right, stupid, fall down!" I don't want to talk. I don't want to look. G'bye! *(He disappears)*

TOMMY: What does "stupid" mean?

MOE *(Invisible)*: I won't tell. *(Surging up, showing his fingers; a rapid-fire jumble)* Do you know what these are? Sometimes you call them fingers; sometimes you call them piggies. One, two, six, five, four, two, ten. This little piggie stayed at home, I don't know why that is. Do you know what you do when the loud bell rings? You do this: *(Telephone business)* "Hello . . . jugga . . . jugga . . . jugga," and when you don't like it any more you say, "G'bye!" Maybe I am stupid. —But that's because MY MOUTH HURTS ALL THE TIME and they don't give me enough to eat and I'm hungry all the time and that's the end of it, that's the end of it. *(He disappears)*

TOMMY: Moe, tell me some more things.

MOE *(Surging up again)*: "Stupid, come here!" "Stupid, get your goddamn tail out of here!" *(Shaking his carriage)* I hate him. I hate him. But I watch him and I learn. *You see:* I learn. And when I get to walk I'm going to do something so that he won't *be* any more. He'll be away—away where people can walk on him. —Don't you hate your father?

TOMMY: Well . . . I don't see him much. Like, once a year.

MOE: You mean: once a day.

TOMMY: Moe, what does "year" mean?

MOE: Year is when it's cold.

TOMMY *(Brightening)*: Yes, I know.

MOE: Sometimes he holds out his hands and says: "How's the little fella? How's the little champ?" And I give him a look! I wasn't born yesterday. He hasn't got anything to sell to me.

TOMMY: Moe—where's your mommy? *(Silence)* Moe, she's not here. Where's your mommy? You don't hate your mommy, do you?

MOE *(Turning his face sideways, cold and proud)*: I don't care about her. She's always away. She goes away for years. She laughs at me . . . with that *man*. He says: "All right, fall down, stupid," and she laughs. I try to talk to her and she goes away all the time and does, "Hello—jugga—jugga—jugga—goo-*bye!*" If she don't care about me any more, I don't care about her any more. Goo-*bye!* *(Silence)*

TOMMY: Say some more, Moe, say some more things.

MOE *(Low and intense)*: Maybe I am stupid. Maybe I'll never be able to walk or make talk. Maybe they didn't give me good feet or a good mouth. —You know what I think? I think they don't want us to walk and to get good and get better. They want us to *stop*. That's what I think. *(His voice has risen to a hysterical wail)* Goddam! Hell! *(He starts throwing cloth elephants and giraffes out of the carriage)* I'm not going to try. Nobody wants to help me and lots of time is passing and I'm not getting bigger, and . . . and . . . *(Anticlimax)* I'm sleepeee . . . *(He continues to whimper)*

(Millie wakes up. She goes gingerly to Moe's carriage and joggles it.)

MILLIE: Moe! What's the matter, Moe? "Rockabye, baby, in the treetop—" *(Moe wails more loudly)* Oh, goodness, gracious me. *(In desperation)* Moe! Do you know that *that* street is called Central Park West? And then there's Columbus Avenue? And then there's Amsterdam Avenue? And then there's Broadway? *(Moe has hushed)* And then there's West End Avenue. *(She can hardly believe her luck; she whispers)* And then there's Riverside Drive. *(She peers into the carriage a long time, then tiptoes to the other end of the stage; with clenched fists)* I hate babies. *(Toward Tommy)* I hate you—sticking your crazy face into my business—frightening Officer Avonzino, the only man I've talked to in six months. I hate you—always butting in. I have a right to my own life, haven't I? *My own life!* I'm sick to death of squalling, smelling, gawking babies . . . I'd be a stenographer only I don't know anything; nobody ever taught me anything . . . "Manhattan, the Bronx"—what do I care what keeps you quiet? You can yell your heads off for all I care! I don't know why nature didn't make it so that people came into the world already grown-up—

instead of a dozen and more years of screaming and diapers and falling down and breaking everything . . . and *asking questions*! "What's that?" "Why-y-y?" "Why-y-y?" . . . Officer Avonzino will never come back, that's certain! . . . Oh, what do I care? You're going to grow up to be *men*—nasty, selfish men. You're all alike. *(Drying her eyes, she picks up her novel from Tommy's carriage and strolls off the stage at the back)*

(Moe's head, now solemn and resolute, rises slowly.)

MOE: Tommy! . . . Tommy!

TOMMY *(Appearing)*: I'm tired.

MOE: You know what I'm going to do, do you?

TOMMY: No—what, Moe?

MOE: I'm just going to lie still.

TOMMY: What do you mean, Moe?

MOE: I'll shut my eyes and do nothing. I won't eat. I'll just go away-away. Like I want Daddy to do.

TOMMY *(Alarm)*: No, Moe! Don't go where people can walk on you!

MOE: Well, I *will* . . . You know what I think? I think people aren't SERIOUS about us. "Little piggie went to market, cradle will fall, Manhattan, the Bronx"—that's not serious. They don't want us to get better.

TOMMY: *Maybe* they do.

MOE: Old people are only interested in old people. Like kiss-kiss-kiss; that's all they do; that's all they think about.

TOMMY *(Eagerly)*: Ye-e-es! Miss'a Millie, all the time, kiss-kiss-kiss, but she don't mean me; she means the policerman.

MOE: We're in the way, see? We're too little, that's how. I don't want to be a man—it's too hard! *(He disappears)*

TOMMY *(With increasing alarm)*: Moe! . . . Moe! . . . Don't stop talking, Moe! . . . MOE!

(Millie returns hastily.)

MILLIE: Now what's the matter with you? I'll spank you. Always crying and making a baby of yourself.

TOMMY *(At the same time; frantic)*: Moe's going away-away. He's not going to eat any more. Go look at Moe . . . *Do* something. *Do* something!

MILLIE: What is the matter with you? Why can't you be quiet like Moe? *(She goes and looks in Moe's carriage and is terrified by what she sees)* Help! . . . Hellllp! The baby's turned purple! Moe! Have you swallowed something?— *(She dashes to the audience exit)* Officer Avonzino! Officer! Hellllp! —Oh, they'll kill me. What'll I do?

(Officer Avonzino rushes in from the audience.)

AVONZINO: What'a matter, Miss Wilchick; you gone crazy today?

MILLIE *(Gasping)*: . . . look . . . he's turned black, Officer Avonzino . . . His mother's over at the museum. Oh . . . I don't know what to do.

(Officer Avonzino, efficient but unhurried, opens his tunic and takes out his handbook. He hunts for the correct page.)

AVONZINO: First, don't scream, Miss Wilchick. Nobody scream. Babies die every day. Always new babies. Nothing to scream about . . . Babies turn black—so! Babies turn blue, black, purple, all the time. Hmph: "Turn baby over, lift middle . . ." *(He does these things)* "Water . . ." *(To Millie)* Go to nurses over there . . . twenty nurses . . . Bring back some ippycack.

MILLIE: Oh, Officer . . . help me. I'm fainting.

AVONZINO *(Furious)*: Faintings on *Sundays*—not workdays, Miss Wilchick.

MILLIE *(Hand to head)*: Oh . . . oh . . .

(Officer Avonzino catches her just in time and drapes her over the bench like a puppet.)

AVONZINO: "Lesson Thirty-Two: Let Mother Die. Save Baby." I get water. *(He dashes off)*

(Tommy raises his head.)

TOMMY: Moe! Don't be black. Don't be black. You're going to walk soon. And by and by you can go to school. And even if they don't teach you good, you can kind of teach yourself. *(Moe is sobbing)* Moe, what's that noise you're making? Make a crying like a baby, Moe. —Soon you can be big and shave. And be a policerman. And you can make kiss-kiss-kiss . . . and make babies. And, Moe—

MOE *(Appearing)*: Don't talk to me. I'm tired. I'm tired.

TOMMY: And you can show your babies how to walk and talk.

MOE *(Yawning)*: I'm . . . tire' . . . *(He sinks back)*

TOMMY *(Yawning)*: I'm tired, tooooo. *(He sinks back)*

(Officer Avonzino returns with a child's pail of water. He leans over Moe.)

AVONZINO *(Astonished)*: What'a matter with you!! You all red again. You not sick. Goddamn! Tricks. Babies always doing tricks. *(Shakes Millie)* Miss Wilchick! Wake up! Falsa alarm. Baby's okay.

MILLIE *(Coming to, dreamily)*: Oh, Officer . . . *(Extending her arms amorously)* Oh you're so . . . handsome . . . Officer . . .

AVONZINO *(Sternly)*: "Lesson Eleven: No Personal Remarks with Public." *(Shouts)* It's going to rain: better take George Washington home . . . and Dr. Einstein, too.

MILLIE: Oh! How *is* the Boker baby?

AVONZINO: Boker baby's a great actor. Dies every performance. Thousands cheer.

MILLIE *(Pushes Tommy toward exit)*: Oh, I can't go until Mrs. Boker comes back. *(Peers out)* —Oh, there she comes, running. See her?

AVONZINO: You *go*. I take care of baby til a'momma comes. *(At exit Millie turns for a heartfelt farewell; he points billy stick and commands her)* Go *faint,* Miss Wilchick! *(She goes out. Avonzino addresses Moe)* I'd like to make your damn bottom red. I know you. All you babies want the whole world. Well, I tell you, you've got a long hard road before you. Pretty soon you'll find that you can cry all you want and turn every color there is—and nobody'll pay *no* attention at all. Your best days are over; you've had'm. From now on it's all up to you— George Washington, or whatever your name is.

(Enter Mrs. Boker, breathless.)

MRS. BOKER: Oh!!

AVONZINO: I sent Miss Wilchick home. *(Pointing toward rain)* You better start off yourself.

MRS. BOKER *(Pushing the carriage to the exit)*: Has every- thing been all right, Officer?

AVONZINO: Just fine, lady, just fine. Like usual: babies act- ing like growed-ups; growed-ups acting like babies.

MRS. BOKER: *Thank* you, Officer. *(She goes out)*

(Officer Avonzino, shading his eyes, peers down the aisle through the audience. Suddenly he sees something that out- rages him. Like a Keystone cop he does a double take and starts running through the audience, shouting:)

AVONZINO: Hey there!! You leave that baby carriage alone! Don't you know what's inside them baby carriages? . . .

END OF PLAY

Childhood

A COMEDY

CHARACTERS

CAROLINE, the oldest daughter, twelve
DODIE, her sister, ten
BILLEE, her brother, eight
MOTHER
FATHER

SETTING

A suburban house and yard.

*Some low chairs at the edges of the arena. These at first repre-
sent some bushes in the yard of the children's home. At the back,
the door to the house; the aisle through the audience serves as a
path to the street. Enter from the house Caroline, twelve; Dodie,
ten; and, with a rush, Billee, eight.*

DODIE: Shh! Shh! Don't let Mama hear you! Car'line, Car'-line, play the game. Let's play the game.

CAROLINE: There's no time, silly. It takes time to play the game.

BILLEE: Play Goin' to China.

CAROLINE: Don't talk so loud; we don't want Mama to hear us. Papa'll be here soon, and we can't play the game when Papa's here.

DODIE: Well, let's play a little. We can play Going to a Hotel.

BILLEE *(Clamorously)*: I want to be Room Service. I want to be Room Service.

CAROLINE: You know Going to a Hotel takes *hours*. It's awful when you have to stop for something.

DODIE *(Quickly)*: Car'line, listen, I heard Mama telephoning Papa and the car's got to be fixed and Papa's got to come home by a bus, and maybe he'll never get here and we can play for a long time.

CAROLINE: Did she say that? Well, come behind the bushes and think.

(They squat on their haunches behind the bushes.)

BILLEE: Let's play Hospital and take everything out of Dodie.

CAROLINE: Let me think a minute.

MOTHER *(At the door)*: Caroline! Dodie!

(Silence.)

Dodie, how often do I have to tell you to hang your coat up properly? Do you know what happened? It fell and got caught under the cupboard door and was dragged back and forth. I hope it's warm Sunday, because you can't wear that coat. Billee, stand out for a moment where I can see you. Are you ready for your father when he comes home? Come out of the bushes, Billee, come out.

(Billee, a stoic already, comes to the center of the stage and stands for inspection. Mother shakes her head in silence; then:)

I simply despair. Look at you! What are you children doing anyway? Now, Caroline, you're not playing one of those games of yours? I absolutely forbid you to play that the house is on fire. You have nightmares all night long. Or those awful games about hospitals. Really, Caroline, why can't you play Shopping or Going to School? *(Silence)* I declare. I give up. I really do. *(False exit)* Now remember, it's Friday night, the end of the week, and you give your father a good big kiss when he comes home. *(She goes out)*

(Billee rejoins his sisters.)

DODIE *(Dramatic whisper)*: Car'line, let's play Funeral! *(Climax)* Car'line, let's play ORPHANS!

CAROLINE: We haven't time—*that* takes all day. Besides, I haven't got the black gloves.

(Billee sees his father coming through the audience. Utter and final dismay.)

BILLEE: Look't! Look!

DODIE: What?

ALL THREE: It's Papa! It's Papa!

(They fly into the house like frightened pigeons. Father enters jauntily through the audience. It's warm, and he carries his coat over his shoulder. Arriving at the center of the stage, he places his coat on the ground, whistles a signal call to his wife, and swinging an imaginary golf club, executes a mighty and very successful shot.)

FATHER: Two hundred and fifty yards!

MOTHER *(Enters, kisses him and picks up the coat)*: Why, you're early, after all.

FATHER: Jerry drove me to the corner. Picked up a little flask for the weekend.

MOTHER: Well, I wish you wouldn't open your little flask when the children are around.

FATHER *(Preparing a difficult shot)*: Eleventh hole . . . Where *are* the children?

MOTHER: They were here a minute ago. They're out playing somewhere . . . Your coat on the ground! Really, you're as bad as Dodie.

FATHER: Well, you should teach the children—little trouble with the dandelions here—that it's their first duty . . . when their father comes home on Friday nights . . . *(Shouts)* Fore, you bastards! . . . to rush toward their father . . . to grovel . . . abject thanks to him who gave them life.

MOTHER *(Amused exasperation)*: Oh, stop that nonsense!

FATHER: On Friday nights . . . after a week of toil at the office . . . a man wants to see . . . *(He swings)* his wives and children clinging to his knees, tears pouring down their cheeks. *(He stands up very straight, holding an enormous silver cup)* Gentlemen, I accept this championship cup, but I wish also to give credit to my wife and children, who drove me out of the house every Sunday morning . . . Where *are* the children? Caroline! Dodie!

MOTHER: Oh, they're hiding somewhere.

FATHER: Hiding? Hiding from their father?

MOTHER: They're playing one of those awful games of theirs. Listen to me, Fred: those games are morbid; they're dangerous.

FATHER: How do you mean, dangerous?

MOTHER: Really! No one told me when I was a bride that children are half crazy. I only hear fragments of the games, naturally, but do you realize that they like nothing better than to imagine us—away?

FATHER: Away?

MOTHER: Yes—dead?

FATHER *(His eye on the shot)*: One . . . two . . . *three*! Well, you know what *you* said.

MOTHER: What did I say?

FATHER: *Your* dream.

MOTHER: Pshaw!

FATHER (*Softly, with lowest insinuation*): Your dream that . . . you and I . . . on a Mediterranean cruise . . .

MOTHER: It was Hawaii.

FATHER: And that we were—ahem!—somehow . . . *alone*.

MOTHER: Well, I didn't imagine them *dead*! I imagined them with Mother . . . or Paul . . . or their Aunt Henrietta.

FATHER (*Piously*): I hope so.

MOTHER: You're a brute, and everybody knows it . . . It's Caroline. She's the one who starts it all. And afterwards she has those nightmares. Come in. You'll see the children at supper.

FATHER (*Looking upward*): What has the weatherman predicted for tomorrow?

MOTHER (*Starting for the house*): Floods. Torrents. You're going to stay home from the golf club and take care of the children. And I'm going to the Rocky Mountains . . . and to China.

FATHER: You'll be back by noon. What does Caroline say in her nightmares?

MOTHER: Oh! When she's awake, too. You and I are—away. Do you realize that that girl is mad about black gloves?

FATHER: Nonsense.

MOTHER: Caroline would be in constant mourning if she could manage it. Come in, come in. You'll see them at supper. (*She goes out*)

FATHER (*He strolls to the end of the stage farthest from the house and calls*): Caroline! (*Pause*) Dodie! (*Pause*) Bill-eeee!

(*Silence. He broods aloud, his eyes on the distance.*)

No instrument has yet been discovered that can read what goes on in another's mind, asleep or awake. And I hope there never will be. But once in a while, it would help a lot. Is it wrong of me to wish that . . . just once . . . I could be an invisible witness to one of my children's dreams, to one of their games? (*He calls again*) Caroline!

(We are in the game which is a dream. The children enter as he calls them, but he does not see them and they do not see him. They come in and stand shoulder to shoulder as though they were about to sing a song before an audience. Caroline carries a child's suitcase and one of her mother's handbags; she is wearing black gloves. Dodie also has a suitcase and handbag, but no gloves.)

CAROLINE: Dodie! Hurry before they see us.

FATHER: Dodie!

DODIE: Where's Billee gone?

FATHER *(Being bumped into by Billee as he joins his sisters)*: Billee!

(Father enters the house. Mother glides out of the house and takes her place at the farther end of the stage and turns and faces the children. She is wearing a black hat, deep black veil and black gloves. Her air is one of mute acquiescent grief. Caroline glances frequently at her mother as though for prompting. A slight formal pause.)

CAROLINE: I guess, first, we have to say how sorry we are. *(To Mother)* Shall we begin? *(Mother lowers her head slightly)* This first part is in church. Well, in a kind of church. And there's been a perfectly terrible accydent, an airplane accydent.

DODIE *(Quickly)*: No, it was an automobile accydent.

CAROLINE *(Ditto)*: It was an airplane.

DODIE *(Ditto)*: I don't want it to be an airplane.

BILLEE *(Fiercely)*: It was on a ship. It was a *big* shipwreck.

CAROLINE: Now, I'm not going to play this game unless you be quiet. It was an airplane accydent. And . . . They were on it, and they're not here any more.

BILLEE: They got *dead*.

CAROLINE *(Glaring at him)*: Don't say that *word*. You promised you wouldn't say that word. *(Uncomfortable pause)* And we're very sad. And . . .

DODIE *(Brightly)*: We didn't see it, though.

CAROLINE: And we'd have put on black dresses, only we haven't got any. But we want to thank Miss Wilkerson for coming today and for wearing black like she's wearing. *(Mother again lowers her head)* Miss Wilkerson is the best teacher in Benjamin Franklin School, and she's the grown-up we like best.

BILLEE *(Suddenly getting excited)*: That's not Miss Wilkerson. That's—I mean—*look*!

CAROLINE: I can't hear a word you're saying, and anyway, don't talk now!

BILLEE *(Too young to enter the dream; pulling at his sisters' sleeves urgently)*: That's not Miss Wilkerson. That's *Mama*!

DODIE: What's the matter with your eyes?

CAROLINE: Mama's not here any more. She went away.

BILLEE *(Staring at Mother, and beginning to doubt)*: It's . . . Mrs. Fenwick!

CAROLINE *(Low but strongly)*: No-o-o-o! *(Resuming the ceremony)* It wasn't so sad about Grandma, because she was more'n a hundred anyway.

DODIE: And she used to say all the time, "I won't be with you always," and things like that, and how she'd give Mama her pearl pin.

BILLEE: I guess she's glad she isn't any more.

CAROLINE *(Uncertainly)*: So . . .

DODIE *(To Mother, with happy excitement)*: Are we orphans now—real orphans? *(Mother, always with lowered eyes, nods slightly)* And we don't have to *do things* any more?

CAROLINE *(Severely)*: Dodie! Don't *say* everything. *(She consults her mother)* What do I say now?

MOTHER *(Almost inaudibly)*: About your father . . .

CAROLINE: Yes. Papa was a very fine man. And . . .

DODIE *(Quickly)*: He used to swear bad words.

BILLEE *(Excitedly)*: All the *time*! He'd swear swearwords.

CAROLINE: Well, maybe a little.

DODIE: He *did*. I used to want to *die*.

CAROLINE: Well, nobody's perfeck *(Slower)* He was all right, sometimes.

DODIE: He used to laugh too loud in front of people. And he didn't give Mama enough money to buy clothes. She had to go to town in rags, in terrible old rags.

BILLEE *(Always excited)*: Papa'd go like this, *(Pumping his arms up and down in desperation)* "I haven't got it! I haven't got it! You can't squeeze blood out of a stone."

DODIE: Yes, he did.

BILLEE: And Mama'd say: "I'm ashamed to go out in the street." It was awful. And then he'd say, "I'll have to mortgage, that's what I'll have to do."

CAROLINE: Billee! How can you say such an awful word? Don't you ever say that again. Papa wasn't perfeck, but he would never have done a mortgage.

BILLEE: Well, that's what he said.

CAROLINE *(Emphatically)*: Most times Papa did his best. Everybody makes some mistakes.

DODIE *(Demurely)*: He used to drink some, too.

BILLEE *(Beside himself again)*: He used to drink *oceans*. And Mama'd say, "Don't you think you've had enough?" and he'd say, "Down the hatch!"

DODIE: Yes, he did. And, "Just a hair of the dog that bit him." And Mama'd say, "Well, if you want to kill yourself before our eyes!" I used to want to die.

CAROLINE: Billee, don't get so excited; and you too, Dodie. Papa was a very fine man, and he *tried*. Only . . . only . . . *(Reluctantly)* he didn't ever say anything very inneresting.

DODIE: He was inneresting when he told about the automobile accydent he'd seen and all the blood.

BILLEE: Yes, he was. But he stopped in the middle when Mama said, "Not before the children."

DODIE: Yes, he stopped then.

CAROLINE: Anyway, we're very sad. And . . . *(She looks to her mother for prompting)*

MOTHER *(Almost inaudibly)*: Your mother . . .

CAROLINE: Yes. About Mama.

BILLEE *(Hot indignation)*: Mama's almost never home. She's always shopping and having her hair made. And one time she was away *years,* to see Grandma in Boston.

DODIE: It was only five days, and Grandma was very sick.

BILLEE: No, it wasn't. It was years and years.

DODIE: Well, when she was away she didn't have to say Don't—Don't—Don't all the time, all day and night, Don't—Don't—Don't.

BILLEE *(Tentatively defending her)*: Sometimes she makes good things to eat.

DODIE: Beans and mash potatoes, and I just hate them. "Now, you eat every mouthful, or you don't leave the table." Ugh!

CAROLINE *(Recalling them to the ceremony)*: It wasn't her fault! Only she didn't unnerstand children. I guess there's not one in a hundred hundred that unnerstands children. *(To Mother)* Is that enough, Miss Wilkerson? I can't think of anything else to say. And we've got to hurry, or Uncle Paul will come to get us, or Aunt Henrietta, or somebody even worse. So can we go now?

MOTHER *(A whisper)*: I think it would be nice, you know, if you said how you loved them, and how they loved you.

CAROLINE: Yes—uh . . .

DODIE: It was awful when they got huggy and kissy. And when we got back an hour late, from Mary Louise's picnic, and Mama said, "I was frantic! I was frantic! I didn't know what had become of you."

CAROLINE *(Slowly)*: She liked us best when we were sick and when I broke my arm.

DODIE: Yes. *(Exhausted pause)* Miss Wilkerson, orphans don't have to be sad *all* the time, do they?

(Mother shakes her head slightly.)

BILLEE: Do we get any money for being orphans?

CAROLINE: We won't need it. Papa used to keep an envelope behind the clock with money in it, for accydents and times like that. I have it here. *(She goes to Mother, like a hostess getting rid of a guest)* Thank you for coming, Miss Wilkerson. We have to go now. And thank you for wearing black.

DODIE *(Also shaking hands; conventionally)*: Thank you very much.

(Mother, with bowed head, glides into the house.)

CAROLINE: Now be quiet, and I'll tell you what we're going to do. We've got to hurry, so don't interrup me. We're orphans and we don't have anybody around us or near us and we're going to take a bus. *(Sensation)* All over the world. We're going to be different persons and we're going to change our names. *(Gravely she opens her suitcase. She takes out and puts on a hat and fur neckpiece of her mother's. She looks adorable)* I'm Mrs. Arizona. Miss Wilson, please get ready for the trip.

DODIE: Wha-a-t?

CAROLINE: *Miss Wilson!* Will you put your hat on, please.

DODIE: Oh! *(She puts on a hat from her suitcase)* I want to be married, too. I want to be Mrs. Wilson.

CAROLINE: You're too young. People would laugh at you. We'll be gone for years and years, and by and by, in China or somewhere, you can gradually be Mrs. Wilson.

BILLEE: I want to be somebody, too.

CAROLINE: You're only *eight*! If you don't cry all the time and say awful things, I'll give you a real name. Now we can start.

BILLEE: But aren't Papa and Mama coming? *(The girls turn and glare at him)* Oh! they're *dead*. *(More glaring)*

CAROLINE: All right. S-s-stay at home and go to s-s-school, if you want to. Papa and Mama are *happy*. Papa's playing golf and Mama's shopping. Are you ready, Miss Wilson?

DODIE: Yes, Mrs. Arizona, thank you.

CAROLINE: Don't run, but if we hurry we can each get a seat by the window.

(Father enters, wearing a bus conductor's cap and big dark glasses. He casually arranges the chairs so as to indicate some of the seats of a long bus pointing toward the exit through the audience. The children form a line at the door of the bus, tickets in hand.)

FATHER: Take your places in line, please. The first stop, ladies and gentlemen, will be Ashagorra-Kallapalla, where there will be twenty minutes for lunch. That's the place where you get to eat the famous heaven-fruit sandwich.

(He starts punching the tickets of some imaginary passengers who precede the children.)

That cat won't be happy, madam. That's our experience. *(Severely, palping a passenger)* You haven't got mumps, have you? Well, I'd appreciate it if you sat at a distance from the other passengers.

BILLEE *(Staggered)*: But that's Papa!

DODIE: Don't be silly, Papa's *away.*

BILLEE: But it looks like Papa . . . and . . . *(Losing assurance)* it looks like Dr. Summers, too.

CAROLINE: Billee, I don't know what's the matter with you. Papa wouldn't be working as a bus conductor. Papa's a man that's got more money than that.

FATHER *(To Caroline)*: Your ticket, please, madam.

CAROLINE: We want to go to all the places you're going to, please.

FATHER: But you mean this to be a round-trip ticket, don't you? You're coming back, aren't you?

CAROLINE *(None too sure; her eyes avoiding his)*: Well, maybe I won't.

FATHER *(Lowering his voice, confidentially)*: I'll punch it on the side here. That'll mean you can use it, whenever you want, to come back here. *(Caroline takes her place on the bus.)*

(Mother glides in and takes her place in the line behind Billee. She is now wearing a brown hat and a deep brown veil. Father punches Dodie's ticket.)

Why, I think I've seen your face before, madam. Weren't you in that terrible automobile accident— blood all over the road and everything?

DODIE *(Embarrassed; low)*: No, no, I wasn't.

FATHER: Well, I'm glad to hear that. *(Dodie takes her seat behind Caroline)*

(To Billee, punching his ticket) And what's your name, sir, if I may ask?

BILLEE: Billee.

CAROLINE *(Officiously)*: His name is Mr. Wentworth.

FATHER: Mr. Wentworth. Good morning. *(Man to man, with a touch of severity)* No smoking in the first six rows, watch that, and . . . *(Significant whisper)* there'll be no liquor drinking on this bus. I hope that's understood. *(Billee, considerably intimidated, takes his place behind Dodie. During the following he sees Mother and stares at her in amazement)*

(Father punches Mother's ticket, saying in sad condolence:) I hope you have a good trip, ma'am. I hope you have a good trip.

MOTHER *(A whisper)*: Thank you. *(She takes a place in the last row)*

CAROLINE *(Rummaging in her handbag)*: Would you like a candy bar, Miss Wilson . . . and Mr. Wentworth?

DODIE: Thank you, Mrs. Arizona, I would.

BILLEE: Look! LOOK! That's Mama!

DODIE: Stop poking me. It's not. It's *not*.

FATHER: Well, now, all aboard that's going to go. *(He climbs on the bus, takes his seat, tries his gears, then rises and addresses the passengers weightily)* Before we start, there are some things I want to say about this trip. *Bus travel is not easy.* I think you'll know what I mean, Mrs. Arizona, when I say that it's like family life: we're all stuck in this vehicle together. We go through some pretty dangerous country, and I want you all to keep your heads. Like when we go through the Black Snake Indian territory, for instance. I've just heard they're getting a little—restless. And along the Kappikappi River, where all those lions and tigers are, and other things. Now, I'm a pretty good driver, but nobody's perfect and everybody can make a mistake once in a while. But I don't want any complaints afterward that you weren't warned. If anybody wants to get off this bus and go home, this is the moment to do it, and I'll give you your money back. *(Indicating Mother)* There's one passenger here I know can be counted on. She's made the trip before and she's a regular crackerjack. Excuse me praising you to your face, ma'am, but I mean every word of it. Now, how many of you have been trained in first aid—will you hold up your hands? *(Billee and Mother raise their hands promptly. Caroline and Dodie look at one another uncertainly but do not raise their hands)* Well, we may have to hold some classes later—go to school, so to speak. Accidents are always likely to happen when we get to the tops of the mountains. So! I guess we're ready to start. When we start, we often have a word of prayer if there's a minister of the gospel on board. *(To Billee)* May I ask if you're a minister of the gospel, Mr. Wentworth?

BILLEE: N-no.

FATHER: Then we'll just have to *think* it. *(Lowering his voice, to Billee)* And, may I add, I hope that there won't be any bad language used on this bus. There are ladies present—and some very fine ladies, too, if I may say so. Well, here we go! Forward march.

CAROLINE *(To Dodie, confidentially)*: If it's going to be so dangerous, I think we'd better move up a little nearer *him*.

(They slip across the aisle and slide, side by side, into the second row behind Father. Billee has gone to the back of the car and stands staring at Mother.)

BILLEE *(Indicating the veil)*: Do you ever take that off?

MOTHER *(Softly, lowered eyes)*: Sometimes I do.

CAROLINE: Billee! Don't disturb the lady. Come and sit by us.

MOTHER: Oh, he's not disturbing me at all.

(Soon he takes the seat beside her, and she puts her arm around him.)

FATHER *(As he drives, talking to the girls over his shoulder)*: It's hard work driving a bus, ladies. Did you ever think of that?

CAROLINE: Oh, yes. It must be hard.

FATHER: Sometimes I wonder why I do it. Mornings . . . leave my house and family and get on the bus. And it's no fun, believe me. *(Jerk)* See that? Almost ran over that soldier. And—would you believe it—I don't get much money for it.

CAROLINE *(Breathless interest)*: Don't they pay you a *lot*?

FATHER: Mrs. Arizona, I'm telling you the truth: sometimes I wonder if we're going to have enough to eat.

DODIE: Why, I think that's terrible!

FATHER: And if I can get enough clothes to wear. I see that's a nice fur piece you have on, Mrs. Arizona.

CAROLINE: Oh, this is *old*.

DODIE *(Very earnestly)*: But at your house you do have breakfast and lunch and supper, don't you?

FATHER: Miss Wilson, you're awfully kind to ask. So far we have. Sometimes it's just, you know, beans and things like that. Life's not easy, Mrs. Arizona. You must have noticed that.

BILLEE *(Big alarm)*: Mr. Bus Conductor, look't. Look over there!

FATHER *(Galvanized; all stare toward the left)*: Ladies and gentlemen, there are those goldarn Indians again! I want you to put your heads right down on the floor! Right down! *(All except Father crouch on the floor)* I don't want any of them arrows to come in the windows and hit you. *(Father fires masterfully from the hip)* They'll be sorry for this. BANG! BANG! That'll teach them. BANG! *(Billee rises and whirls, shooting splendidly in all directions)* There! The danger's over, ladies and gentlemen. You can get in your seats now. I'll report that to the Man Up There in Washington, D.C., you see if I don't. *(To Mother)* May I ask if you're all right back there?

MOTHER: Yes, thank you, Mr. Bus Conductor. I want to say that Mr. Wentworth behaved splendidly. I don't think that I'd be here except for him.

FATHER: Good! Minute I saw him I knew he had the old stuff in him! Ladies, I think you did A-number-one, too.

CAROLINE: Does that happen often, Mr. Bus Conductor?

FATHER: Well, you know what a man's life is like, Mrs. Arizona. Fight. Struggle. Survive. Struggle. Survive. Always was.

DODIE: What if—what if you *didn't* come back?

FATHER: Do you mean, if I died? We don't think of that, Miss Wilson. But when we come home Friday nights we like to see the look on the faces of our wives and children. Another week, and we're still there. And do you know what I do on my free days, Miss Wilson, after sitting cooped up behind this wheel?

DODIE *(Sudden inspiration)*: Play golf.

FATHER: You're bright, Miss Wilson, bright as a penny.

CAROLINE *(Who has been glancing at Mother)*: Mr. Bus Conductor, can I ask you why that lady—why she's so sad?

FATHER: You don't know?

CAROLINE: No.

FATHER *(Lowering his voice)*: She just got some bad news. Her children left the house.

CAROLINE: Did they?

FATHER: Don't mention it to her, will you?

CAROLINE *(Insecurely)*: Why did they do that?

FATHER: Well, children are funny. Funny. Now I come to think of it, it'd be nice if, a little later, you went back and sort of comforted her. Like Mr. Wentworth's doing.

DODIE: Wasn't she good to them?

FATHER: What's that?

DODIE: Wasn't she a *good* mother?

FATHER: Well, let me ask *you* a question: is there any such thing as a good mother or a good father? Look at me: I do the best I can for my family—things to eat, you know, and dresses and shoes. I see you've got some real pretty shoes on, ladies. But, well, *children don't understand,* and that's all you can say about it. Do you know what one of my daughters said to me last week? She said she wished she was an orphan. Hard. Very hard.

CAROLINE *(Struggling)*: Lots of times parents don't understand children, either.

FATHER *(Abruptly breaking the mood)*: But now, ladies and gentlemen, I have a treat for you. *(Stops the bus and points dramatically to the front right. All gaze in awe)* Isn't that a sight! The Mississippi River! Isn't that a lot of water!

MOTHER *(After a moment's gaze, with increasing concern)*: But—but—Mr. Bus Conductor.

FATHER *(Looking back at her and sharing her anxiety)*: Madam, I think I know what you're thinking, and it troubles me too. *(Mother has come halfway down the aisle, her eyes on the river)* Ladies and gentlemen, the river's in flood. I don't think I've ever seen it so high. The question is: would it be safe to cross it today? Look yourselves—would that bridge hold?

MOTHER *(Returning to her seat)*: Mr. Bus Conductor, may I make a suggestion?

FATHER: You certainly may.

MOTHER: I suggest that you ask the passengers to raise their hands if they think it's best that we don't cross the Mississippi today.

FATHER: *Very* good idea! That'll mean we turn around and go back to where we came from. Now think it over, ladies and gentlemen. All who are ready to do that raise their hands. *(Mother and Billee raise their hands at once. Then Dodie. Finally, unhappily, Caroline. Father earnestly counts the twenty hands in the bus)* All right! Everybody wants to go back. So, here we go. *(He starts the bus)* Now, I'm going to go pretty fast, so sit square in your seats.

(After a pause, confidentially over his shoulder to Caroline) I hope you really meant it when you put your hand up, Mrs. Arizona.

CAROLINE: Well . . .

FATHER: You *do* have some folks waiting for you at home, don't you?

DODIE *(Quickly)*: Yes, we do.

CAROLINE *(Slowly, near to tears)*: But we didn't get to China or to that river where the lions and tigers are. It's too soon to go back to where I come from, where everybody says silly things they don't mean one bit, and where nobody treats you like a real person. And we didn't get to eat the famous heaven-fruit sandwich at that place.

DODIE *(Embarrassed)*: Car'line, you can do it another time.

(Caroline's lowered head shows that she doesn't believe this.)

FATHER *(Confidentially)*: Mrs. Arizona, I'll honor that ticket *at any time,* and I'll be looking for you.

CAROLINE *(Raises her eyes to him gravely; after a minute she says, also in a low voice)*: Mr. Bus Conductor—

FATHER: Yes, Mrs. Arizona.

CAROLINE: Do you get paid just the same, even if you didn't go the whole way?

FATHER: I? Oh, don't you think of that, ma'am. We can tighten our belts. There's always something.

CAROLINE *(Groping feverishly in her handbag, with a quick sob)*: No! I haven't got a *lot* of money, but—here! Here's more'n two dollars, and you can buy a lot of things to eat with that.

FATHER *(Quietly and slowly, his eyes on the road)*: That's real thoughtful of you, Mrs. Arizona, and I thank you. But you put that away and keep it. I feel sure that this is going to be my good year. *(After a pause)* Excuse me, may I put my hand on your hand a minute to show you know I appreciate what you did?

CAROLINE *(Shy)*: Yes, you may.

(He does so, very respectfully; then returns to his wheel.)

DODIE: Car'line, what're you crying about?

CAROLINE: When . . . you try to *do* something for somebody . . . and . . .

FATHER *(Very cheerful and loud)*: Gee whillikers! My wife will be surprised to see me back home so soon. Poor old thing, she doesn't have many pleasures. Just a little shopping now and then. *(He tosses off a snatch of song)* "The son of a, son of a, son of a gambolier . . ." I think this would be a good time to go back and say a nice word to that lady who's had a little disappointment in her home, don't you?

CAROLINE: Well, uh . . . Come, Dodie *(Caroline goes back and sits in front of Mother, talking to her over the back of the seat; Dodie stands beside her)* The bus conductor says that everybody isn't in your house any more.

MOTHER *(Lowered eyes)*: Did he? That's true.

CAROLINE: They'll come back. I know they will.

MOTHER: Oh, do you think so?

CAROLINE: Children don't like being treated as children *all the time*. And I think it isn't worthwhile being born into the world if you have to do the same things every day.

DODIE: The reason I don't like grown-ups is that they don't ever think any inneresting thoughts. I guess they're so old that they just get tired of expecting anything to be different or exciting. So they just do the same old golfing and shopping.

CAROLINE *(Suddenly seeing a landmark through the window)*: Mr. Bus Conductor! Mr. Bus Conductor! Please, will you please stop at the next corner? This is where we have to get off.

(Under her voice, commandingly) Come, Dodie, Billee. Come quick!

(They start up the aisle toward the bus exit, then turn back to Mother. Their farewells are their best party manners.)

THE CHILDREN *(Shaking hands with both parents)*: I'm very glad to have met you. Thank you very much. I'm very glad to have met you.

FATHER *(As Mother joins him at the bus exit)*: But you'll come on my bus again? We'll see you again?

CAROLINE *(To Dodie and Billee, low)*: Now, run!

(They run into the house like rabbits. She stands at the bus door, with lowered eyes.)

Well . . . you see . . . you're just people in our game. You're not *really* alive. That's why we could talk to you. *(A quick glance at her father, then she looks down again)* Besides, we've found that it's best not to make friends with grown-ups, because . . . in the end . . . they don't act fair to you . . . But thank you; I'm very glad to have met you.

(She goes into the house. Father takes off his cap and glasses; Mother her hat and veil. They place them on chairs. Father prepares to make a difficult golf stroke.)

FATHER: Where *are* the children?

MOTHER: Oh, they're hiding somewhere, as usual.

FATHER: Hiding! Hiding from their father!

MOTHER: Or they're playing one of those awful games of theirs. Come in, come in. You'll see them at supper. *(She goes into the house)*

FATHER *(He stands at the end of the stage farthest from the house and calls)*: Caroline! Dodie! Billee-ee-ee!

(Silence, of course. He goes into the house.)

END OF PLAY

Youth

CHARACTERS

LEMUEL GULLIVER, a shipwrecked sea captain, forty-six
MISTRESS BELINDA JENKINS, a commoner, eighteen
LADY SIBYL PONSONBY, a noble lady, twenty-four
THE DUKE OF CORNWALL, the island's governor, twenty-eight
SIMPSON, a commoner and builder, twenty
[TWO BOY GUARDS, fifteen]

SETTING

A tropical island.

At the back, an opening through a thicket leads to the principal town. Forward on the stage is a palm-thatched summer house without walls. Under its roof is a rustic table and bench; on the table some worn books. On the floor at one side of the stage is a piece of glass, fringed with moss; this represents a spring.

Gulliver, forty-six, drags himself on in the last stages of hunger and exhaustion. He sees the spring and avidly laps at it with hand and tongue. Somewhat refreshed, he lies down and closes his eyes. Then rising to a sitting position, he becomes aware of the summer house. He goes to it and opens one of the books. In great amazement he murmurs: "English! In English!"

In the distance a young woman's voice is heard lilting a kind of yodel. It ceases and is resumed several times.

Gulliver makes a shell of his hands and calls:

GULLIVER: Anyone? . . . Is anyone there?

BELINDA'S VOICE: What? . . . Wha . . . a . . . t?

GULLIVER: Is anyone there?

VOICE: *(Nearer)*: 'Oo are *you*?

GULLIVER *(Still calling)*: I am an Englishman, madam, shipwrecked on this island.

VOICE: 'Oo? . . . 'Ooh?

GULLIVER: I am Captain Gulliver, at your service, madam.

VOICE: 'Ooh?

GULLIVER: Captain Gulliver—Lemuel Gulliver of the fourmaster *Arcturus*, Port of London, at your service, madam.

VOICE: Oh! Lord. 'Ow old are you?

(Gulliver, nonplussed, does not answer.)

'Ow *old* are you?

GULLIVER: I'm forty-six years of age.

VOICE *(Just offstage)*: No!! No!! *Forty*-six! 'Ow did you get here?

GULLIVER: I was shipwrecked, madam. I have been in the sea for three days, pushing a spar. I am sorely in need of food and am much dependent on your kindness.

(Enter Mistress Belinda Jenkins, eighteen. She gazes at Gulliver with growing abhorrence, covers her face with her hands and turns to the entrance through which she came.)

BELINDA: Oh, Lady Sibyl! 'Ow 'ideous! 'Ow unbearable!

(Enter Lady Sibyl Ponsonby, twenty-four. Both are charmingly dressed as of the eighteenth century in some textile-like tapa cloth. Lady Sibyl is a great lady, however, and carries a parasol tufted with seagulls' feathers.)

LADY SIBYL *(Staring at Gulliver, but with more controlled repulsion; as though to herself)*: It's hall true! Then it's hall true, wot they say! *(Pronounced "si")*

BELINDA *(To Gulliver, spitefully)*: Turn your fice awigh! How can you look at Lady Sibyl?

LADY SIBYL *(With authority)*: 'Old your tongue, Jenkins.

BELINDA *(Pointing)*: But he's terrible! He's terrible!

LADY SIBYL *(Coldly)*: Yes. —You are 'ideous to behold.

GULLIVER: I'm a plain man, madam; and in addition I have been without food and drink for three days—and with very little sleep.

LADY SIBYL *(Again as though to herself)*: I have never seen an old man before. *Forty*-six, you say? It's hall true, too true.

BELINDA *(Peeking from behind Lady Sibyl)*: The wrinkles, your ladyship. Nobody could count them! —Can he see? Can he hear?

LADY SIBYL *(From curiosity not kindness)*: You must be suffering in every part of your body?

GULLIVER: I have suffered, madam, principally from thirst until I found this spring here; and I would be most beholden to you if *you* could also graciously give me something to eat.

LADY SIBYL: I shall never forget this moment. You are, indeed, a most pitiable spectacle.

GULLIVER *(With dignity)*: I shall turn my face away if it distresses you, madam.

BELINDA: All of you is as repulsive as your face.

GULLIVER: I am as God made me and the hardships I have endured. —If you would graciously provide me with the means I could catch fish to [assuage] my hunger. I have been shipwrecked before and have sustained myself in many ways.

LADY SIBYL *(Musing)*: At your age everything must be painful—exceedingly—breathing . . . and walking . . .

GULLIVER *(Loud)*: Young woman, are you indeed deaf *(Pronounced "deef")* or do you lack humanity? I am starving.

BELINDA: "Young woman!" You are talking to Lady Sibyl Ponsonby.

LADY SIBYL: Be quiet, Jenkins. —Old man, you will be given something to eat. There have been other old men on this island. They were given something to eat before they departed.

GULLIVER: I hope that will not be long.

LADY SIBYL: That will not be long.

GULLIVER: Did I understand you, madam, did I hear correctly: that you have never seen a man of forty-six before?

BELINDA: Forty-six! No one has ever seen anyone older than twenty-nine—except one that floated up from the sea, like yourself. There is no one on this island older than twenty-nine and there never will be.

GULLIVER: Merciful Heavens! What do you do with your older persons?

LADY SIBYL: I will now go and call someone to attend to your needs. You will not follow me! You will not leave this place. Today is a day of festival and it is of the highest importance that no one sees you—that is, as few as possible see you. —Jenkins, stay near him.

BELINDA: I, your ladyship!!

LADY SIBYL: Do not enter into conversation with him. *(Appraising him coldly)* I do not think he could progress far.

BELINDA *(Becoming hysterical)*: Oh, your ladyship, your ladyship—do not leave me alone with him. I will become ill with the sight. *(She falls on her knees, clinging to Lady Sibyl)* I will become ill. I will become ill.

LADY SIBYL: Get up, Jenkins! —Very well, I will stay with this man. Go to the Duke of Cornwall. Draw him aside and speak to him in a low voice. Tell him that we have come upon this . . . foreigner. 'E will know what to do.

GULLIVER (*Gesturing as though bringing food to his mouth*): And tell him—

LADY SIBYL: Tell him the old man is hungry. —But, Jenkins, hold your tongue. Do not speak of it to anyone else.

BELINDA: To think that this should happen *today*—of all days! (*She sidles up toward Gulliver and examines him intently. Softly*) Think of all the years he has lived!

LADY SIBYL: Jenkins!

BELINDA (*Still scanning Gulliver; half answering*): Yes, milady.

LADY SIBYL: Jenkins! Do as I tell you!

BELINDA: Yes, milady; but I shall never see an old man again. I want to look at him . . . (*Lower*) . . . he is not as abominable as he was at first. One gets used to him, a little. —Old man, have you wives . . . and children?

LADY SIBYL: Belinda! I shall have you jailed!

BELINDA (*Turning to her, with spirit*): Your ladyship, with all due respect to your ladyship, your ladyship has been extremely severe with me for many weeks. I care not if I go to jail. As I was the first person to see this old man I ask to be permitted to have a few words with him.

LADY SIBYL: Two minutes, Belinda . . . No more.

(*Lady Sibyl turns her back on them and moves to the rear of the scene, striking her parasol on the floor.*)

GULLIVER: Yes, Mistress Jenkins, I have a wife Mary, a son John, and a daughter Betsy.

BELINDA (*Slowly, scarcely a question*): And are you very cruel to them?

GULLIVER: Madam?

BELINDA: *Old* men are cruel and nasty tempered. Everyone knows that.

(Gulliver gazes deep into her eyes with a faint smile, slowly shaking his head. She continues, as if to herself.)

Your eyes are different from our eyes. Maybe some old men are a *little bit* kind.

(Gulliver, as though in friendly complicity, rubs his stomach with one hand and conveys the other to his mouth.)

Yes, I will hurry. —I am going, your ladyship.

LADY SIBYL: And remember, no blabbing. *(She looks toward the sun, almost directly overhead)* The games are about to begin. When you have delivered your message, take your place in silence.

BELINDA *(Curtsies)*: Yes, your ladyship.

(Belinda goes out. Lady Sibyl starts strolling about with great self-possession.)

GULLIVER: Surely, I did not hear correctly—*no* older men?

LADY SIBYL: I have no wish to enter into conversation with you.

GULLIVER *(After a short pause, no longer able to contain himself)*: By God's body, madam, you cannot be of stone! You are not a child! I have not hitherto been regarded as a contemptible being. I have been received by kings and queens and have been their guest at meat . . . I am Captain Lemuel Gulliver. I am not a dog.

LADY SIBYL: I have never seen a dog, but I think you must greatly resemble one.

GULLIVER: Madam, you have seen nothing but one small island. You are not in a position to say that you have seen anything. I am astonished that you have no questions to put to me about the world that surrounds you.

LADY SIBYL *(Lofty smile)*: What questions would those be, Captain Gullibo?

GULLIVER: Madam, ignorance is a misery, but there is one still greater: a lack of any desire to increase one's knowledge.

LADY SIBYL: But I have learned much from you in this short time. You have come from that world out there *(She indicates it lightly with her parasol; her voice turns suddenly vindictive)* and you have brought its poisons with you. Your visible infirmities are also marks of the country from which you came. They must be as painful for you to bear as for us to behold. However, you will not have to bear them much longer.

(Gulliver gives up trying to understand her. He sinks down on the bench by the table. He is about to fall asleep.)

Captain, it is not our custom for a commoner to be seated in the presence of the nobility. *(Gulliver, uncomprehending, raises his head)* I see; you are deaf *(Pronounced "deef ")*. I said: it is not the custom for a commoner to be seated in the presence of the nobility.

GULLIVER *(Dragging himself to his feet; with ironic deference)*: Oh . . . oh . . . your ladyship will forgive me . . . my fatigue . . . and my hunger.

(Lady Sibyl puts her hand into her reticule and brings out some lozenges, which she places on the table.)

LADY SIBYL: While you are waiting, here are some comfits which I have been keeping . . . for my children.
GULLIVER: For your children, Lady Sibyl?
LADY SIBYL: Our children on this island live in a village of their own. They are well tended. They are happy. That is our custom here.

(In astonishment, Gulliver is about to ask a question. He corrects himself, and, bowing, says in a low voice:)

GULLIVER: I thank your ladyship.

(He puts two into his mouth ravenously; then takes one out for decorum's sake. A musical sound, like a rolling chord from many harps, is heard from the city. Gulliver listens in astonishment.)

May I ask your ladyship the source of that music?

LADY SIBYL: You forget everything you are told. Today is a day of great festival. *(She looks at the sun)* It is beginning with the children's Morris Dance and—

GULLIVER: Oh, milady, I would greatly wish to see this festival—

LADY SIBYL *(Slight laugh, "how unthinkable")*: These will be followed by the Hoop Dance and the Dagger Dance. The Duke of Cornwall—who will be here in a moment—is the greatest victor in the Hoop Dance that has ever been known. He has won eight garlands. Moreover, he is the only man who has ever kept a kite in the air for an entire day.

GULLIVER: Ah!! He must indeed be remarkable! . . . An entire day! . . . I trust that the duke is of mature years?

LADY SIBYL *(Sharply)*: I did not hear you correctly. *(Gulliver does not repeat the question)* He is naturally of mature years. He is our governor. He is twenty-eight *(Pronounced "ite")*.

GULLIVER *(Stares at her; then with dawning horror)*: Great Heavens, girl! What do you do with your older persons?

LADY SIBYL: Captain Gullibo, there is no profit in pursuing a conversation on matters you are not capable of understanding.

GULLIVER *(Shouting)*: You kill them. You murder them when they reach the age of twenty-nine?

LADY SIBYL: How dare you address me in that manner? —Vulgar brutish Englander! Barbarian! How could you understand customs that are based on wisdom and reason.

GULLIVER: I dread to hear them! *(Louder)* Are you able to answer me: what do you do to those who reach the age of twenty-nine?

LADY SIBYL *(Slowly; with serene assurance)*: We drink the wine. We sleep. We are placed in a boat. The current carries us away.

GULLIVER: Thunder! This is hellish!

LADY SIBYL *(Putting a hand delicately on her ear)*: Restrine your senile violence, Captain Gullibo.

GULLIVER: And *you*, your ladyship—are you going to drink that wine and go to sleep in that boat?

LADY SIBYL: When I am old—readily, gladly. I have four years to live. That is a very long time.

GULLIVER: And no one ever rebels? No one twenty-nine years old ever wishes to live longer?

LADY SIBYL: Captain Gullibo, you prate. You rive. You forget that you are old—very old. What I have told you is the custom of this island! Do you understand the word "custom"? . . . Would any of us *wish* to be . . .

GULLIVER *(Hand to head)*: Your ladyship must permit me to sit down. *(He does)*

LADY SIBYL *(Strolling about and fanning herself)*: It is understandable that the duke is occupied today. *(Severely)* Your arrival is most inopportune.

GULLIVER: The matter was beyond my control, Lady Sibyl. Little did I know that I was arriving on this happy island on the great day of the Hoop Dance. On future occasions I shall arrange it with greater propriety.

LADY SIBYL *(Looks at him and raises her eyebrows)*: Future occasions, Captain Gullibo? At your age, Captain, you cannot speak with certainty of future occasions.

GULLIVER *(Returning her glance; in a low voice)*: Lady Sibyl, I am thinking of your children. You will never know the joys of seeing them grow into young manhood and womanhood. You will never hold grandchildren on your knees.

LADY SIBYL: You are tedious, Captain Gullibo. I have read of those things in books.

GULLIVER: Ah, madam. —You have books, I see.

LADY SIBYL: We have one hundred and twenty-seven books, Captain.

GULLIVER *(Lowers his head in admiration; after a pause, suddenly humble and earnest)*: Lady Sibyl, let me throw myself upon your mercy. You are a woman, and women in all times have tempered this rough world with mercy and compassion. I have arrived a stranger and an interloper here; I do not wish to intrude upon this happy existence. I can see that you have much influence on this island; graciously exert it on my behalf. I saw that there were boats drawn up along the shore. I am a seaman of experience. When I have been given some food to stay my hunger, be my advocate with this Duke of Cornwall—

LADY SIBYL *(Purest amazement)*: Where would you go?

GULLIVER *(Pointing)*: . . . That island or continent . . . those mountains . . .

LADY SIBYL *(Harshly)*: I have nothing to do with such matters. Those fishing boats and their sails are fixed to the shore. They are locked with thongs that only a few nobles can undo. —You forget that you are old—very old. Your life is over. Anyone can see that. *(She turns away)*

GULLIVER: I have a wife and children. —You said you have children?

LADY SIBYL: Naturally I have children.

GULLIVER: Look in your heart. Enable me to—

LADY SIBYL: Be silent!

GULLIVER *(Sinking onto the bench; to himself, in despair)*: Yes . . . yes . . . Humanity is the last thing that will be learned by man. *(He puts his head on his arms and is about to fall asleep)*

LADY SIBYL *(Walking up and down, loftily)*: You may be certain that nothing will be done here that is not for the wisest and the best. We are enlightened here; and we are Christians. That strain of music you heard came from Westminster Abbey. The Archbishop of Canterbury is addressing the contestants in the games. If you were a *young* man we would be proud to show you how happy our existence is, and how perfect our institutions. This perfection is rendered possible by the fact that here we have no—

(Gulliver has fallen asleep.)

GULLIVER *(Mumbling)*: . . . steep . . . the steep streets . . . Redriff, home! . . . Mary—Polly! . . . Polly, forgive me . . .

(He falls silent. Lady Sibyl gazes at him for a moment with repugnance, then draws nearer and scans his face intently— a long gaze. When he stirs and seems about to wake, she moves away and, opening her parasol, strolls off the stage.

In deep stupor Gulliver slips off the bench and rolls under the table.

Lady Sibyl returns hurriedly; there is a suggestion of walking backward as though royalty were approaching. Enter the Duke of Cornwall, twenty-eight, very splendid in festival dress. To the early eighteenth-century costume have been added feathers and colored shells, etc. He is followed by Simpson, twenty, a commoner, carrying a tray of food. The Duke gazes fixedly at Gulliver.)

LADY SIBYL: He has fallen into a swound, your grace.

DUKE: Simpson—throw some water on his face.

(Simpson scoops some water from the mirror pool and throws it on Gulliver's face. Gulliver recovers consciousness, stirs and cumbrously extricates himself from under the table. Finally, he grasps the situation and, standing erect, confronts the Duke, eye to eye.)

Who are you?

GULLIVER: Lemuel Gulliver, your grace, captain of the fourmaster *Arcturus*, Port of London.

DUKE: How old are you?

GULLIVER: I am in my middle years; I am forty-six.

DUKE: They tell me you have been three days without food—Simpson, place the food on the table. Eat!

GULLIVER: I thank your grace. Commoners do not sit in the presence of the nobility. I shall eat when you have left to take part in the festival.

(Pause.)

Sir, I have visited many countries and have been ship-wrecked on the shores of several. In all of them, save one, I have been treated with courtesy as a citizen of England and a subject of our gracious sovereign, Queen Anne. I am indebted to you for this relief from my hunger. I trust that hereafter I may see your cities and learn of your customs. In return I shall gladly tell you of other parts of the world that I have visited; and above all of the country whose language you speak and from which your ancestors came.

DUKE *(Again a short contemptuous pause; then with a curt gesture of the hand)*: You are tedious, old man. —Simpson!

SIMPSON: Yes, your grace?

DUKE: Withdraw to a distance. It is not suitable that a commoner hear this nonsense. I shall call you when it is time for you to stand watch over the captain.

(Simpson bows and goes out. Gulliver begins to laugh to himself and, turning away, sits down.)

LADY SIBYL *(Revolted)*: He is laughing!!

GULLIVER: To be young, and yet ask no questions about the country from which your ancestors came! To be young, and yet have no curiosity concerning the shore that lies upon the horizon! To be young, and yet—oh, ye immortal Gods!—to be without adventure of mind or generosity of spirit! Now it is clear to me why you so gladly bring your lives to a close at the age of twenty-nine—*gladly* was Lady Sibyl's word.

DUKE *(Bitingly)*: That should not be difficult for you to understand—you, with this decay of mind and body—

GULLIVER *(Interrupting)*: No! No, it is not the advance of age that frightens you on this island. *(With a sardonic smile)* A greater enemy threatens you. *(Abruptly changing the subject)* I do not wish to detain your grace from the festival and from your trophies.

DUKE: Come, Lady Sibyl.

GULLIVER: Permit me, however, one question. *(The Duke nods)* What is the name of this island and this country?

DUKE: Name? Why should it have a name?

GULLIVER: I have visited twenty countries. Each has borne a name in which it takes pride.

DUKE: Proud? All of them were proud?

GULLIVER: They were. They are.

DUKE: Among those twenty countries was there *one* that was not governed by old men—governed, misgoverned, burdened, oppressed by old men? By the pride and avarice, and the lust for power of old men? One which did not constantly war at the instigation of old men like *yourself*, to enlarge its boundaries; to enslave others; to enrich itself? We know of the War of the Roses. Or by the religious bigotry of old men—we know of the Saint Bartholomew Massacre, [the] murder of Charles, king and martyr. And when these prides of yours have obtained their lands, whose bodies are those lying upon the field of battle? —They are the bodies of men under thirty. We need no name to distinguish this country from others. Say that you are in the Country of the Young.

GULLIVER: So be it! —Since you do not wish me to encumber you longer, I request some boat with which I may rid you of my presence. *(In amazement)* How did you come here? Who brought you here?

DUKE: God!

GULLIVER: God! —Where did you acquire this distrust and hatred of the old?

DUKE: We have no boats for that purpose.

GULLIVER: The smallest would serve me.

DUKE: No boat of ours has ever made that journey and never will.

GULLIVER: Perhaps your grace will let me purchase a boat. This ring was given to me by the King of Laputa. It is of pure alchemist's gold.

DUKE: You have been here a few hours. Lady Sibyl has told me that already you have offered us insult and have spoken of our customs with contempt; and now you wish to introduce barter and trafficking, and gold!— gold, which is above all the instrument by which old men keep the younger in subjection. There is no gold and no trading here. You shall never leave this island and you shall not long envenom it. We shall make you a present for which we ask no return. We shall give you the only happiness that still lies open to you.

GULLIVER: Duke of Cornwall—Duke of Palm Trees and Sand! I wish you a happy twenty-ninth birthday. I can understand that you will gladly drink the wine and welcome the long sleep. Twenty-nine years of jumping through hoops and flying kites will have been enough. Already you are advancing toward a decay worse than age—yes, toward boredom, infinite boredom. Youth left to itself is a cork upon the waves. As we say of the young: they do not know what to do with themselves. It is only under the severity—the well-wishing severity—of your elders that you can shake from yourselves the misery of your aimless state. You elect yourselves into societies and call yourselves dukes and earls; did I hear correctly that each man on this island has several wives? You play games. What more can you ask of a thirtieth birthday than a deep slumber!

LADY SIBYL *(Ablaze)*: Your grace! How can you let him speak to you so?!

DUKE: *(With a smile)*: But this is what we knew; foul and embittered age! Envy and jealousy! Despising those things of which he is no longer capable. *(Whimsically to Lady Sibyl)* Perhaps we should take this man and exhibit him for all to see.

LADY SIBYL *(Covering her face)*: Your grace!

GULLIVER: Yes, and for all to hear, your grace.

DUKE: And to hear. —What would you say to them?

GULLIVER: Why, I should tell them that if a man is not civilized between the ages of twelve and twenty—civilized by his elders—he will never be civilized at all.

(Lady Sibyl covers her ears.)

And oh, it is not an easy task. To educate young men is like rolling boulders up to the tops of mountains; the whole community is engaged in the work and with what doubtful success! For every *one* Isaac Newton or Christopher Wren there are thousands who roll to the bottom of the mountain and occupy themselves with jumping through hoops.

(He sways from weakness, his hand to his head and heart.)

Go to your dances and garlands. I can see that your happiness has begun to stale already. You are weary of life. Old age has marked you already.

DUKE *(With supreme complaisance)*: Oh, I'm young enough!
(He calls) Mr. Simpson! Mr. Simpson!!

(The sound of music has been rising from the distance. Enter Simpson.)

SIMPSON: Yes, your grace?

DUKE: Simpson, you are in charge of this man. See that he does not leave this clearing. Do not enter into conversation with him. It would suffocate you. Later I shall send someone to replace you—Lady Sibyl!

(Lady Sibyl's hand has gone to her forehead; her parasol and reticule fall. She is about to faint.)

LADY SIBYL: Oh, your grace . . . this sight . . . has sickened me.

DUKE *(Cold fury)*: Take command of yourself!

(With a gesture he orders Simpson to pick up the fallen objects. Simpson does so and holds them ready for Lady Sibyl.)

LADY SIBYL *(Swaying; with closed eyes)*: I must breathe a moment.

DUKE: Fool! *(He strikes her sharply on both cheeks)* Go to the city!

GULLIVER *(Taking two steps forward)*: You strike her!! You *strike* her!

DUKE: We permit no weakness here—neither ours nor *yours.*

GULLIVER *(Turns and seats himself on the bench by the table)*: Humanity is the last thing that will be learned by man; it will not be learned from the young.

(Lady Sibyl has taken her parasol and reticule. She collects her dignity, but is scarcely able to leave the stage.)

DUKE: Simpson!

SIMPSON: Your grice!

DUKE: If you fail at any point in your guard over this man, you will be put to the press—and you know what press I mean. And you will be removed from your hoffice as builder and constructor. *(He looks appraisingly at Gulliver)* If he tries to leave the clearing, kick him strongly at the shinbones.

(He goes out. Simpson takes his stand at a distance from Gulliver whom he watches intently. Gulliver returns to his meal, but seems to have lost his appetite. Again there is a sound of music from the city. Gulliver rises and listens.)

GULLIVER: Is there no way, Mr. Simpson, that I may view the games from a distance? *(Simpson shakes his head)* I am sorry. *(He eats a little)* They must be a wonderful sight . . . wonderful. Hoops and kites. *(Pause)* You strike women . . . is that often, Mr. Simpson? . . . Do you strike women frequently, Mr. Simpson? *(No reply)* . . . You are very proud of your civilization . . . when you are angry you *strike* and you *torture* . . .

(Simpson mutters something.)

I did not hear what you said, Mr. Simpson.

SIMPSON: He is old. Strikes and tortures because 'e is old. 'E will die next year.

GULLIVER: He will be killed next year. That is not quite the same thing as merely dying. He will be killed. No wonder he is excitable, Mr. Simpson. In the normal way of life we grow of a more mild and kindly disposition with the years. *(He eats)* So you are a builder and constructor, Mr. Simpson. You are an architect. Lady Sibyl spoke of a Westminster Abbey. I would like to see it. Did you build this Westminster Abbey, sir? *(No answer)* You have great storms in this part of the world—far greater than London has. You must build very—solidly. Have you rock here? *(Simpson points off. Gulliver rises and peers in the direction)* Coral limestone, I presume. Not easy. Arches and a vaulted roof. Ah, you should see the dome of St. Paul's. There's a sight, Mr. Simpson . . . *(He eats)* I am glad that you feel no disposition to talk, sir. I was afraid that you might ask me questions about the life led by young men like yourself in my country. *(Pause)* It would fill me with shame to describe it to you. *(He lowers his voice as though imparting a discreditable secret)* Imagine it! You would be working all the time to acquire more knowledge: from morning to night—and at night by lamplight. Think: to be a better doctor, to govern the people more wisely, *to be a better builder*, Mr. Simpson. Go down on your knees, sir, and thank your Maker that you live on this happy island where learning never penetrates, where young men are not encouraged by old men to extend their knowledge and their skill.

SIMPSON *(Loudly)*: The old men drive them like slaves; the old men take the credit and the profit.

GULLIVER: The young men succeed them. They are not killed at twenty-nine. They become master builders themselves and may decide whether they will be just or unjust. However, I do not wish to talk about it. I reproach myself that I am preventing you from taking part in the games.

SIMPSON: Commoners do not take part in the games.

GULLIVER: Ah! *(He eats)*

(Simpson gazes at him, brooding.)

SIMPSON: I'm a builder.

GULLIVER *(Looking up at the summerhouse)*: Ah!—you made *this*?

SIMPSON: Aye—and the new Westminster Abbey.

GULLIVER: Westminster Abbey! Then you are the chief builder.

SIMPSON: The chief builder is an earl. He has no time to build.

GULLIVER: The new Abbey is of stone—of sandstone or coral?

SIMPSON: The pillars at the corners are.

GULLIVER: And the roof? *(Simpson shakes his head. Gulliver points to the thatch)* Of thatch?—of palm boughs?

(Simpson nods.)

But, man, you have severe storms here. Ah! *(He looks up)* Mr. Simpson, the storm that cast me on your shores has damaged this charming . . . shelter, this pagoda. Was your Westminster Abbey able to sustain the fury of that wind and rain? *(Simpson stares straight before him)* You will not answer me, man! Your Abbey seats—what?—four hundred. Of what is your roof?

Of palm fronds? *(Simpson, without moving his eyes, nods)* I see! When storm destroys your Westminster Abbey you build another. I see! I see! You don't know how to make an arch or a buttress. Oh, Mr. Simpson, do not ask me the secrets of the arch, the buttress and the dome. You are happy. Remain happy. Do not let us think of all the labor that went into those discoveries.

SIMPSON *(Taking steps toward Gulliver; in a low voice)*: Sir . . . Mr. Captain . . . *(His hands describe an arch)* Do you know how to pile stone . . . so they will not fall?

GULLIVER: Believe me. Mr. Simpson, I did not arrive in this paradise in order to poison it with thoughts of progress and industry.

SIMPSON: But you *do* know?

GULLIVER: Perhaps in a hundred years some unhappy youth will be born with talent—with genius. *He* will light upon the laws of the arch. He will prove that youth stands in no need of its elders, no need of the accumulated wisdom of its ancestors. *He will make a roof* . . . Bring your ear nearer, young man: the dome of St. Paul's . . . *(His hand describes a high dome)*

SIMPSON: How high is it?

GULLIVER: How high? Sixty men standing on one another's shoulders could not touch the top of it.

SIMPSON *(Back three yards)*: You are lying! All old men lie. Eat your food. Go to sleep. I ask you a question and you give me a lie. *(Simpson has raised his head)*

GULLIVER: What I said is true, but your rebuke is justified. There is no greater unkindness than to arouse ambition in a young man. —But *you* are to blame. You asked me a question. *(With assumed indignation)* A few more questions like that and you'll be proposing that we take a *boat* and cross to that shore. No I'll not go, I tell you.

SIMPSON *(Sullenly)*: The boats are tied and we cannot untie them.

GULLIVER: Yes, those thongs the nobles keep . . . *(His eyes are looking off speculatively)*

SIMPSON: They're twisted and untwisted with hooks of iron.

GULLIVER: Iron?

SIMPSON: Aye, they're the only pieces of metal on the island. The nobles keep them.

GULLIVER: Very wise! Some fool might think of journeying out there . . . for knowledge and science. —Understand, young man, I'll not leave this island. Give me this day here; then bring the wine and the long sleep. Why should a man trouble his head raising domes? Fly kites, jump through hoops, beget children and sleep.

SIMPSON *(After a pause, grumbling unintelligibly)*: These things you call secrets . . .

GULLIVER: I cannot understand you, sir.

SIMPSON: These things you call the secrets of the arch and the . . . batless—old men keep these secrets to themselves, that's certain.

GULLIVER *(Sternly)*: Cease, Mr. Simpson, to talk of things you know nothing about.

SIMPSON: How would a young man learn them?

GULLIVER: You are asking dangerous questions, Mr. Simpson. —Let me bid you again to go down on your knees and thank your Maker that you do not live in a country where older men would urge you and struggle with you and encourage you to enrich yourself with all learning and skill.

SIMPSON: I don't believe you.

GULLIVER: —A young man would learn them by crossing that water and finding his way into a world that does not spend all its time in games and dances.

SIMPSON *(Mumbles)*: I do not believe you. *(Suddenly loud)* All old men are wicked.

GULLIVER *(Simply)*: I am the only old man you have ever seen.

SIMPSON *(Approaching Gulliver, the beginning of violence)*: Then tell me—

GULLIVER: What?

SIMPSON: The secrets: the arch and the batless.

GULLIVER *(Backing away)*: I do not know them.

SIMPSON *(Seizing Gulliver's throat)*: Tell me them! Wicked old man, tell me them!

GULLIVER *(Forced to his knees)*: I am not a builder. I am a doctor and a seaman.

SIMPSON *(As they struggle)*: I will not let you go before you tell me—

(Gulliver faints. Pause. Simpson leans over him and calls:)

Old man! Old man!

(Enter Belinda carrying a tray and more fruit. She starts back in consternation.)

BELINDA *(Whispering)*: Is he dead? . . . Have *you* killed him?

SIMPSON *(Sullenly)*: No . . . he has died of his old age.

(Belinda puts her ear to Gulliver's mouth.)

BELINDA: I think he is still breathing. It is a swound.

(Both are on their knees gazing at Gulliver.)

Now I do not think he is ugly at all. I think he is a friend.

SIMPSON *(Moves away in inner turmoil)*: I do not understand a word he says. He should not have come here.

BELINDA *(As before)*: What a strange thing wrinkles are. *(Unconsciously she strokes her face . . . softly)* I could ask him questions all day. —Mr. Simpson, let him go back to his own people.

SIMPSON *(Harshly)*: How could he do that?

(Belinda slowly draws from her apron pocket a hook of iron. Simpson draws back in horror.)

BELINDA *(Lowering her voice)*: This is the hook that was lost last year. It was on Lady Sibyl's dressing table. I think she put it there for me to find it. I think she has hidden it to spite the Duke of Cornwall. *(She holds it out toward Simpson)* Unlock the boat and let the man go.

SIMPSON: No!

BELINDA *(Gazes at Gulliver. Pause. Low, with energy)*: Go with him! . . . He is not strong enough to sail the boat alone. Go.

SIMPSON: Do not speak to me! No, I will not go . . . among other men . . . I do not know anything. *He* does not know that we commoners cannot read. Every—*over there*—would see that I am a booby.

BELINDA: Mr. Simpson! Look at him. Come close and look at him! He would be your friend . . . I think *some* old people are good.

SIMPSON: No, I will not go.

BELINDA: He is waking up. Go away and think; but take the hook.

(Simpson takes the hook and goes off.)

GULLIVER *(Opens his eyes. Pause. Sees Belinda)*: Oh! You are here . . . Where is the young man?

BELINDA: He is nearby . . . Will you tell me your name again?

GULLIVER: Captain Gulliver.

BELINDA: Captain Gulliver. If you came to your home again what would you do first?

GULLIVER: Mistress Jenkins, I would go up the steep street—you have never seen a steep street!—I think it would be at sunset . . . I would knock at the door . . . My wife or one of my children would come to the door . . . *(Pause)* . . . Soon we would sit down at the table, and give thanks to God . . . and eat . . .

BELINDA *(Laughing, scandalized)*: Captain Gulliver, you would sit down with your wife!!

GULLIVER: Do not husband and wives—

BELINDA: No—!! *(She laughs)* Sit down! No man has ever eaten with a woman—! The men eat all by themselves.

The nobles in one place. The commoners in another.
And the boys when they are six by themselves.

GULLIVER: And if I lived on this happy island, when would
I see my daughter? *(She does not answer)* You remember your father?

BELINDA: Yes.

GULLIVER: You saw him often? You loved him?

BELINDA: But . . . men live . . . *over there* . . .

GULLIVER: The childhood of the race . . . You have slipped
five—ten thousand years . . .

(Simpson has returned, and half hidden, is listening.)

In a thousand years, Mistress Jenkins, gradually on this
island things will change. A man will have one wife and
only one wife. I think when your father died at twenty-
nine he was just beginning to understand *(Gulliver
points to his forehead)* what the joys of being *your* father
could be—but it was too late. *(Gulliver clasps Belinda
by her shoulders, sadly)* You all die here just before a new
world of mind and heart is open to you.

[*(The music and sounds of celebration have increased, as
if approaching. Simpson breaks from his hiding place and
rushes to Gulliver with the iron hook. Simpson pulls at
Gulliver's arm and points toward the sea. Gulliver grasps
the situation immediately, starts to go with Simpson, but
looks back at Belinda. She remains motionless, staring
straight ahead, and does not meet his glance. Simpson
drags Gulliver off.*

*Music is louder. Belinda gazes front; intense, conflicted.
Pause.*

*Simpson reappears running. He takes both of Belinda's
hands in his. They look at each other. A decision passes
between them. Belinda casts one glance back over her shoulder
at all she has ever known; and they run off to join Gulliver.*

Music increases.

Two Boy Guards, fifteen, rush in with ropes to bind Gulliver for his ceremonial death. The Duke enters behind. They look about, see that Gulliver, Simpson and Belinda are gone. The Duke is the first to realize the implication of this absence. He stands upstage center as the Guards roughly search everywhere. Convinced that the man they were after has escaped, they turn to the Duke.

Music takes on a wild, threatening sound.

The Duke has been gazing out toward a horizon, perhaps seeing the boat moving off, perhaps contemplating his own soon wasted mortality. The Boy Guards gaze intently at him as the lights fade.)]

END OF PLAY

This play became available through the research and editing of F. J. O'Neil of manuscripts in the Thornton Wilder Collection at Yale University.

The author's manuscript existed in a partial typescript, which contained Wilder's handwritten corrections interleaved with several handwritten pages of clearly indicated revised material. The author's manuscript ended with Gulliver's speech to Belinda, spoken while Simpson listens hidden from their view. To conclude the play for production, I felt it would be helpful to take into account Wilder's most plausible intention: that Swift's Gulliver, only borrowed for this adventure, be returned safely to London and his place in English literature.

What then of Simpson and Belinda? Belinda had earlier insisted to Simpson that Gulliver was not strong enough to make the trip alone. Her plea that Simpson accompany Gulliver in the escape strongly suggests that Wilder intended Simpson and Gulliver to leave the island together. Simpson had been sent off with the tool that unlocks the boats. Further, there is the duke's threat that Simpson will be put to the press if he fails in his guard duties. Will Belinda stay behind to face the wrath of the duke?

Gulliver has developed a strong paternal feeling for her and, in addition, she and Simpson are commoners, both of age, both bright and interested and curious by nature: a matched set to be saved on Gulliver's "ark."

And the duke? Wilder often placed characters in a position where, experiencing an epiphany, they catch a glimpse of what lies ahead. *Youth* seems constructed for just such a moment. The twenty-eight-year-old duke, himself within a year of his enforced demise, returns as he must, accompanied by his callow bullyish guards. Might Wilder perhaps have wanted us to wonder what the duke feels about the defeat of his will and authority in the light of what he will not be able to avoid in a year's time? Those questions hang in the added final tableau.

F. J. O'Neil
April 1997

The Rivers Under the Earth

(? Middle Age)

CHARACTERS

MRS. CARTER, mother, thirty-eight
TOM, her son, sixteen
FRANCESCA, her daughter, seventeen
MR. CARTER, their father, forty-three

SETTING

A few years ago. A point of land near a lake in southern Wisconsin.

At both sides of the stage are boxes of various sizes, but none very large—orange boxes, canned goods boxes, covered with burlap or bits of rug. These are rocks. The action of this play takes place in the dark, but I wish it to be played in bright light. Mrs. Carter, very attractive and looking less than her thirty-eight years, enters tentatively feeling her way in the dark. She is followed by her son, Tom, sixteen.

MRS. CARTER: Take my hand, Tom. I don't know where you children inherited your ability to see in the dark.

(Tom passes her and starts slowly leading her forward.)

TOM: It isn't dark at all. All these stars reflected in the lake. —There's a sort of path here, Mother. The rocks are at the side of it.

MRS. CARTER *(Stopping)*: Fireflies. All those fireflies. *(Pause)* I don't know why it is that when I see fireflies I think of *horses*—no, of an old horse named Billy that we used to have when we were children.

TOM: Fireflies—and a horse!!

MRS. CARTER *(Still standing and smiling)*: There are many associations like that one can't explain. —Why does your father dislike the color green? Why do I always make a mistake when I add a six and a seven? Why have I an ever so faint tiny prejudice against people whose name begins with B—Blodgetts and Burnses and Binghams and even dear old Mrs. Becket.

(Tom leads her a step forward.)

TOM: I haven't got any quirks like that.

MRS. CARTER *(Stopping again)*: Why have we never been able to make you eat rice?

TOM: Ugh!—I just don't like it!

MRS. CARTER: Why does your sister hate to sit in the back-seat of automobiles?

TOM: Oh, Francesca's crazy, anyway.

MRS. CARTER: Oh, no she isn't. She's the most reasonable and logical of us all.

TOM: Why does Francesca hate to come here?

MRS. CARTER: What?

TOM: She hates to come out on this point of land. She told me once—but then she was sorry she told me. She told me that every now and then she dreamed that she was on this point of land, and that when she dreamed it, it was a nightmare and she woke up crying or screaming or something.

MRS. CARTER *(Thoughtful)*: You mustn't tease her about it. Promise me you won't tease her about it.

TOM: All right.

MRS. CARTER: Now take my elbow and lead me to a rock that I can remember at the very tip of the point. *(As they progress)* No—all those quirks, as you call them, are like wrecks at the bottom of the sea. They mark the place where there was once a naval battle—or a storm. Why did my dear father always become angry whenever anybody mentioned . . .

—Thank you, Tom. Here it is! I used to come and sit here when I was a girl. There aren't any snakes are there?

TOM *(Competent)*: One: snakes don't like this kind of pine needles; two: snakes in America don't come out at night.

MRS. CARTER: You're such a pleasure, Tom; you know everything. What I mean is: you know everything comforting. —Now you go back and do whatever it is you were doing.

(Tom stands irresolute in the middle of the stage, looking up.)

TOM: When do you want me to come and lead you back?

MRS. CARTER: Forget me, Tom. I can find my way back now.

(Girl's voice off: "T-o-o-m! . . . Tom C-a-a-arter.")

TOM *(Warningly, to his mother)*: Hsh!

(The voice, passing in the distance: "T-o-o-m!")

TOM: Polly Springer's always wanting something. Golly, those girls are helpless. They can't even stick a marshmallow on a fork . . . The moon will rise over *there* . . . You came to this very place?

MRS. CARTER: In those days we knew everyone in all the houses around the lake. Many times I'd come and spend the night with the Wilsons . . . or the Kimballs. *(She indicates first the right, then the left)* And I'd slip away from them, and come here; and think . . . We were told that this point had been some sort of Indian ceremonial campground . . . and a burial place, I suppose. Your father used to find arrowheads here.

TOM: What did you used to think about?

MRS. CARTER: Oh, what do young girls think about? . . . I remember once . . . I made a vow: never to marry. Yes. I was going to be a doctor. And at the same time I was going to be a singer. But I wasn't going to sing in concerts . . . for money. I was going to sing to my patients in the wards just before they turned out the lights for the night. That's the kind of thing young girls think about.

(Tom has been taking this in very gravely, his eyes on the distance. He says abruptly:)

TOM: But you *did* get married. And you almost never sing anymore. —I brought your guitar.

MRS. CARTER: What!?

TOM: Yes. I knew they'd ask you to sing later—around the bonfire.

MRS. CARTER: Why, Tom, you little devil. They would never have thought of it. Now don't you go putting the idea into their heads.

TOM: I didn't. I heard them talking about it. I canoed back across the lake and got your guitar . . . You don't *hate* to sing.

MRS. CARTER: Oh, I'll sing, if anybody asks me to. It's not important enough to make any discussion about.

(Silence. Tom lies down in the path facing the sky, his head on his folded arms.)

TOM: Right up there ... in the Milky Way ... There's something called a Coal Hole.

MRS. CARTER: What?

TOM: A Coal Hole. It's sort of a deep empty stocking. If Father gave me a Jaguar; and I started driving five thousand miles a minute—*starting* from up there—it'd take me hundreds of millions of years to get halfway through it. —Lake water has a completely different sound of slapping—or lapping—than water at the seashore, hasn't it? I like it best.

(He shuts his eyes. Girls' voices, giggling and talking excitedly, are heard near the entrance. Tom sits up energetically and calls:)

TOM: Mildred! Constance! —Is that you, Constance?

VOICE: Ye-e-s!

TOM: Get me a hamburger! Be a sweetie!

VOICE *(Sweetly)*: Get it yourself, deeeer bo-oo-y.

TOM *(Lying down again; darkly)*: The slaves are getting uppish at the end of the summer.

MRS. CARTER: Would these be the same trees that were here twenty years ago?

TOM: Yes. Red pines grow fast the first five years, then they settle down and grow about a foot a year. *(He turns to lie on his stomach, leaning on his elbow. He explains simply and casually)* This is really a sand dune here. Until recently there was a great big lake over all this area. When the lake shrunk, there were these dunes. Ordinarily, it takes about five thousand years for the first grasses to get their roots in and to make enough humus for small bushes to grow. Then it takes about 10,000 years for the bushes to make enough humus for the white pines. Then come the red pines. Probably it was faster here because of these rocks. They prevented the top sand from being blown away every few days. That's why the trees are so much bigger here, and over at the Cavanaughs, and around the boat club . . . Rocks.

FRANCESCA'S VOICE *(Off)*: Mo-o-ther!

MRS. CARTER: Yes, dear, here I am.

(Enter Francesca, seventeen, with a scarf.)

FRANCESCA: Father said you'd probably be here.

TOM *(Rolling to one side)*: Don't step on me, you galoot!

FRANCESCA: Oh, *you're* here. —Goodness, a regular jungle. —Father said you're to put this shawl on. He's bringing a blanket.

MRS. CARTER: I'm too warm as it is. Well, give it to me. Thank you, dear.

FRANCESCA: What are you *doing* out here?

TOM *(Bitingly)*: We're talking about you. *(Imitating a teacher)* "I was just saying to Mrs. Carter: I don't know what's to become of Francesca. In all my ninety years of teaching I've never known such a problem child."

FRANCESCA *(Airily; leaving)*: Tz-tz-tz.

TOM *(Urgently)*: Be a sweet little flower box and get me a hamburger.

FRANCESCA: Mother, don't you let Tom have another. Everybody's laughing at him. James Wilson says he had eight. —If you want to make a howling pig of yourself, you can just get up and fetch your own. *(Leaning over him maliciously)* Of course, I don't know what Miss What's-Her-Name will think of you— gorging yourself like that. —Mother, Tom has been making a perfect fool of himself over a new girl—a cousin of the Richardsons. Anybody can see she's a perfect nothing, but there's Tom: "Violet, you didn't get any peach ice cream. Violet . . ."

TOM *(Covering her speech)*: Quack-quack-quack. Honk-honk-honk.

FRANCESCA: Violet this and Violet that. *(Louder)* He even started a fight over her.

TOM *(Rising and starting off)*: Quack-quack-quack! I'll be back. Honk-honk-honk.

[*(Tom leaves.)*]

MRS. CARTER: When you're by yourself, Francesca, you're of course much older than Tom. But when you're *with* Tom, you're younger—and *much* younger. I wish someone could explain that to me.

FRANCESCA: Well, as far as I'm concerned, he's been an eight-year-old for years. And always will be.

MRS. CARTER: To get to know the best of Tom, you must learn to *(She puts her hand on her lips)* hold your tongue. It's always a pleasure to be silent with Tom. You try it someday.

FRANCESCA: Why should I hold my tongue with him?

MRS. CARTER: Have you noticed how your father holds his tongue with you?

FRANCESCA: I don't talk *all the time* when I'm with Father.

MRS. CARTER: No. But when you do, you talk so *well*.

FRANCESCA *(Softened; with wonder)*: Do I? *(Kneeling before her mother)* Do I, really?

MRS. CARTER: I shouldn't have to tell you that.

FRANCESCA: Thank you.

(Enter Mr. Carter, forty-three, lawyer, with a blanket.)

MR. CARTER: Mary?

MRS. CARTER: Here I am, Fred.

MR. CARTER: Try this rock. It's drier. *(He puts the blanket on a rock)* Can you see?

MRS. CARTER *(Crossing)*: Yes. —What's this about a fight Tom had?

FRANCESCA: He's in a terrible mood tonight. First, that fight with the MacDougal boy—I wasn't there. Just some craziness or other.

MRS. CARTER: Do you know anything about it, Fred?

MR. CARTER: Yes. I'll tell you about it later.

FRANCESCA: But that's not really what upset him. A very funny thing happened. Before supper we were all lying around the dock and somebody said that you were going to sing tonight at the bonfire. And that boy from Milwaukee said: "Mrs. Carter sing! *She's too old!*" *(Francesca thinks this is very funny. Gales of laughter)* He'd mixed you up with Mrs. Cavanaugh!! And Paul or Herb said: "She isn't *old*. She isn't any older than . . ." their own mothers. And the boy from Milwaukee said: "Sure, she's old. She's nice and all that, but she oughtn't to be allowed to sing." He thought Mrs. Cavanaugh was *you*!! *(More laughter)* But you should have seen Tom's face!

MRS. CARTER: What?

FRANCESCA: Tom's face. You'd have thought he was seeing a ghost. And the boy from Milwaukee said: "Why, she's got all those gray hairs." *(Gales of laughter)* You remember how at breakfast a few days ago you said you'd found some more gray hairs?

MRS. CARTER: Yes.

FRANCESCA: And Tom was *believing* all this was about you. Well, I thought he'd either . . . jump on the boy and kill him, or go away and . . . maybe throw up.

MR. CARTER: What did he do?

MRS. CARTER: He canoed back across the lake to get my guitar.

MR. CARTER: Francesca, I want to talk to your mother alone a moment.

FRANCESCA *(Touch of pique)*: All right . . . but kindly don't . . . mention . . . *me*.

(She goes out; very queenly. Pause.)

MR. CARTER: Well, what do you think about that? . . . I suppose in the code, a boy can't strike another boy for calling his mother an old woman . . . Tom learns about old age.

MRS. CARTER: What was this other story about a fight?

MR. CARTER: Very odd. Very odd. Tom is not a bulldog type. There's a new girl here—a cousin of the Richardsons. I don't know her name.

MRS. CARTER: Violet.

MR. CARTER: Yes, Violet Richardson. It looks as though Tom had taken a sudden fancy to her. She doesn't seem interesting to me—neither pretty nor individual. Anyway, he was sitting beside her—and the MacDougal boy—the bigger one—Ben—came up and began pulling at her arm . . . to get her to go over where some of them were dancing. Suddenly Tom got up in an awful rage. Told him to let her alone. She was talking to him. Not to stick his nose in where he wasn't wanted. It all flared up in a second: two furious roosters; two stags fighting over a doe. The MacDougal boy backed down. I think he went home. It was all over in a second, too—but it was *real* . . . it was very real and hot.

(Slight pause.)

MRS. CARTER: And I thought this was going to be just one more dull picnic!

(Mr. Carter lights a pipe and goes to sit on the rock where his wife had been sitting.)

Fred, Tom just told me that Francesca hated to come *here*—that she had bad dreams about it? Did you ever know that?

MR. CARTER: What? —Here, this point of land!

MRS. CARTER: Can you think of any reason for it?

MR. CARTER: No!

MRS. CARTER: I'll give you a hint: a robin redbreast.

MR. CARTER: What are you getting at?

MRS. CARTER: A dead robin? . . . The children were about six and seven. We had told them there had been an

Indian graveyard here. They had found a dead robin in the woods, and they set out to bury it . . . I came on: such solemn hymn singing and preaching and praying . . . That night Francesca was deathly ill—

MR. CARTER: Do I remember!! It was one of the most shattering experiences in my life!!

MRS. CARTER: Dr. Macintosh kept asking us what she had eaten, and I—stupidly, stupidly—failed to connect convulsions and hysterics with the burial of Robin Red Breast. Francesca had learned about death . . . You sat soothing her and reading aloud to her until the sun rose.

MR. CARTER: And ever since she dislikes the color red.

MRS. CARTER: And the same experience had no effect on Tom, whatever. Yet we always think of Tom as the sensitive one and Francesca as the sensible one.

MR. CARTER: I guess, growing up is one long walk among perils—among yawning abysses . . .

(Silence.)

Well, since you're talking about old times—I'm going to interrogate you. We've just heard that Tom had a fight. A fight over a girl named Violet. Does the name Violet bring back anything to you?

MRS. CARTER: No . . . No, why?

MR. CARTER: The color?

MRS. CARTER: No.

MR. CARTER: Think a minute.

(She shakes her head.)

A dress you wore?

MRS. CARTER: Fred, you wouldn't remember that! Your sister brought me back from Italy that beautiful silk. I had a dress made from it.

MR. CARTER: Go on.

MRS. CARTER: Then I bought various things to match it . . . beads . . .

MR. CARTER: I called it "your violet year" . . . perfume! . . .

MRS. CARTER: Absurd . . . just before the war . . . 1940 and '41. *(Pause)* What are you implying? Tom wouldn't have known anything about that!

MR. CARTER *(Dismissing it unhesitatingly)*: Of course not. He would have been only two. *(With teasing, flirtatious intention)* It was *myself* I was thinking of. He is infatuated with a Violet, just as I was.

MRS. CARTER: Now, go away . . . to think wives wear . . . you're in the way, Fred.

MR. CARTER *(With a low laugh)*: Well, I've had my troubles on that rock, too.

(Tom appears at the entrance, carrying a guitar.)

TOM: I could have found my way here by the smell of Father's pipe. *(He stops, closes his eyes and smells it)* Christmas is coming. You'll need some more of that tobacco. *(He gropes)* I know its name. No, don't help me . . . ah! "Bonny Prince Charlie." *(He puts the guitar on his mother's lap)*

MRS. CARTER: What's this? Oh—my guitar. Maybe they won't call for me.

MR. CARTER *(Starting off)*: Are you sure you're warm enough? —Tom, do you remember coming out here with Francesca when you were six and holding a funeral over a robin redbreast?

TOM *(Lightly)*: No, did I? Did I, really? —Why?

MRS. CARTER: We were just wondering, Tom.

(Exit Mr. Carter.
Tom gets down on his knees preparatory to lying down again.)

TOM: I helped the squad that was picking up the trash. I rolled the ice cream cans to the truck. I showed Polly Springer how to put a marshmallow on a fork. —I've done my duty. I can rest.

(Silence.)

Mother, make one chord on the guitar.

(She does a slow arpeggiated chord. Silence.)

TOM: One note of music out of doors is worth ten thousand in a building. *(He again turns over on his stomach, raises himself on his elbows)* Mother, I'm going to be the doctor that you planned to be.

MRS. CARTER: Oh! —Not an astronomer? Or a physicist?

TOM: No. That's all too far away. I'm going to be a research doctor.

MRS. CARTER *(Not hurrying)*: Well, you don't have to decide now.

TOM *(Decisively)*: I've decided.—Last month I thought maybe I'd be one of those new physicists. I'd find something that could stop every atomic bomb . . . I think others'll get there before me . . . Besides, that's not hard enough. Any Joe will be able to find that one of these days. I want something harder . . . something nearer. For instance—

(Voice offstage: "MRS. CAAAR-TER." Nearer: "MRS. CAAAR-TER!")

MRS. CARTER *(Raising her voice)*: Ye-es. Here I am.

VOICE: The bonfire's starting. They want you to come and sing.

MRS. CARTER: Is that you, Gladys? Tell them to start singing. I'll come soon.

VOICE: All-riiight.

MRS. CARTER: You were saying you wanted to do something harder.

TOM: Harder and *nearer. (Beating the ground)* There's no reason people have got to grow old so fast. I guess everybody's got to grow old some day. But I'll bet you we can discover lots of things that will put it off. I'll bet you that three hundred years from now people will think that we were just stupid about, well, about growing old so soon . . . I haven't any crazy idea about people living forever; but . . . it's funny: I don't mind getting old, but I don't like it to happen to other people. Anyway, that's decided. *(He puts his head in his arms and closes his eyes as though going to sleep)* It's great to have something decided. *(Pause)* Mother, what was the name of that nurse I had when I was real young, the southern one?

MRS. CARTER: Miss . . . Miss Forbes.

TOM: What was her first name?

MRS. CARTER: Let me think a minute . . . Maude? No. *(Trouvé)* Madeleine!

TOM: Do you remember any teacher I had back then that was named . . . Violet?

MRS. CARTER: . . . N-n-n-o.

TOM *(Dreamily)*: There must have been somebody . . . I remember . . . it was like floating . . . and the smell of violets. Golly, I go crazy when I smell them. I'll tell you why I was so polite to old Mrs. Morris—you remember? She had perfume of violets on her. Why don't you ever wear that, Mother? Don't you like it?

MRS. CARTER *(Caught)*: Why, it . . . never occurred to me.

TOM: That's an idea for a Christmas present, maybe.

(Voices: "MRS. CAAAR-TER!")

MRS. CARTER: Here they come.

(Enter Mr. Carter.)

MR. CARTER: Do you feel like singing or not? They're making a fuss about you down there.

MRS. CARTER: Why not?

(Enter Francesca, running.)

FRANCESCA: Mother, they're stamping their feet and—

MRS. CARTER: I'm coming. —I . . . *(She starts tuning the guitar. Going out)* What'll I do, Tom? I'll do . . .

([They are] out. Silence.)

FRANCESCA: The fireflies . . . the moon.

(Mr. Carter takes the blanket from the rock, carries it across the stage and wraps it around the rock he formerly sat on; then, sitting on the floor, leans his back against it.)

Your pipe smells so wonderful in the open air. *(She starts quietly laughing)* Papa, I'll tell you a secret. *Years* ago—when I went away to summer camp—do you know what I did? I went into your study, and I stole some of that tobacco. I put it in an envelope. And in the tent after lights out, I'd take it out and smell it . . . Why do they call it "Bonny Prince Charlie"? *(Pause; dreamily)* I like the name of Charlie . . . I've never known a stupid boy named Charles. Isn't that funny? They all have something about them that's interesting. *(She starts laughing again)* But I'll tell you something else: all Freds are terrible. Really terrible. You're the only Fred *(Laughing and scarcely audible)* that I can *stand*.

MR. CARTER: Look at the moonlight just hitting the top of the boat club. *(She turns on her knees and draws in her breath, rapt. Mr. Carter drawing his fingers over the ground)* When I was a boy I found all sorts of things here. I made a collection and got a prize for it. Arrowheads and ax heads . . . I used to come out here and think—on this very rock.

FRANCESCA *(Glowing)*: Did you?—What did you think *about*?

MR. CARTER: That someday maybe I'd have a family. That someday maybe I'd go into politics.

FRANCESCA: And now you're senator!

MR. CARTER: Tom's not interested in this place as a *human* place. He's always talking about it as a place before there were any human beings here. But even as boy, I used to think all that must have gone on here. —Initiations—

FRANCESCA: What?

MR. CARTER: Initiations into the tribe. And councils about those awful whiteskins. And buryings. *(Pause)* On this very rock I decided to become a lawyer.

FRANCESCA *(Moving a few feet toward him on her knees)*: Papa, why was I so mean to Mother?

MR. CARTER: Mean?

FRANCESCA *(Bent head, slowly)*: Yes, I was. When I was telling that story about the boy from Milwaukee . . . mistaking Mother for an old woman, like Mrs. Cavanaugh. I knew I was mean while I was doing it. *(She sobs)* And why am I mean about Tom? I *am*. I *am*. *(Sinking lower on her heels)* I'm terrible. I'm unforgivable. —But *why*?

MR. CARTER: Are you mean about yourself? *(She stares at him)* Yes, now you're being mean toward yourself! —Could you imagine building a house on this point?

FRANCESCA: No . . .

MR. CARTER: Because you'd have to cut down so many trees?

FRANCESCA *(Slight pause)*: No . . . I could do it without cutting down the best trees.

MR. CARTER: Why couldn't you imagine building here?

FRANCESCA *(Lightly)*: I wouldn't.

MR. CARTER: No *reason*?

FRANCESCA *(Affectionately)*: Why do you keep asking me when you can *see* that I don't want to answer.

MR. CARTER: Oh, I beg your pardon.

FRANCESCA *(In a loud whisper)*: I don't like this point. I've never liked it.

MR. CARTER *(Walking back and forth, right to left)*: Well, isn't that funny—people feeling so differently about things.

[*(Mr. Carter holds out his hand and Francesca moves closer and takes his hand. They both look into the distance, lost in their thoughts and feelings, as the lights fade.)*]

END OF PLAY

This play became available through the research and editing of F. J. O'Neil of manuscripts in the Thornton Wilder Collection at Yale University.

The place of *The Rivers Under the Earth* in Wilder's schema of short plays is ambiguous. In its first draft it was entitled *Children*. That title was dropped in later drafts. Students of Wilder have speculated that he finally meant the play to represent middle age, since *Childhood* was the title given to one of the three "Plays for Bleecker Street," produced in 1962 at Circle in the Square in New York City.

Wilder had written in his journal[1]: "I planned [*Rivers*] to arrive at a culmination illustrating—so recurrent in me—the relations between a daughter and a father." I added the final stage direction (in brackets) to illustrate this idea in a concluding tableau. The author's manuscript had ended with the line:

MR. CARTER *(Walking back and forth, right to left)*: Well, isn't that funny—people feeling so differently about things.

F. J. O'Neil
April 1997

---

[1] *The Journals of Thornton Wilder 1939–1961*, entry 749, page 265, selected and edited by Donald Gallup, Yale University Press, 1985.

THE TWO WORLDS OF
THORNTON WILDER

by John Gassner

This was previously published as the introduction to The Long Christmas Dinner and Other Plays in One Act, *Harper & Row Publishers, New York, 1963.*

I N RECOMMENDING a volume of short plays by Thornton Wilder published as long ago as 1931, it is tempting to lean on his subsequently achieved reputation as the author of *Our Town* and *The Skin of Our Teeth*, two of the outstanding American plays of the century, and on the fame of several novels since the publication of *The Bridge of San Luis Rey* in 1927 that contain some of the best writing to be found in contemporary American fiction. But the author of these works is interesting to us not as a reputation but as a living artist, and the pleasure derived from the plays in the present volume is sure to be instant and self-sufficient. I trust it is not a momentary judgment of mine that *The Long Christmas Dinner* is the most beautiful one-act play in English prose; at this writing its only rival in my affections is Synge's radically different masterpiece *Riders to the Sea*.

If *Pullman Car Hiawatha* is bound to suffer by comparison with *Our Town*, it is questionable whether the comparison should be allowed to carry any weight. Since Wilder did not compose the shorter and earlier play as a mere preparatory exercise, it has its own distinct substance and style. The presence of an omniscient Stage Manager in both *Pullman Car Hiawatha* and *Our Town* leaves large areas of difference after the technical resemblance has been duly noted. A third experiment in imaginative theatre, *The Happy Journey to Trenton and Camden*, is a deservedly well-known and frequently performed *tour de force*. And even the conventional realistic dramatic structure of the remaining plays, *Queens of France*, an affecting genre painting of social pretensions in old New Orleans, and *Love and How to Cure It*, a non-stagy glance at stage folk, has unique features gratifying to those who know how to read dramatic literature. [Editor's note: The edition to which this introduction originally appeared did not include *Such Things Only Happen in Books*.]

Still, it is within the frame of Wilder's total endeavor as playwright and novelist that these short pieces stand out most meaningfully. And, conversely, these little masterworks help to define their author, concerning whom opinions have been frequently divided and rarely cogent despite the attention paid to his writings and the regard in which he is held on two continents. In this collection of early plays we find (not unexpectedly in the case of so disciplined and self-aware an artist) the configurations of a talent that combines sensitivity with a strong awareness of form and embraces both the commonplaces of life and the life of the imagination, which fluctuates between fantasy and philosophy, skepticism and mysticism, playfulness and sobriety. We see him poised between "life" and "theatre," and this not merely as a beguiling technician but as an observer of reality who does not hesitate to throw off the shackles of realistic play construction in order to come closer to reality.

For assembling the scattered endeavors of the author the present collection was extremely well situated in time. When it appeared rather inconspicuously in 1931, its thirty-four-year-old author (Thornton Wilder was born in Madison, Wisconsin, on April 17, 1897) had already published three novels—*The Cabala* in 1926, *The Bridge of San Luis Rey* in 1927 and *The Woman of Andros* in 1930. This early period of his career was marked by considerable fluctuation. *The Cabala*, a Proustian or Jamesian work rich in characterization if not in unity and clarity, was an impressive but hardly successful novel. *The Bridge of San Luis Rey*, a beautifully written philosophical novel, was enthusiastically received as a relief from semidocumentary, naturalistic fiction in America as well as from the pseudosophistication of the literature of the 1920s. One literary critic (Harry Salpeter) wrote that readers "were tired of realistic novels and were rotten ripe for a book like *The Bridge*"; Alexander Woollcott, in the prime of his reputation as an arbiter of taste, called it a novel of "aloof and untruckling beauty," and the book brought its author his first Pulitzer Prize. But the next novel, *The Woman of Andros*, published in 1930, was a failure and, according to his critics, reflected in the most unfavorable light his special limitations of abstruseness, preciosity, and remoteness from the contemporary world. In the fall of that year, in fact, Wilder became the object of a violent assault by the left-wing journalist Michael Gold in the *New Republic*, and although he found so powerful a defender as Edmund Wilson, it was quite evident that the vein of cultivated fiction for which he had evinced a strong affinity was virtually exhausted. It was no longer considered viable art during the "socially conscious" depression period of the 1930s to which volcanic eruptions in Europe were continually adding new challenges.

The Woman of Andros may not be a substantial novel; it is nonetheless an enchanting and affecting book, and it is more satisfying in my opinion than many an acclaimed contemporary novel. But the historical situation was plainly unfavorable to the reflective and tastefully distanced artistry which is one of the two worlds of art Wilder has inhabited in the course of his distinguished literary career.

He would have to move into the other world of common reality which he had fastidiously avoided but with which he soon made a successful compromise that accounts for much of his originality and his special genius—the compromise of combining intensive observation of the common world with uncommon transcendence or sublimation of that world. Wilder himself was apparently aware of a limitation in his art when he declared some years later (in 1938) that he had shrunk from describing the modern world and was "alarmed at finding a way of casting into generalization the world of doorbells and telephones." He was ready, he believed, "to accept the twentieth century, not only as a fascinating age to live in, but as assimilable stuff to think with."

He still had to accept the theatre as well. His first plays, published in 1928 under the collective title *The Angel That Troubled the Waters*, were three-minute-long dramatic pieces. They possess some of the literary conversation in the manner of Walter Savage Landor but without Landor's prolixity in prose; there is considerably less dramatic pressure in them than in the miniature verse plays of Pushkin and the short pieces Musset wrote to illustrate proverbs. They are extremely beautiful pieces of writing and I particularly treasure *Now the Servant's Name Was Malchus* in which "Our Lord" in heaven receives the servant of the High Priest whose ear was lopped off by Peter's sword when Christ was arrested. Malchus would like to have his name expunged from the New Testament because the episode makes him look ridiculous. Christ invites him to stay in heaven with Him, saying, "Malchus, will you stay and be ridiculous with me?" Malchus says he will be glad to stay but isn't sure he merits all that attention: "I wasn't even the High Priest's servant; I only held his horse every now and then." Besides, it was his left ear and not his right that was the casualty of that fateful encounter; whereupon "Our Lord" assures him that "the book isn't always true about me, either."

The affirmative counterpart to this rather bitter one-acter is another miniature masterpiece, *The Flight into*

Egypt, in which Hepzibah, the talkative donkey that carries the Holy Family fleeing from Herod's massacre of the children, loiters dangerously on the road to Egypt. On being ordered to move ahead, Hepzibah reflects that "it's a queer world where the survival of the Lord is dependent on donkeys," and, requesting some answers to the puzzle of faith and reason, is told by Our Lady that there will be an answer perhaps someday, but "For the present just do as I do and bear your master on." A third dramatic capsule, *Hast Thou Considered My Servant Job,* asserts faith in man himself. Wilder's often noted optimistic view of man is expressed with unusual warmth when Judas renounces Satan, who has been awaiting his favorite son, confident that he has defeated Christ, "For I build not on intermittent dreams and timid aspirations, but on the unshakable passions and lust and self-love." The stage direction that answers this boast reads: "Suddenly the thirty pieces of silver are cast upward from the revolted hand of Judas. They hurtle across the stars and continue falling forever through the vast funnel of space." Christ and Judas then "mount upward to their due place and Satan remains to this day, uncomprehending, upon the pavement of Hell."

Still, the world of art that Wilder inhabited with the writing of some forty three-minute plays (and this activity went as far back as 1915, when he wrote the first of these in California) was the same reflective and literary world that had served him in the novels. It was a strong enticement for one who had studied the classics in his youth, written ambitious undergraduate literature, pursued the study of archaeology at the American Academy in Rome after graduation from Yale in 1920, taught from 1921 to 1928 at the Lawrenceville boys' preparatory school near Princeton, and was to teach again for over half a decade, from 1930 to 1936, at the University of Chicago under the classically inspired regime of his former Yale classmate Robert Hutchins. Characteristically, in writing the foreword to *The Angel That Troubled the Waters* in 1928, Wilder declared that "beauty is the only persuasion." But with the writing of *The Long Christmas Dinner* and the other dramatically active one-act plays in the present volume he was plainly intent on achieving something more than "beauty." He aimed here for the truth of common life, on the one hand, and its theatrical expression, on the other.

Henceforth he was to inhabit two worlds, the real and the imaginary, or to blend the two in the same work. This was apparent in his later fiction—in *Heaven's My Destination*, an amusing yet rueful novel about a moralistic innocent adrift in American society, published in 1935, and in *The Ides of March* (1948), in which he combined a novel of manners in Julius Caesar's time with a penetrating portrait of Caesar and exquisitely reflective prose often intensified with emotion and lightened with humor. (In the invented letters and diary that make up this semi-Shavian novel one comes across well-turned observations such as Caesar's statements that "The Gods hide themselves even in their choice of instruments," that "Hope has never changed tomorrow's weather," and that "Wickedness may be the exploration of one's liberty" and "The search for a limit that one can respect.") But it is especially in the plays published after *The Angel That Troubled the Waters* that Wilder effected the reconciliation of reality and imagination which proved so rewarding in *Our Town* in 1938 and *The Skin of Our Teeth* in 1942.*

---

*Mr. Wilder, I should add, has been a more prolific playwright since 1931 than the above reference to his major plays would suggest. *The Merchant of Yonkers*, a Max Reinhardt production in 1938, was revised and entitled *The Matchmaker*. In this version the play was produced at the Edinburgh Festival in 1954 and in New York in 1955. He adapted André Obey's poetic drama *Le Viol de Lucrèce* for Katharine Cornell and *A Doll's House* for a Jed Harris presentation featuring Ruth Gordon as Nora, and he wrote an Alcestis drama, *The Alcestiad,* performed at the Edinburgh Festival of 1955 under the title *A Life in the Sun*. Mr. Wilder is now at work on two cycles of one-act plays, *The Seven Ages of Man* and *The Seven Deadly Sins,* from which three pieces were put together for a Circle in the Square Off-Broadway production in 1962. In the best of these, *Childhood*, one finds the same fusion of homely reality and piquant fantasy that characterizes the major stage productions.

To the plays in the present volume belongs the distinction of introducing their author as an original and effective playwright, and three of these will introduce the reader to the essence of his craftsmanship. Thus, the omniscient Stage Manager so important to the structure of *Our Town* first appears in *Pullman Car Hiawatha* and serves the same purpose of introducing the dramatic action and functioning within it. He is both the *raisonneur,* or commentator, and, in speaking the lines of several minor figures, a veritable constellation of characters. The Stage Manager is, so to speak, both a one-man chorus and a multiple "second character," or deuteragonist, in the play, which reflects conventions of both Greek and Oriental drama in this respect while the dialogue and the characterizations are unmistakably American.

Time is telescoped in *The Long Christmas Dinner*, so that ninety years of family life flow through the play without interruption in a sequence of merging scenes. Thornton Wilder was to telescope time again on a more historically significant plane in *The Skin of Our Teeth* a decade later. In *The Long Christmas Dinner* the author's imaginative management of time is simple and persuasive. We feel as though we were floating in the flux of life and of time itself, in a broad and never-ending stream which is both "real" and "unreal." We move ahead and are nevertheless becalmed by the sameness of the things that ultimately matter most to us, the quotidian realities that underlie the course of nations and even the ardors and endurances of men and women celebrated in history, saga, and high tragedy. And the marvel is that this effect of simplicity was achieved by the author with some of the most sophisticated strategies of dramaturgy within the competence of modern theatrical art.

The same simplicity of subject and style combined with modernistic structural departures from realism also appears in *The Happy Journey to Trenton and Camden,* in which the author again resorts to a Stage Manager who sets up the visible action and participates in the play in several small roles.

In *Pullman Car Hiawatha*, moreover, the author's resources of dramatic construction and symbolic visualization even enable him to move into a world of fancy, allowing him to give a speech to a dead woman (Harriet) as affecting as Emily's lines in the last act of *Our Town* and to personify places such as "Grover's Corners" and "The Field" (too archly, perhaps) in the dramatic action. He even feels free to indulge in the playful histrionics of bringing "The Hours" onstage as "beautiful girls dressed like Elihu Vedder's Pleiades," each carrying a great gold Roman numeral; this, after a whimsical introduction by the Stage Manager to the effect that the minutes are "gossips," the hours "philosophers," and the years "theologians." And following this, anticipating a procession of the hours in *The Skin of Our Teeth*, Ten O'Clock, Eleven O'Clock, and Twelve O'Clock quote Plato, Epictetus, and St. Augustine, while "the planets appear on the balcony." Nothing less than a wistful mysticism relating our insignificant species to the universe satisfies Wilder's imagination once he elects for histrionic freedom or "theatricalism."

It is to be noted, finally, that with this roving kind of dramaturgy he brings us to one more paradoxical attribute of his virtuosity. He is at once a radical and a traditionalist in employing a form of stylization that proclaims the theatrical nature of the drama instead of sedulously sustaining the so-called illusion of reality required by the conventions of modern realism. The artificial nature of the theatre was the established convention of classic, Oriental, Renaissance, Elizabethan, Neoclassic, and Romantic theatre; realistic convention, which became firmly established only in the second half of the nineteenth century, is a very late development. In returning to "theatricalism" or "theatre for theatre's sake" (rather than "theatre for the sake of illusion"), Wilder associated himself with tradition in dramatic art. But returning to tradition in the twentieth century was an innovation, and Wilder's manner of returning to it was personal and unique. It came about not without some dangers, the

greatest of these being in his case some frolicsome bookish-
ness and self-conscious skittishness, but it amounted to a
minor revolution in the American theatre.

   Both its revolutionary character and its risks were, however, minimized by the persuasive humanity, natural tact,
and good taste of the well-bred and well-educated author
of short and long plays that quickly established themselves
as classics of the American theatre in so far as this jittery
institution can lay claim to any classics at all. A nearly infal-
lible sense of theatre, moreover, overcame the antidramatic
tendencies of Thornton Wilder's temperament, giving
liveliness to his reflectiveness and life to his artifices. In a little essay entitled *Some Thoughts on Playwriting,* published
in 1941, he set down his creed and awareness of craft suc-
cinctly. He declared that "the stage is a fundamental pre-
tense" and that it thrives on the acceptance of that fact and
"in the multiplication of additional pretenses." But he went
on to affirm the immediacy of life in the drama despite the
pretenses of the stage by writing that, "A play is what takes
place. A novel is what one person tells us took place. A play
visibly represents pure existing." He did not have to defend
the paradox as his own plays, beginning with *The Long
Christmas Dinner* in 1931, provided sufficient proof of its
truth and gratifying results.†

---

†Readers curious enough about the nature and justification of this paradox, this dual character of dramatic art, may refer to the following para-
graph in John Gassner's *Form and Idea in Modern Theatre* (pp. 141–42)
The Dryden Press, New York, 1956:

   The fundamental premise of realism is the Aristotelian one
   that drama is an imitation of an action; realists held, therefore, that
   the most desirable theatre is that which imitation is closest. The
   fundamental premise of theatricalism is that theatre is not imitation in the narrow sense, which Aristotle never could have held,
   since the Greek drama upon which he based conclusions in his
   Poetics was not realistically imitative. For the theatricalist, the
   object of action and of all other "imitative" elements is not imi-

tation but creativeness, and a special kind of creativeness at that. The realists would agree, of course, as to the value of creativeness. But the theatricalist goes one step further, and that step is the truly decisive one for the theory and practice of pure theatricalism. He maintains that there is never any sense in pretending that one is not in the theatre; that no amount of make-believe is reality itself; that in short, theatre is the medium of dramatic art, and that effectiveness in art consists in *using* the medium rather than concealing it.

And Thornton Wilder provided conclusive evidence of the compatibility of convention and emotional conviction with an example in *Some Thoughts on Playwriting*. Starting with the statement that the theatre "lives by conventions: a convention is an agreed-upon falsehood, a permitted lie," he cited the case of Euripides' *Medea*. According to an ancient report, the passage in the play where Medea contemplates the murder of her children nearly produced a riot. Yet Medea was "played by a man," "he wore a large mask on his face," "he wore shoes with soles and heels half a foot high," he spoke in metric lines and "all poetry is an 'agreed-upon falsehood' in regard to speech" and "the lines were sung in a kind of recitative"—as in opera, which "involves this 'permitted lie' in regard to speech." Wilder rightly concluded that the mask, the costume and the mode of declamation were "a series of signs which the spectator interpreted and reassembled in his own mind." That is, "Medea was being recreated within the imagination of each of the spectators."

JOHN GASSNER (1903–1967) was Sterling Professor of Playwriting and Dramatic Literature at Yale from 1956 to 1965.

BIBLIOGRAPHIC AND PRODUCTION NOTES

THE LONG CHRISTMAS DINNER AND OTHER PLAYS IN ONE ACT

The Long Christmas Dinner and Other Plays in One Act was first published 5 November 1931 in New York by Coward-McCann in a trade edition of 5,900 copies and in New Haven by Yale University Press in a special limited signed edition of 525 copies.

In March 1931, Thornton Wilder arranged with Samuel French, Inc., New York, Los Angeles, London, Toronto (hereafter called SF) to manage all dramatic rights to the plays in this volume. Until after WWII, performances of the plays were mounted principally by amateur groups, using the book or typescript copies of the plays if an acting edition had not yet been published. After the war, several of the plays were produced professionally in this country and abroad. New York City productions over the last thirty years include: *The Long Christmas Dinner*, *The Happy Journey to Trenton and Camden* and *Queens of France* at Cherry Lane Theater in 1966; and "Wilder, Wilder, Wilder: Three by Thornton Wilder" (*The Long Christmas Dinner*, *The Happy Journey to Trenton and Camden* and *Pullman Car Hiawatha*) at Circle in the Square in 1993.

The Long Christmas Dinner. First produced by the Yale Dramatic Association and the Vassar College Philaletheis at the Yale University theatre in New Haven, CT, on 25 November 1931. Some revisions in stage directions and text were made by Alexander

Dean, the director, and were apparently sanctioned by the author, and later incorporated into the acting edition published by SF in 1934, and are included in this volume's edition. First licensed productions occurred on 19 December 1931 at Antioch College in Yellow Springs, OH, and in New York (site unidentified). An opera based on this play, composed by Paul Hindemith with a libretto by Wilder, premiered in Mannheim, Germany, on 12 December 1961.

Queens of France. First printed in the *Yale Review*, XXI.1 (Sept. 1931) 72–85. First licensed production occurred 9 March 1932 at the Hill School, Pottstown, PA, and the Miss Masters' School, Dobbs Ferry, NY. SF acting edition was published in 1958.

Pullman Car Hiawatha. First licensed production occurred 19 March 1932 at Antioch College in Yellow Springs, OH. SF acting edition was published in London in 1952.

Love and How to Cure It. First produced with *The Long Christmas Dinner* on 25 November 1931 (see above). First licensed production occurred in Washington, D.C., on 17 March 1932 (site unidentified). SF acting edition was published in London in 1932.

Such Things Only Happen in Books. First produced with *The Long Christmas Dinner* on 25 November 1931 (see above). First licensed production occurred in Plattsburgh, NY, on 5 March 1932 (site unidentified). Withdrawn from production and print by the author no later, and probably much earlier, than 1946. No acting edition was ever printed.

The Happy Journey to Trenton and Camden. First produced with *The Long Christmas Dinner* on 25 November 1931 (see above). First licensed production occurred 19 December 1931 at Antioch College in Yellow Springs, OH. SF acting edition, with revisions, was published in 1934. Those revisions are incorporated in this volume's edition.

The production licensing information for the six plays cited above was taken from SF's 25 October 1932 royalty statement to Thornton Wilder.

PLAYS FOR BLEECKER STREET
(PLAYS IN ONE ACT FOR AN ARENA STAGE)

"The Seven Deadly Sins"

The Drunken Sisters (Gluttony). First printed in the *Atlantic Monthly*, CC.5 (Nov. 1957) 92–95. A revised text was published in *The Alcestiad or A Life in the Sun: A Play in Three Acts—With a Satyr Play: The Drunken Sisters* by Harper & Row, New York, Hagerstown, San Francisco, London, in 1977. SF acting edition published in 1978. The SF acting edition of *The Alcestiad* version was published in 1980.

Bernice (Pride). First produced in English at the Congress Hall, West Berlin, Germany, in September 1957. Printed in German translation as *Berenike* in *Die Neue Rundschau*, LXXI.4 (1960) 585–95. First printed in English in the *Yale Review*, LXXXV.2 (Apr. 1997) 19–38. American premiere production occurred at "The Thornton Wilder Play Festival" at the Hill School, Pottstown, PA, on 18 February 1997.

The Wreck on the Five-Twenty-Five (Sloth). The world premiere in English was produced at the Congress Hall, West Berlin, Germany, in September 1957. First printed in the *Yale Review*, LXXXII. 4 (Oct. 1994) 17–41. American premiere in May 1995 as part of "Marathon '95," the Ensemble Studio Theatre series. Reprinted in *The Best American Short Plays 1994–1995* by Applause Theatre Book Publishers, New York, London, 1995, and in *EST Marathon '95: The Complete One-Act Plays* by Smith & Kraus, Lyme, NH, 1995.

A Ringing of Doorbells (Envy). First printed here from the author's manuscripts in the Thornton Wilder Archive of the Yale Collection of American Literature, Beinecke Rare Book and Manuscript Library (hereafter called TWYCAL).

In Shakespeare and the Bible (Wrath). First printed here from the author's manuscripts in the TWYCAL.

Someone from Assisi (Lust). First produced in New York as one of the three "Plays for Bleecker Street" in 1962. The script, reproduced from typed copy, was distributed by SF in 1964.

Cement Hands (Avarice). First printed here from the author's manuscripts in the TWYCAL. World premiere reading was held on 15 April 1997 at the University Club in New York City as part of "A Wilder Evening," The MacDowell Colony's celebration of the Thornton Wilder Centennial.

"The Seven Ages of Man"

Infancy. First produced in New York as one of the three "Plays for Bleecker Street" in 1962. Amateur licenses became available through SF in 1964. SF acting edition was published in June 1970.

Childhood. First published in the *Atlantic Monthly*, CCVI.5 (Nov. 1960) 78–84. First produced in New York as one of the three "Plays for Bleecker Street" in 1962. Amateur licenses became available through SF in 1964. SF acting edition was published in June 1970.

Youth. First printed here from the author's manuscripts and typescripts in the TWYCAL.

The Rivers Under the Earth (? Middle Age). First published in *American Theatre*, XIV.3 (Mar. 1997) 25–30, and here from the author's manuscripts in the TWYCAL.